Puppet 5 Beginner's Guide

Third Edition

Go from newbie to pro with Puppet 5

John Arundel

BIRMINGHAM - MUMBAI

Puppet 5 Beginner's Guide

Third Edition

First published: April 2013

Second edition: May 2017

Third edition: October 2017

Production reference: 1031017

Published by Packt Publishing Ltd.
Livery Place
35 Livery Street
Birmingham B3 2PB, UK.

ISBN 978-1-78847-290-6

www.packtpub.com

Credits

Author
John Arundel

Reviewer
Jo Rhett

Acquisition Editor
Ben Renow-Clarke

Project Editor
Alish Firasta

Content Development Editor
Monika Sangwan

Technical Editors
Bhagyashree Rai
Gaurav Gavas

Copy Editor
Gladson Monteiro

Indexer
Mariammal Chettiyar

Graphics
Kirk D'Penha

Production Coordinator
Arvindkumar Gupta

Cover Work
Arvindkumar Gupta

About the Author

John Arundel is a DevOps consultant, which means he helps people build world-class web operations teams and infrastructure and has fun doing it. He was formerly a senior operations engineer at global telco Verizon, designing resilient, high-performance infrastructures for major corporations such as Ford, McDonald's, and Bank of America. He is now an independent consultant, working closely with selected clients to deliver web-scale performance and enterprise-grade resilience on a startup budget.

He likes writing books, especially about Puppet (*Puppet 2.7 Cookbook* and *Puppet 3 Cookbook* are available from Packt as well). It seems that at least some people enjoy reading them, or maybe they just like the pictures. He also provides training and coaching on Puppet and DevOps, which, it turns out, is far harder than simply doing the work himself.

Off the clock, he is a medal-winning competitive rifle and pistol shooter and a decidedly uncompetitive piano player. He lives in a small cottage in Cornwall, England and believes, like Cicero, that if you have a garden and a library, then you have everything you need.

You may like to follow him on Twitter at `@bitfield`.

Acknowledgments

My grateful thanks are due to Jo Rhett, who made innumerable improvements and suggestions to this book, and whose Puppet expertise and clarity of writing I can only strive to emulate. Also to the original Puppet master, Luke Kanies, who created a configuration management tool that sucks less, and my many other friends at Puppet. Many of the key ideas in this book came from them and others including Przemyslaw 'SoboL' Sobieski, Peter Bleeck, and Igor Galić.

The techniques and examples in the book come largely from real production codebases, of my consulting clients and others, and were developed with the indispensable assistance of my friends and colleagues Jon Larkowski, Justin Domingus, Walter Smith, Ian Shaw, and Mike Thomas. Special thanks are also due to the Perseids Project at Tufts University, and most of all to the inestimable Bridget Almas, who patiently read and tested everything in the book several times and made many valuable suggestions, not to mention providing continuous moral support, love, and guidance throughout the writing process. This book is for her.

About the Reviewer

Jo Rhett is a DevOps architect with more than 25 years of experience conceptualizing and delivering large-scale Internet services. He creates automation and infrastructure to accelerate deployment and minimize outages.

Jo has been using, promoting, and enhancing configuration management systems for over 20 years. He builds improvements and plugins for Puppet, Mcollective, Chef, Ansible, Docker, and many other DevOps tools.

Jo is the author of the following books:

- *Learning Puppet 4* by *O'Reilly*
- *Learning MCollective* by *O'Reilly*
- *Instant Puppet 3 Starter* by *Packt Publishing*

I'd like to thank the Puppet community for their never-ending inspiration and support.

www.PacktPub.com

eBooks, discount offers, and more

Did you know that Packt offers eBook versions of every book published, with PDF and ePub files available? You can upgrade to the eBook version at `www.PacktPub.com` and as a print book customer, you are entitled to a discount on the eBook copy. Get in touch with us at `customercare@packtpub.com` for more details.

At `www.PacktPub.com`, you can also read a collection of free technical articles, sign up for a range of free newsletters and receive exclusive discounts and offers on Packt books and eBooks.

`https://www.packtpub.com/mapt`

Do you need instant solutions to your IT questions? PacktLib is Packt's online digital book library. Here, you can search, access, and read Packt's entire library of books.

Why subscribe?

- Fully searchable across every book published by Packt
- Copy and paste, print, and bookmark content
- On demand and accessible via a web browser

Customer Feedback

Thanks for purchasing this Packt book. At Packt, quality is at the heart of our editorial process. To help us improve, please leave us an honest review on this book's Amazon page at `https://www.amazon.com/dp/178847290X`.

If you'd like to join our team of regular reviewers, you can e-mail us at `customerreviews@packtpub.com`. We award our regular reviewers with free eBooks and videos in exchange for their valuable feedback. Help us be relentless in improving our products!

Table of Contents

Preface

There are many bad ways to write a technical book. One simply rehashes the official documentation. Another walks the reader through a large and complex example, which doesn't necessarily do anything useful, except show how clever the author is. Yet another exhaustively sets out every available feature of the technology, and every possible way you can use them, without much guidance as to which features you'll really use, or which are best avoided.

Like you, I read a lot of technical books as part of my job. I don't need a paraphrase of the documentation: I can read it online. I also don't want huge blocks of code for something that I don't need to do. And I certainly don't want an uncritical exposition of every single feature.

What I do want is for the author to give me a cogent and readable explanation of how the tool works, in enough detail that I can get started using it straight away, but not so much detail that I get bogged down. I want to learn about features in the order in which I'm likely to use them, and I want to be able to start building something that runs and delivers business value from the very first chapters.

That's what you can expect from this book. Whether you're a developer, a system administrator, or merely Puppet-curious, you're going to learn Puppet skills you can put into practice right away. Without going into lots of theory or background detail, I'll show you how to install packages and config files, create users, set up scheduled jobs, provision cloud instances, build containers, and so on. Every example deals with something real and practical that you're likely to need in your work, and you'll see the complete Puppet code to make it happen, along with step-by-step instructions for what to type and what output you'll see. All the examples are available in a GitHub repo for you to download and adapt.

After each exercise, I'll explain in detail what each line of code does and how it works, so that you can adapt it to your own purposes, and feel confident that you understand everything that's happened. By the end of the book, you will have all the skills you need to do real, useful, everyday work with Puppet, and there's a complete demo Puppet repository you can use to get your infrastructure up and running with minimum effort.

So let's get started.

What this book covers

Chapter 1, Getting started with Puppet, introduces Puppet and gets you up and running with the Vagrant virtual machine that accompanies this book.

Chapter 2, Creating your first manifests, shows you how Puppet works, and how to write code to manage packages, files, and services.

Chapter 3, Managing your Puppet code with Git, introduces the Git version control tool, shows you how to create a repository to store your code, and how to distribute it to your Puppet-managed nodes.

Chapter 4, Understanding Puppet resources, goes into more detail about the `package`, `file`, and `service` resources, as well as introducing resources to manage users, SSH keys, scheduled jobs, and commands.

Chapter 5, Variables, expressions, and facts, introduces Puppet's variables, data types, expressions, and conditional statements, shows you how to get data about the node using Facter, and how to create your own custom facts.

Chapter 6, Managing data with Hiera, explains Puppet's key-value database and how to use it to store and retrieve data, including secrets, and how to create Puppet resources from Hiera data.

Chapter 7, Mastering modules, teaches you how to install ready-to-use modules from the Puppet Forge using the `r10k` tool, introduces you to four key modules including the standard library, and shows you how to build your own modules.

Chapter 8, Classes, roles, and profiles, introduces you to classes and defined resource types, and shows you the best way to organize your Puppet code using roles and profiles.

Chapter 9, Managing files with templates, shows you how to build complex configuration files with dynamic data using Puppet's EPP template mechanism.

Chapter 10, Controlling containers, introduces Puppet's powerful new support for Docker containers, and shows you how to download, build, and run containers using Puppet resources.

Chapter 11, Orchestrating cloud resources, explains how you can use Puppet to provision cloud servers on Amazon AWS, and introduces a fully-automated cloud infrastructure based on Hiera data.

Chapter 12, Putting it all together, takes you through a complete example Puppet infrastructure that you can download and modify for your own projects, using ideas from all the previous chapters.

What you need for this book

You'll need a reasonably modern computer system and access to the Internet. You won't need to be a Unix expert or an experienced sysadmin; I'll assume you can install software, run commands, and edit files, but otherwise I'll explain everything you need as we go.

Who this book is for

The main audience for this book are those who are new to Puppet, including system administrators and developers who are looking to manage computer server systems for configuration management. No prior programming or system administration experience is assumed. However, if you have used Puppet before, you'll get a thorough grounding in all the latest features and modules, and I hope you'll still find plenty of new things to learn.

Conventions

In this book, you will find a number of styles of text that distinguish between different kinds of information. Here are some examples of these styles, and an explanation of their meaning.

Code words in text, database table names, folder names, filenames, file extensions, pathnames, dummy URLs, user input, and Twitter handles are shown as follows: "Puppet can manage files on a node using the `file` resource"

A block of code is set as follows:

```
file { '/tmp/hello.txt':
  ensure  => file,
  content => "hello, world\n",
}
```

When we wish to draw your attention to a particular part of a code block, the relevant lines or items are set in bold:

```
file { '/tmp/hello.txt':
  ensure  => file,
  content => "hello, world\n",
}
```

Any command-line input or output is written as follows:

```
sudo puppet apply /vagrant/examples/file_hello.pp
Notice: Compiled catalog for ubuntu-xenial in environment production
in 0.07 seconds
```

New terms and **important words** are shown in bold. Words that you see on the screen, in menus or dialog boxes for example, appear in the text like this: "In the AWS console, select **VPC** from the **Services** menu".

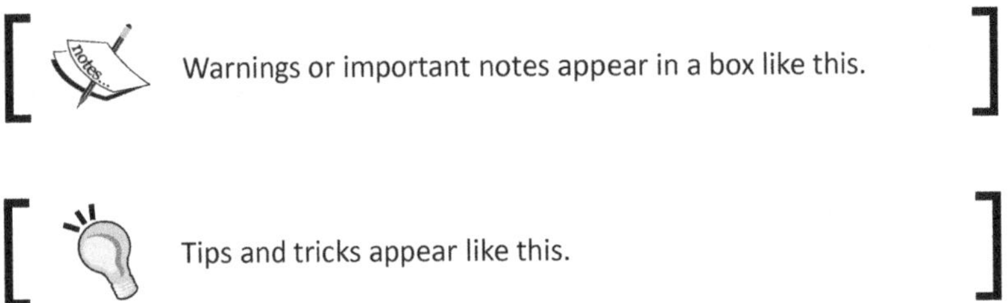

Warnings or important notes appear in a box like this.

Tips and tricks appear like this.

Reader feedback

Feedback from our readers is always welcome. Let us know what you think about this book—what you liked or disliked. Reader feedback is important for us as it helps us develop titles that you will really get the most out of.

To send us general feedback, simply e-mail `feedback@packtpub.com`, and mention the book's title in the subject of your message.

If there is a topic that you have expertise in and you are interested in either writing or contributing to a book, see our author guide at `www.packtpub.com/authors`.

Customer support

Now that you are the proud owner of a Packt book, we have a number of things to help you to get the most from your purchase.

Downloading the example code

You can download the example code files for this book from your account at `http://www.packtpub.com`. If you purchased this book elsewhere, you can visit `http://www.packtpub.com/support` and register to have the files e-mailed directly to you.

You can download the code files by following these steps:

1. Log in or register to our website using your e-mail address and password.
2. Hover the mouse pointer on the **SUPPORT** tab at the top.
3. Click on **Code Downloads & Errata**.
4. Enter the name of the book in the **Search** box.
5. Select the book for which you're looking to download the code files.
6. Choose from the drop-down menu where you purchased this book from.
7. Click on **Code Download**.

You can also download the code files by clicking on the **Code Files** button on the book's webpage at the Packt Publishing website. This page can be accessed by entering the book's name in the **Search** box. Please note that you need to be logged in to your Packt account.

Once the file is downloaded, please make sure that you unzip or extract the folder using the latest version of:

- WinRAR / 7-Zip for Windows
- Zipeg / iZip / UnRarX for Mac
- 7-Zip / PeaZip for Linux

The code bundle for the book is also hosted on GitHub at the following URLs:

- `https://github.com/bitfield/puppet-beginners-guide-3.git`
- `https://github.com/bitfield/pbg_ntp.git`
- `https://github.com/bitfield/control-repo-3.git`

You can use the code bundle on GitHub from the Packt Publishing repository as well:

`https://github.com/PacktPublishing/Puppet-5-Beginners-Guide-Third-Edition`

We also have other code bundles from our rich catalog of books and videos available at `https://github.com/PacktPublishing/`. Check them out!

Errata

Although we have taken every care to ensure the accuracy of our content, mistakes do happen. If you find a mistake in one of our books—maybe a mistake in the text or the code—we would be grateful if you could report this to us. By doing so, you can save other readers from frustration and help us improve subsequent versions of this book. If you find any errata, please report them by visiting `http://www.packtpub.com/submit-errata`, selecting your book, clicking on the **Errata Submission Form** link, and entering the details of your errata. Once your errata are verified, your submission will be accepted and the errata will be uploaded to our website or added to any list of existing errata under the Errata section of that title.

To view the previously submitted errata, go to `https://www.packtpub.com/books/content/support` and enter the name of the book in the search field. The required information will appear under the **Errata** section.

Piracy

Piracy of copyrighted material on the Internet is an ongoing problem across all media. At Packt, we take the protection of our copyright and licenses very seriously. If you come across any illegal copies of our works in any form on the Internet, please provide us with the location address or website name immediately so that we can pursue a remedy.

Please contact us at `copyright@packtpub.com` with a link to the suspected pirated material.

We appreciate your help in protecting our authors and our ability to bring you valuable content.

Questions

If you have a problem with any aspect of this book, you can contact us at `questions@packtpub.com`, and we will do our best to address the problem.

1

Getting started with Puppet

> *For a list of all the ways technology has failed to improve the quality of life, please press three.*
>
> —*Alice Kahn*

In this chapter, you'll learn about some of the challenges of managing configuration on servers, some common solutions to these problems, and how automation tools such as Puppet can help. You'll also learn how to download the GitHub repository containing all of the source code and examples in this book, how to set up your own Vagrant virtual machine to run the code, and how to download and install Puppet.

Whether you're a system administrator, a developer who needs to wrangle servers from time to time, or just someone who's annoyed at how long it takes to deploy a new app, you'll have come across the kind of problems Puppet is designed to solve.

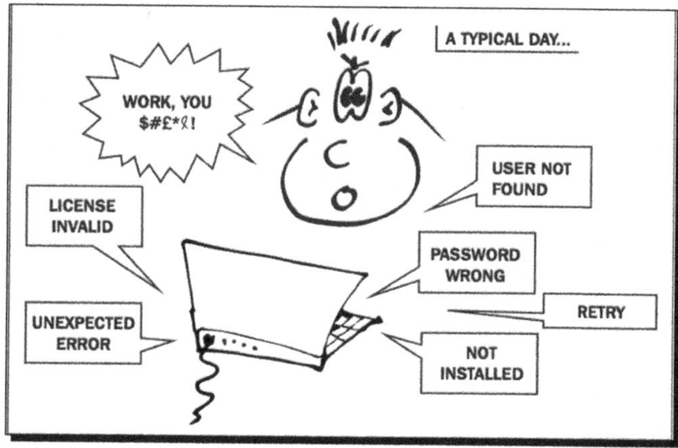

Why do we need Puppet anyway?

Managing applications and services in production is hard work, and there are a lot of steps involved. To start with, you need some servers to serve the services. Luckily, these are readily available from your local cloud provider, at low, low prices. So you've got a server, with a base operating system installed on it, and you can log into it. So now what? Before you can deploy, you need to do a number of things:

- Add user accounts and passwords
- Configure security settings and privileges
- Install all the packages needed to run the app
- Customize the configuration files for each of these packages
- Create databases and database user accounts; load some initial data
- Configure the services that should be running
- Deploy the app code and static assets
- Restart any affected services
- Configure the machine for monitoring

That's a lot to do—and for the next server you build, you'll need to do the exact same things all over again. There's something not right about that. Shouldn't there be an easier solution to this problem?

Wouldn't it be nice if you could write an executable specification of how the server should be set up, and you could apply it to as many machines as you liked?

Keeping the configuration synchronized

Setting up servers manually is tedious. Even if you're the kind of person who enjoys tedium, though, there's another problem to consider. What happens the next time you set up a server, a few weeks or months later?

Your careful notes will no longer be up to date with reality. While you were on vacation, the developers installed a couple of new libraries that the app now depends on—I guess they forgot to tell you! They are under a lot of schedule pressure, of course. You could send out a sternly worded email demanding that people update the build document whenever they change something, and people might even comply with that. But even if they do update the documentation, no-one actually tests the new build process from scratch, so when you come to do it, you'll find it doesn't work anymore. Turns out that if you just upgrade the database in place, it's fine, but if you install the new version on a bare server, it's not.

Also, since the build document was updated, a new version of a critical library was released upstream. Because you always install the latest version as part of the build, your new server is now subtly different to the old one. This will lead to subtle problems which will take you three days, or three bottles of whiskey, to debug.

By the time you have four or five servers, they're all a little different. Which is the authoritative one? Or are they all slightly wrong? The longer they're around, the more they will drift apart. You wouldn't run four or five different versions of your app code at once, so what's up with that? Why is it acceptable for server configuration to be in a mess like this?

Wouldn't it be nice if the state of configuration on all your machines could be regularly checked and synchronized with a central, standard version?

Repeating changes across many servers

Humans just aren't good at accurately repeating complex tasks over and over; that's why we invented robots. It's easy to make mistakes, miss things out, or be interrupted and lose track of what you've done.

Changes happen all the time, and it becomes increasingly difficult to keep things up to date and in sync as your infrastructure grows. Again, when you make a change to your app code, you don't go and make that change manually with a text editor on each server. You change it once and roll it out everywhere. Isn't your firewall setup just as much part of your code as your user model?

Wouldn't it be nice if you only had to make changes in one place, and they rolled out to your whole network automatically?

Self-updating documentation

In real life, we're too busy to stop every five minutes and document what we just did. As we've seen, that documentation is of limited use anyway, even if it's kept fanatically up-to-date.

The only reliable documentation, in fact, is the state of the servers themselves. You can look at a server to see how it's configured, but that only applies while you still have the machine. If something goes wrong and you can't access the machine, or the data on it, your only option is to reconstruct the lost configuration from scratch.

Wouldn't it be nice if you had a clear, human-readable build procedure which was independent of your servers, and was guaranteed to be up to date, because the servers are actually built from it?

Version control and history

When you're making manual, ad hoc changes to systems, you can't roll them back to a point in time. It's hard to undo a whole series of changes; you don't have a way of keeping track of what you did and how things changed.

This is bad enough when there's just one of you. When you're working in a team, it gets even worse, with everybody making independent changes and getting in each other's way.

When you have a problem, you need a way to know what changed and when, and who did it. And you also need to be able to set your configuration back to any previously stable state.

Wouldn't it be nice if you could go back in time?

Why not just write shell scripts?

Many people manage configuration with shell scripts, which is better than doing it manually, but not much. Some of the problems with shell scripts include the following:

- Fragile and non-portable
- Hard to maintain
- Not easy to read as documentation
- Very site-specific
- Not a good programming language
- Hard to apply changes to existing servers

Why not just use containers?

Containers! Is there any word more thrilling to the human soul? Many people feel as though containers are going to make configuration management problems just go away. This feeling rarely lasts beyond the first few hours of trying to containerize an app. Yes, containers make it easy to deploy and manage software, but where do containers come from? It turns out someone has to build and maintain them, and that means managing Dockerfiles, volumes, networks, clusters, image repositories, dependencies, and so on. In other words, configuration. There is an axiom of computer science which I just invented, called *The Law of Conservation of Pain*. If you save yourself pain in one place, it pops up again in another. Whatever cool new technology comes along, it won't solve all our problems; at best, it will replace them with refreshingly different problems.

Yes, containers are great, but the truth is, container-based systems require even more configuration management. You need to configure the nodes that run the containers, build and update the container images based on a central policy, create and maintain the container network and clusters, and so on.

Why not just use serverless?

If containers are powered by magic pixies, serverless architectures are pure fairy dust. The promise is that you just push your app to the cloud, and the cloud takes care of deploying, scaling, load balancing, monitoring, and so forth. Like most things, the reality doesn't quite live up to the marketing. Unfortunately, serverless isn't actually serverless: it just means your business is running on servers you don't have direct control over, plus, you have higher fixed costs because you're paying someone else to run them for you. Serverless can be a good way to get started, but it's not a long-term solution, because ultimately, you need to own your own configuration.

Configuration management tools

Configuration management (**CM**) tools are the modern, sensible way to manage infrastructure as code. There are many such tools available, all of which operate more or less the same way: you specify your desired configuration state, using editable text files and a model of the system's resources, and the tool compares the current state of each **node** (the term we use for configuration-managed servers) with your desired state and makes any changes necessary to bring it in line.

As with most unimportant things, there is a great deal of discussion and argument on the Internet about which CM tool is the best. While there are significant differences in approaches and capabilities between different tools, don't let that obscure the fact that using a tool of any sort to manage configuration is much better than trying to do it by hand.

That said, while there are many CM tools available, Puppet is an excellent choice. No other tool is more powerful, more portable, or more widely adopted. In this book, I'm going to show you what makes Puppet so good and the things that only Puppet can do.

What is Puppet?

Puppet is two things: a language for expressing the desired state (how your nodes should be configured), and an engine that interprets code written in the Puppet language and applies it to the nodes to bring about the desired state.

What does this language look like? It's not exactly a series of instructions, like a shell script or a Ruby program. It's more like a set of declarations about the way things should be. Have a look at the following example:

```
package { 'curl':
  ensure => installed,
}
```

In English, this code says, "The `curl` package should be installed." When you apply this manifest (Puppet programs are called manifests), the tool will do the following:

1. Check the list of installed packages on the node to see if `curl` is already installed.
2. If it is, do nothing.
3. If not, install it.

Here's another example of Puppet code:

```
user { 'bridget':
  ensure => present,
}
```

This is Puppet language for the declaration, "The `bridget` user should be present." (The keyword `ensure` means "the desired state of the resource is..."). Again, this results in Puppet checking for the existence of the `bridget` user on the node, and creating it if necessary. This is also a kind of documentation that expresses human-readable statements about the system in a formal way. The code expresses the author's desire that Bridget should always be present.

So you can see that the Puppet program—the Puppet **manifest**—for your configuration is a set of declarations about what things should exist, and how they should be configured.

You don't give commands, like "Do this, then do that". Rather, you describe how things should be, and let Puppet take care of making it happen. These are two quite different kinds of programming. One kind (so-called procedural style) is the traditional model used by languages such as C, Python, shell, and so on. Puppet's is called declarative style because you declare what the end result should be, rather than specify the steps to get there.

This means that you can apply the same Puppet manifest repeatedly to a node and the end result will be the same, no matter how many times you apply the manifest. It's better to think of Puppet manifests as a kind of specification, or declaration, rather than as a program in the traditional sense.

Resources and attributes

Puppet lets you describe configuration in terms of **resources** (types of things that can exist, such as users, files, or packages) and their **attributes** (appropriate properties for the type of resource, such as the home directory for a user, or the owner and permissions for a file). You don't have to get into the details of how resources are created and configured on different platforms. Puppet takes care of it.

The power of this approach is that a given manifest can be applied to different nodes, all running different operating systems, and the results will be the same everywhere.

Puppet architectures

It's worth noting that there are two different ways to use Puppet. The first way, known as **agent/master architecture**, uses a special node dedicated to running Puppet, which all other nodes contact to get their configuration.

The other way, known as **stand-alone Puppet** or **masterless**, does not need a special Puppet master node. Puppet runs on each individual node and does not need to contact a central location to get its configuration. Instead, you use Git, or any other way of copying files to the node, such as SFTP or `rsync`, to update the Puppet manifests on each node.

Both stand-alone and agent/master architectures are officially supported by Puppet. It's your choice which one you prefer to use. In this book, I will cover only the stand-alone architecture, which is simpler and easier for most organizations, but almost everything in the book will work just the same whether you use agent/master or stand-alone Puppet.

To set up Puppet with an agent/master architecture, consult the official Puppet documentation.

Getting ready for Puppet

Although Puppet is inherently cross-platform and works with many different operating systems, for the purposes of this book, I'm going to focus on just one operating system, namely the **Ubuntu 16.04 LTS** distribution of Linux, and the most recent version of Puppet, Puppet 5. However, all the examples in the book should work on any recent operating system or Puppet version with only minor changes.

You will probably find that the best way to read this book is to follow along with the examples using a Linux machine of your own. It doesn't matter whether this is a physical server, desktop or laptop, cloud instance, or a virtual machine. I'm going to use the popular Vagrant software to run a virtual machine on my own computer, and you can do the same. The public GitHub repository for this book contains a Vagrantfile, which you can use to get up and running with Puppet in just a few steps.

Installing Git and downloading the repo

To get a copy of the repo that accompanies this book, follow these steps:

1. Browse to `https://git-scm.com/downloads`
2. Download and install the right version of Git for your operating system.
3. Run the following command:

```
git clone https://github.com/bitfield/puppet-beginners-guide-3.git
```

Installing VirtualBox and Vagrant

If you already have a Linux machine or cloud server you'd like to use for working through the examples, skip this section and move on to the next chapter. If you'd like to use VirtualBox and Vagrant to run a local **virtual machine (VM)** on your computer to use with the examples, follow these instructions:

1. Browse to `https://www.virtualbox.org/`
2. Download and install the right version of VirtualBox for your operating system
3. Browse to `https://www.vagrantup.com/downloads.html`
4. Select the right version of Vagrant for your operating system: OS X, Windows, and so on
5. Follow the instructions to install the software

Running your Vagrant VM

Once you have installed Vagrant, you can start the Puppet Beginner's Guide virtual machine:

1. Run the following commands:

   ```
   cd puppet-beginners-guide-3
   scripts/start_vagrant.sh
   ```

   Vagrant will begin downloading the base box. Once that has booted, it will install Puppet. This may take a while, but once the installation is complete, the virtual machine will be ready to use.

2. Connect to the VM with the following command:

   ```
   vagrant ssh
   ```

3. You now have a command-line shell on the VM. Check that Puppet is installed and working by running the following command (you may get a different version number, which is fine):

   ```
   puppet --version
   5.2.0
   ```

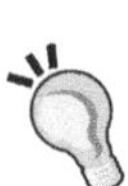

> If you're using Windows, you may need to install the PuTTY software to connect to your VM. There is some helpful advice about using Vagrant on Windows at:
>
> `http://tech.osteel.me/posts/2015/01/25/how-to-use-vagrant-on-windows.html`

Troubleshooting Vagrant

If you have any problems running the VM, look for help on the VirtualBox or Vagrant websites. In particular, if you have an older machine, you may see a message like the following:

```
VT-x/AMD-V hardware acceleration is not available on your system. Your
64-bit guest will fail to detect a 64-bit CPU and will not be able to
boot.
```

Your computer may have a BIOS setting to enable 64-bit hardware virtualization (depending on the manufacturer, the trade name for this is either **VT-x** or **AMD-V**). Enabling this feature may fix the problem. If not, you can try the 32-bit version of the Vagrant box instead. Edit the file named `Vagrantfile` in the Git repository, and comment out the following line with a leading # character:

```
config.vm.box = "ubuntu/xenial64"
```

Uncomment the following line by removing the leading # character:

```
# config.vm.box = "ubuntu/xenial32"
```

Now re-run the `scripts/start_vagrant.sh` command.

Summary

In this chapter, we looked at the various problems that configuration management tools can help solve, and how Puppet in particular models the aspects of system configuration. We checked out the Git repository of example code for this book, installed VirtualBox and Vagrant, started the Vagrant VM, and ran Puppet for the first time.

In the next chapter, we'll write our first Puppet manifests, get some insight into the structure of Puppet resources and how they're applied, and learn about the `package`, `file`, and `service` resources.

2
Creating your first manifests

> *Beginnings are such delicate times.*
>
> *—Frank Herbert, 'Dune'*

In this chapter, you'll learn how to write your first manifest with Puppet, and how to put Puppet to work configuring a server. You'll also understand how Puppet compiles and applies a manifest. You'll see how to use Puppet to manage the contents of files, how to install packages, and how to control services.

Hello, Puppet – your first Puppet manifest

The first example program in any programming language, by tradition, prints `hello, world`. Although we can do that easily in Puppet, let's do something a little more ambitious, and have Puppet create a file on the server containing that text.

On your Vagrant box, run the following command:

```
sudo puppet apply /examples/file_hello.pp
Notice: Compiled catalog for ubuntu-xenial in environment production
in 0.07 seconds
Notice: /Stage[main]/Main/File[/tmp/hello.txt]/ensure: defined content
as '{md5}22c3683b094136c3398391ae71b20f04'
Notice: Applied catalog in 0.01 seconds
```

We can ignore the output from Puppet for the moment, but if all has gone well, we should be able to run the following command:

```
cat /tmp/hello.txt
hello, world
```

Understanding the code

Let's look at the example code to see what's going on (run `cat /example/file_hello.pp`, or open the file in a text editor):

```
file { '/tmp/hello.txt':
  ensure  => file,
  content => "hello, world\n",
}
```

The code term `file` begins a **resource declaration** for a `file` resource. A **resource** is some bit of configuration that you want Puppet to manage: for example, a file, user account, or package. A resource declaration follows this pattern:

```
RESOURCE_TYPE { TITLE:
  ATTRIBUTE => VALUE,
  ...
}
```

Resource declarations will make up almost all of your Puppet manifests, so it's important to understand exactly how they work:

- `RESOURCE_TYPE` indicates the type of resource you're declaring; in this case, it's a `file`.
- `TITLE` is the name that Puppet uses to identify the resource internally. Every resource must have a unique title. With `file` resources, it's usual for this to be the full path to the file: in this case, `/tmp/hello`.

The remainder of this block of code is a list of attributes that describe how the resource should be configured. The attributes available depend on the type of the resource. For a file, you can set attributes such as `content`, `owner`, `group`, and `mode`, but one attribute that every resource supports is `ensure`.

Again, the possible values for `ensure` are specific to the type of resource. In this case, we use `file` to indicate that we want a regular file, as opposed to a directory or symlink:

```
ensure  => file,
```

Next, to put some text in the file, we specify the `content` attribute:

```
content => "hello, world\n",
```

The `content` attribute sets the contents of a file to a string value you provide. Here, the contents of the file are declared to be `hello, world`, followed by a newline character (in Puppet strings, we write the newline character as `\n`).

Note that `content` specifies the entire content of the file; the string you provide will replace anything already in the file, rather than be appended to it.

Modifying existing files

What happens if the file already exists when Puppet runs and it contains something else? Will Puppet change it?

```
sudo sh -c 'echo "goodbye, world" >/tmp/hello.txt'
cat /tmp/hello.txt
goodbye, world
sudo puppet apply /examples/file_hello.pp
cat /tmp/hello.txt
hello, world
```

The answer is yes. If any attribute of the file, including its contents, doesn't match the manifest, Puppet will change it so that it does.

This can lead to some surprising results if you manually edit a file managed by Puppet. If you make changes to a file without also changing the Puppet manifest to match, Puppet will overwrite the file the next time it runs, and your changes will be lost.

So it's a good idea to add a comment to files that Puppet is managing: something like the following:

```
# This file is managed by Puppet - any manual edits will be lost
```

Add this to Puppet's copy of the file when you first deploy it, and it will remind you and others not to make manual changes.

Dry-running Puppet

Because you can't necessarily tell in advance what applying a Puppet manifest will change on the system, it's a good idea to do a dry run first. Adding the `--noop` flag to `puppet apply` will show you what Puppet would have done, without actually changing anything:

```
sudo sh -c 'echo "goodbye, world" >/tmp/hello.txt'
sudo puppet apply --noop /examples/file_hello.pp
Notice: Compiled catalog for ubuntu-xenial in environment production
in 0.04 seconds
Notice: /Stage[main]/Main/File[/tmp/hello.txt]/content: current_value
{md5}7678..., should be {md5}22c3... (noop)
```

Puppet decides whether or not a `file` resource needs updating, based on its MD5 hash sum. In the previous example, Puppet reports that the current value of the hash sum for `/tmp/hello.txt` is `7678...`, whereas according to the manifest, it should be `22c3...`. Accordingly, the file will be changed on the next Puppet run.

If you want to see what change Puppet would actually make to the file, you can use the `--show_diff` option:

```
sudo puppet apply --noop --show_diff /examples/file_hello.pp
Notice: Compiled catalog for ubuntu-xenial in environment production
in 0.04 seconds
Notice: /Stage[main]/Main/File[/tmp/hello.txt]/content:
--- /tmp/hello.txt      2017-02-13 02:27:13.186261355 -0800
+++ /tmp/puppet-file20170213-3671-2yynjt        2017-02-13
02:30:26.561834755 -0800
@@ -1 +1 @@
-goodbye, world
+hello, world
```

These options are very useful when you want to make sure that your Puppet manifest will affect only the things you're expecting it to—or, sometimes, when you want to check if something has been changed outside Puppet without actually undoing the change.

How Puppet applies the manifest

Here's how your manifest is processed. First, Puppet reads the manifest and the list of resources it contains (in this case, there's just one resource), and compiles these into a catalog (an internal representation of the desired state of the node).

Puppet then works through the catalog, applying each resource in turn:

1. First, it checks if the resource exists on the server. If not, Puppet creates it. In the example, we've declared that the file `/tmp/hello.txt` should exist. The first time you run `sudo puppet apply`, this won't be the case, so Puppet will create the file for you.
2. Then, for each resource, it checks the value of each attribute in the catalog against what actually exists on the server. In our example, there's just one attribute: `content`. We've specified that the content of the file should be `hello, world\n`. If the file is empty or contains something else, Puppet will overwrite the file with what the catalog says it should contain.

In this case, the file will be empty the first time you apply the catalog, so Puppet will write the string `hello, world\n` into it.

We'll go on to examine the `file` resource in much more detail in later chapters.

Creating a file of your own

Create your own manifest file (you can name it anything you like, so long as the file extension is `.pp`). Use a `file` resource to create a file on the server with any contents you like. Apply the manifest with Puppet and check that the file is created and contains the text you specified.

Edit the file directly and change the contents, then re-apply Puppet and check that it changes the file back to what the manifest says it should contain.

Managing packages

Another key resource type in Puppet is the **package**. A major part of configuring servers by hand involves installing packages, so we will also be using packages a lot in Puppet manifests. Although every operating system has its own package format, and different formats vary quite a lot in their capabilities, Puppet represents all these possibilities with a single `package` type. If you specify in your Puppet manifest that a given package should be installed, Puppet will use the appropriate package manager commands to install it on whatever platform it's running on.

As you've seen, all resource declarations in Puppet follow this form:

```
RESOURCE_TYPE { TITLE:
  ATTRIBUTE => VALUE,
  ...
}
```

`package` resources are no different. The `RESOURCE_TYPE` is `package`, and the only attribute you usually need to specify is `ensure`, and the only value it usually needs to take is `installed`:

```
package { 'cowsay':
  ensure => installed,
}
```

Try this example:

```
sudo puppet apply /examples/package.pp
Notice: Compiled catalog for ubuntu-xenial in environment production
in 0.52 seconds
Notice: /Stage[main]/Main/Package[cowsay]/ensure: created
Notice: Applied catalog in 29.53 seconds
```

Let's see whether `cowsay` is installed:

```
cowsay Puppet rules!
 _______________
< Puppet rules! >
 ---------------
        \   ^__^
         \  (oo)\_______
            (__)\       )\/\
                ||----w |
                ||     ||
```

Now that's a useful package!

How Puppet applies the manifest

The title of the `package` resource is `cowsay`, so Puppet knows that we're talking about a package named `cowsay`.

The `ensure` attribute governs the installation state of packages: unsurprisingly, `installed` tells Puppet that the package should be installed.

As we saw in the earlier example, Puppet processes this manifest by examining each resource in turn and checking its attributes on the server against those specified in the manifest. In this case, Puppet will look for the `cowsay` package to see whether it's installed. It is not, but the manifest says it should be, so Puppet carries out all the necessary actions to make reality match the manifest, which here means installing the package.

It's still early on in the book, but you can already do a great deal with Puppet! If you can install packages and manage the contents of files, you can get a very long way towards setting up any kind of server configuration you might need. If you were to stop reading right here (which would be a shame, but we're all busy people), you would still be able to use Puppet to automate a large part of the configuration work you will encounter. But Puppet can do much more.

Exercise

Create a manifest that uses the `package` resource to install any software you find useful for managing servers. Here are some suggestions: `tmux`, `sysdig`, `atop`, `htop`, and `dstat`.

Querying resources with the puppet resource

If you want to see what version of a package Puppet thinks you have installed, you can use the `puppet resource` tool:

```
puppet resource package openssl
package { 'openssl':
  ensure => '1.0.2g-1ubuntu4.8',
}
```

`puppet resource TYPE TITLE` will output a Puppet manifest representing the current state of the named resource on the system. If you leave out `TITLE`, you'll get a manifest for all the resources of the type `TYPE`. For example, if you run `puppet resource package`, you'll see the Puppet code for all the packages installed on the system.

`puppet resource` even has an interactive configuration feature. To use it, run the following command:

```
puppet resource -e package openssl
```

If you run this, Puppet will generate a manifest for the current state of the resource, and open it in an editor. If you now make changes and save it, Puppet will apply that manifest to make changes to the system. This is a fun little feature, but it would be rather time-consuming to do your entire configuration this way.

Services

The third most important Puppet resource type is the **service**: a long-running process that either does some continuous kind of work, or waits for requests and then acts on them. For example, on most systems, the `sshd` process runs all the time and listens for SSH login attempts.

Puppet models services with the `service` resource type. The `service` resources look like the following example (you can find this in `service.pp` in the `/examples/` directory. From now on, I'll just give the filename of each example, as they are all in the same directory):

```
service { 'sshd':
  ensure => running,
  enable => true,
}
```

The `ensure` parameter governs whether the service should be running or not. If its value is `running`, then as you might expect, Puppet will start the service if it is not running. If you set `ensure` to `stopped`, Puppet will stop the service if it is running.

Services may also be set to start when the system boots, using the `enable` parameter. If `enable` is set to `true`, the service will start at boot. If, on the other hand, `enable` is set to `false`, it will not. Generally speaking, unless there's a good reason not to, all services should be set to start at boot.

Getting help on resources with puppet describe

If you're struggling to remember all the different attributes of all the different resources, Puppet has a built-in help feature that will remind you. Run the following command, for example:

```
puppet describe service
```

This will give a description of the `service` resource, along with a complete list of attributes and allowed values. This works for all built-in resource types as well as many provided by third-party modules. To see a list of all the available resource types, run the following command:

```
puppet describe --list
```

The package-file-service pattern

It's very common for a given piece of software to require these three Puppet resource types: the `package` resource installs the software, the `file` resource deploys one or more configuration files required for the software, and the `service` resource runs the software itself.

Here's an example using the MySQL database server (`package_file_service.pp`):

```
package { 'mysql-server':
  ensure => installed,
  notify => Service['mysql'],
}

file { '/etc/mysql/mysql.cnf':
  source => '/examples/files/mysql.cnf',
  notify => Service['mysql'],
}

service { 'mysql':
  ensure => running,
  enable => true,
}
```

The `package` resource makes sure the `mysql-server` package is installed.

The config file for MySQL is `/etc/mysql/mysql.cnf`, and we use a `file` resource to copy this file from the Puppet repo so that we can control MySQL settings.

Finally, the `service` resource ensures that the `mysql` service is running.

Notifying a linked resource

You might have noticed a new attribute, called `notify`, in the `file` resource in the previous example:

```
file { '/etc/mysql/mysql.cnf':
  source => '/examples/files/mysql.cnf',
  notify => Service['mysql'],
}
```

What does this do? Imagine you've made a change to the `mysql.cnf` file and applied this change with Puppet. The updated file will be written to a disk, but because the `mysql` service is already running, it has no way of knowing that its config file has changed. Therefore, your changes will not actually take effect until the service is restarted. However, Puppet can do this for you if you specify the `notify` attribute on the `file` resource. The value of `notify` is the resource to notify about the change, and what that involves depends on the type of resource that's being notified. When it's a service, the default action is to restart the service. (We'll find out about the other options in *Chapter 4, Understanding Puppet resources*.)

Usually, with the package-file-service pattern, the file notifies the service, so whenever Puppet changes the contents of the file, it will restart the notified service to pick up the new configuration. If there are several files that affect the service, they should all notify the service, and Puppet is smart enough to only restart the service once, however many dependent resources are changed.

The name of the resource to notify is specified as the resource type, capitalized, followed by the resource title, which is quoted and within square brackets: `Service['mysql']`.

Resource ordering with require

In the package-file-service example, we declared three resources: the `mysql-server` package, the `/etc/mysql/mysql.cnf` file, and the `mysql` service. If you think about it, they need to be applied in that order. Without the `mysql-server` package installed, there will be no `/etc/mysql/` directory to put the `mysql.cnf` file in. Without the package or the config file, the `mysql` service won't be able to run.

A perfectly reasonable question to ask is, "Does Puppet apply resources in the same order in which they're declared in the manifest?" The answer is usually yes, unless you explicitly specify a different order, using the `require` attribute.

All resources support the `require` attribute, and its value is the name of another resource declared somewhere in the manifest, specified in the same way as when using `notify`. Here's the package-file-service example again, this time with the resource ordering specified explicitly using `require` (`package_file_service_require.pp`):

```
package { 'mysql-server':
  ensure => installed,
}

file { '/etc/mysql/mysql.cnf':
  source  => '/examples/files/mysql.cnf',
  notify  => Service['mysql'],
```

```
    require => Package['mysql-server'],
  }

  service { 'mysql':
    ensure  => running,
    enable  => true,
    require => [Package['mysql-server'], File['/etc/mysql/mysql.cnf']],
  }
```

You can see that the `mysql.cnf` resource requires the `mysql-server` package. The `mysql` service requires both the other resources, listed as an array within square brackets.

When resources are already in the right order, you don't need to use `require`, as Puppet will apply the resources in the order you declare them. However, it can be useful to specify an ordering explicitly, for the benefit of those reading the code, especially when there are lots of resources in a manifest file.

In older versions of Puppet, resources were applied in a more or less arbitrary order, so it was much more important to express dependencies using `require`. Nowadays, you won't need to use it very much, and you'll mostly come across it in legacy code.

Summary

In this chapter, we've seen how a manifest is made up of Puppet resources. You've learned how to use Puppet's `file` resource to create and modify files, how to install packages using the `package` resource, and how to manage services with the `service` resource. We've looked at the common package-file-service pattern and seen how to use the `notify` attribute on a resource to send a message to another resource indicating that its configuration has been updated. We've covered the use of the `require` attribute to make dependencies between resources explicit, when necessary.

You've also learned to use `puppet resource` to inspect the current state of the system according to Puppet, and `puppet describe` to get command-line help on all Puppet resources. To check what Puppet would change on the system without actually changing it, we've introduced the `--noop` and `--show_diff` options to `puppet apply`.

In the next chapter, we'll see how to use the version control tool Git to keep track of your manifests, we'll get an introduction to fundamental Git concepts, such as the repo and the commit, and you'll learn how to distribute your code to each of the servers you're going to manage with Puppet.

3

Managing your Puppet code with Git

We define ourselves by our actions. With each decision, we tell ourselves and the world who we are.

—Bill Watterson

In this chapter, you'll learn how to use the Git version control system to manage your Puppet manifests. I'll also show you how to use Git to distribute the manifests to multiple nodes, so that you can start managing your whole network with Puppet.

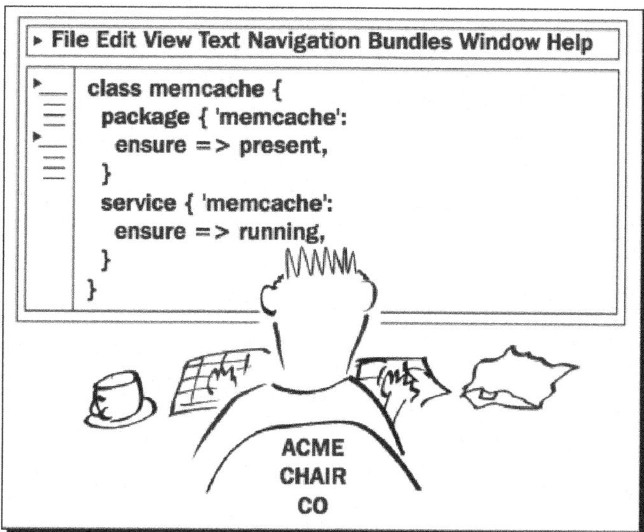

What is version control?

If you're already familiar with Git, you can save some reading by skipping ahead to the *Creating a Git repo* section. If not, here's a gentle introduction.

Even if you're the only person who works on a piece of source code (for example, Puppet manifests), it's still useful to be able to see what changes you made, and when. For example, you might realize that you introduced a bug at some point in the past, and you need to examine exactly when a certain file was modified and exactly what the change was. A version control system lets you do that, by keeping a complete history of the changes you've made to a set of files over time.

Tracking changes

When you're working on code with others, you also need a way to communicate with the rest of the team about your changes. A version control tool such as Git not only tracks everyone's changes, but lets you record a **commit message**, explaining what you did and why. The following example illustrates some aspects of a good commit message:

```
Summarize changes in around 50 characters or less

More detailed explanatory text, if necessary. Wrap it to about 72
characters or so. In some contexts, the first line is treated as
the subject of the commit and the rest of the text as the body.
The blank line separating the summary from the body is critical
(unless you omit the body entirely); various tools like `log`,
`shortlog`, and `rebase` can get confused if you run the two together.

Explain the problem that this commit is solving. Focus on why you
are making this change as opposed to how (the code explains that).
Are there side effects or other unintuitive consequences of this
change? Here's the place to explain them.

Further paragraphs come after blank lines.

 - Bullet points are okay, too

 - Typically a hyphen or asterisk is used for the bullet, preceded
   by a single space, with blank lines in between, but conventions
   vary here

If you use an issue tracker, put references to them at the bottom,
like this:

Resolves: #123
See also: #456, #789
```

> This example is taken from Chris Beams' excellent blog post on *How to Write a Git Commit Message*:
>
> `https://chris.beams.io/posts/git-commit/`
>
> Of course, you won't often need such a long and detailed message; most of the time, a single line will suffice. However, it's better to give more information than less.

Git also records when the change happened, who made it, what files were changed, added, or deleted, and which lines were added, altered, or removed. As you can imagine, if you're trying to track down a bug, and you can see a complete history of changes to the code, that's a big help. It also means you can, if necessary, roll back the state of the code to any point in history and examine it.

You might think this introduces a lot of extra complication. In fact, it's very simple. Git keeps out of your way until you need it, and all you have to do is write a commit message when you decide to record changes to the code.

Sharing code

A set of files under Git version control is called a **repository**, which is usually equivalent to a project. A Git repository (from now on, just **repo**) is also a great way to distribute your code to others, whether privately or publicly, so that they can use it, modify it, contribute changes back to you, or develop it in a different direction for their own requirements. The public GitHub repo for this book which we looked at in *Chapter 1, Getting started with Puppet* is a good example of this. You'll be able to use this repo for working through examples throughout the book, but you can also use it for help and inspiration when building Puppet manifests for your own infrastructure.

Because Git is so important for managing Puppet code, it's a good idea to get familiar with it, and the only way to do that is to use it for real. So let's start a new Git repo we can use to experiment with.

Creating a Git repo

It's very easy to create a Git repo. Follow these steps:

1. Make a directory to hold your versioned files using the following commands:

   ```
   cd
   mkdir puppet
   ```

2. Now run the following commands to turn the directory into a Git repo:

   ```
   cd puppet
   git init
   Initialized empty Git repository in /home/ubuntu/puppet/.git/
   ```

Making your first commit

You can change the files in your repo as much as you like, but Git will not know about the changes until you make what's called a **commit**. You can think of a commit as being like a snapshot of the repo at a particular moment, but it also stores information about what changed in the repo since the previous commit. Commits are stored forever, so you will always be able to roll back the repo to the state it was in at a certain commit, or show what files were changed in a past commit and compare them to the state of the repo at any other commit.

Let's make our first commit to the new repo:

1. Because Git records not only changes to the code, but also who made them, it needs to know who you are. Set your identification details for Git (use your own name and email address, unless you particularly prefer mine) using the following commands:

   ```
   git config --global user.name "John Arundel"
   git config --global user.email john@bitfieldconsulting.com
   ```

2. It's traditional for Git repos to have a `README` file, which explains what's in the repo and how to use it. For the moment, let's just create this file with a placeholder message:

   ```
   echo "Watch this space... coming soon!" >README.md
   ```

3. Run the following command:

   ```
   git status
   On branch master
   Initial commit
   Untracked files:
     (use "git add <file>..." to include in what will be committed)
          README.md
   nothing added to commit but untracked files present (use "git add"
   to track)
   ```

4. Because we've added a new file to the repo, changes to it won't be tracked by Git unless we explicitly tell it to. We do this by using the `git add` command, as follows:

   ```
   git add README.md
   ```

5. Git now knows about this file, and changes to it will be included in the next commit. We can check this by running `git status` again:

```
git status
On branch master
Initial commit
Changes to be committed:
  (use "git rm --cached <file>..." to unstage)
        new file:   README.md
```

6. The file is listed under `Changes to be committed`, so we can now actually make the commit:

```
git commit -m 'Add README file'
[master (root-commit) ee21595] Add README file
 1 file changed, 1 insertion(+)
 create mode 100644 README.md
```

7. You can always see the complete history of commits in a repo by using the `git log` command. Try it now to see the commit you just made:

```
git log
commit ee215951199158ef28dd78197d8fa9ff078b3579
Author: John Arundel <john@bitfieldconsulting.com>
Date:   Tue Aug 30 05:59:42 2016 -0700
    Add README file
```

How often should I commit?

A common practice is to commit when the code is in a consistent, working state, and have the commit include a set of related changes made for some particular purpose. So, for example, if you are working to fix bug number 75 in your issue-tracking system, you might make changes to quite a few separate files and then, once you're happy the work is complete, make a single commit with a message such as:

```
Make nginx restart more reliable (fixes issue #75)
```

On the other hand, if you are making a large number of complicated changes and you are not sure when you'll be done, it might be wise to make a few separate commits along the way, so that if necessary you can roll the code back to a previous state. Commits cost nothing, so when you feel a commit is needed, go ahead and make it.

Branching

Git has a powerful feature called **branching**, which lets you create a parallel copy of the code (a branch) and make changes to it independently. At any time, you can choose to merge those changes back into the master branch. Or, if changes have been made to the master branch in the meantime, you can incorporate those into your working branch and carry on.

This is extremely useful when working with Puppet, because it means you can switch a single node to your branch while you're testing it and working on it. The changes you make won't be visible to other nodes which aren't on your branch, so there's no danger of accidentally rolling out changes before you're ready.

Once you're done, you can merge your changes back into master and have them roll out to all nodes.

Similarly, two or more people can work independently on their own branches, exchanging individual commits with each other and with the master branch as they choose. This is a very flexible and useful way of working.

> For more information about Git branching, and indeed about Git in general, I recommend the excellent book '*Pro Git*', by *Scott Chacon* and *Ben Straub*, published by *Apress*. The whole book is available for free at: `https://git-scm.com/book/en/v2`

Distributing Puppet manifests

So far in this book we've only applied Puppet manifests to one node, using `puppet apply` with a local copy of the manifest. To manage several nodes at once, we need to distribute the Puppet manifests to each node so that they can be applied.

There are several ways to do this, and as we saw in *Chapter 1, Getting started with Puppet*, one approach is to use the **agent/master** architecture, where a central Puppet master server compiles your manifests and distributes the **catalog** (the desired node state) to all nodes.

Another way to use Puppet is to do without the master server altogether, and use Git to distribute manifests to client nodes, which then runs `puppet apply` to update their configuration. This **stand-alone** Puppet architecture doesn't require a dedicated Puppet master server, and there's no single point of failure.

Both agent/master and stand-alone architectures are officially supported by Puppet, and it's possible to change from one to the other if you decide you need to. The examples in this book were developed with the stand-alone architecture, but will work just as well with agent/master if you prefer it. There is no difference in the Puppet manifests, language, or structure; the only difference is in the way the manifests are applied.

All you need for a stand-alone Puppet architecture is a Git server which each node can connect to and clone the repo. You can run your own Git server if you like, or use a public Git hosting service such as GitHub. For ease of explanation, I'm going to use GitHub for this example setup.

In the following sections, we'll create a GitHub account, push our new Puppet repo to GitHub, and then set up our virtual machine to automatically pull any changes from the GitHub repo and apply them with Puppet.

Creating a GitHub account and project

If you already have a GitHub account, or you're using another Git server, you can skip this section.

1. Browse to `https://github.com/`
2. Enter the username you want to use, your email address, and a password.
3. Choose the **Unlimited public repositories for free** plan.
4. GitHub will send you an email to verify your email address. When you get the email, click on the verification link.
5. Select **Start a project**.
6. Enter a name for your repo (I suggest `puppet`, but it doesn't matter).
7. Free GitHub accounts can only create public repos, so select **Public**.

> Be careful what information you put into a public Git repo, because it can be read by anybody. Never put passwords, login credentials, private keys, or other confidential information into a repo like this unless it is encrypted. We'll see how to encrypt secret information in your Puppet repo in *Chapter 6, Managing data with Hiera*.

8. Click **Create repository**.

9. GitHub will show you a page of instructions about how to initialize or import code into your new repository. Look for the `https` URL which identifies your repo; it will be something like this (`https://github.com/pbgtest/puppet.git`):

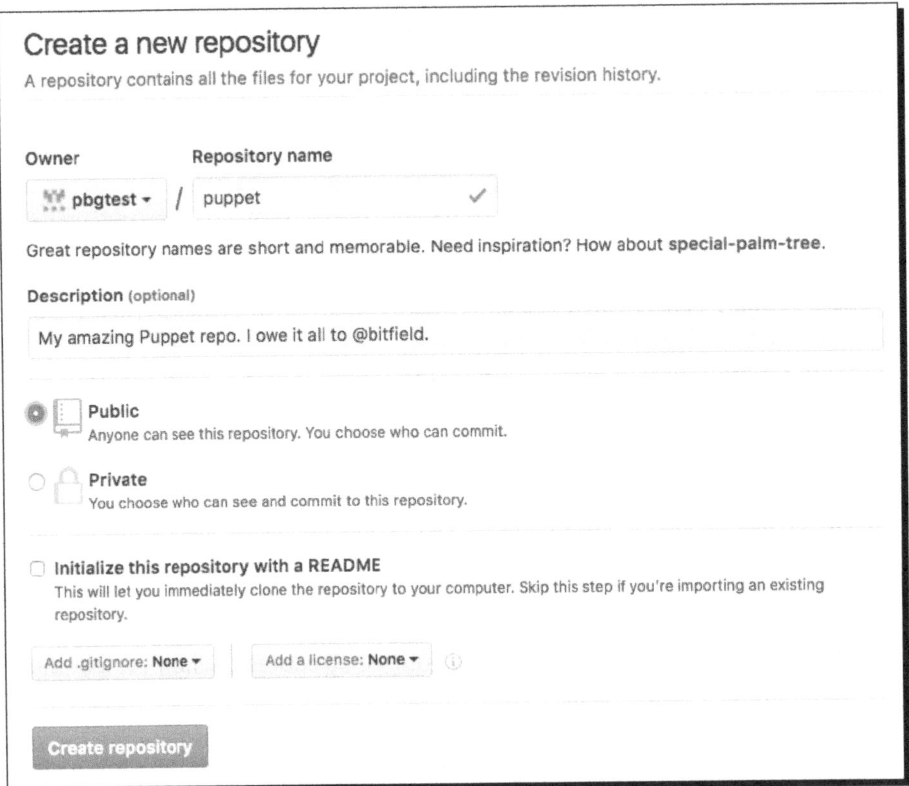

Pushing your repo to GitHub

You're now ready to take the Git repo you created locally earlier in this chapter and push it to GitHub so that you can share it with other nodes.

1. In your repo directory, run the following commands. After `git remote add origin`, specify the URL to your GitHub repo:

```
git remote add origin YOUR_REPO_URL
git push -u origin master
```

2. GitHub will prompt you for your username and password:

```
Username for 'https://github.com': pbgtest
Password for 'https://pbgtest@github.com':
Counting objects: 3, done.
Writing objects: 100% (3/3), 262 bytes | 0 bytes/s, done.
```

```
Total 3 (delta 0), reused 0 (delta 0)
To https://github.com/pbgtest/puppet.git
 * [new branch]      master -> master
Branch master set up to track remote branch master from origin.
```

3. You can check that everything has worked properly by visiting the repo URL in your browser. It should look something like this:

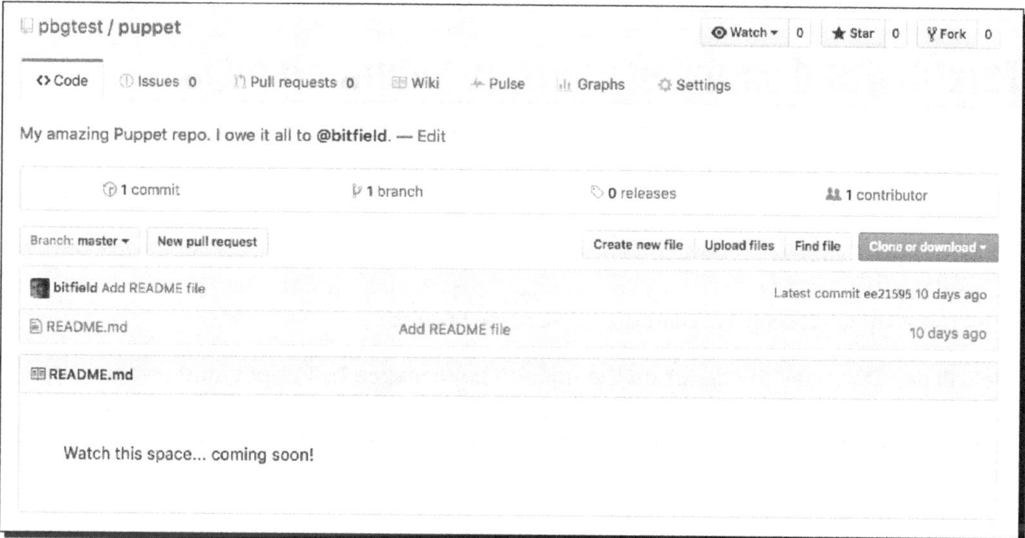

Cloning the repo

In order to manage multiple nodes with Puppet, you will need a copy of the repo on each node. If you have a node you'd like to manage with Puppet, you can use it in this example. Otherwise, use the Vagrant box we've been working with in previous chapters.

Run the following commands (replace the argument to `git clone` with the URL of your own GitHub repo, but don't lose the `production` at the end):

```
cd /etc/puppetlabs/code/environments
sudo mv production production.sample
sudo git clone YOUR_REPO_URL production
Cloning into 'production'...
remote: Counting objects: 3, done.
remote: Total 3 (delta 0), reused 3 (delta 0), pack-reused 0
Unpacking objects: 100% (3/3), done.
Checking connectivity... done.
```

How does this work? The standard place for Puppet manifests in a production environment is the `/etc/puppetlabs/code/environments/production/` directory, so that's where our cloned repo needs to end up. However, the Puppet package installs some sample manifests in that directory, and Git will refuse to clone into a directory that already exists, so we move that directory out of the way with the `mv production production.sample` command. The `git clone` command then recreates that directory, but this time it contains our manifests from the repo.

Fetching and applying changes automatically

In a stand-alone Puppet architecture, each node needs to automatically fetch any changes from the Git repo at regular intervals, and apply them with Puppet. We can use a simple shell script for this, and there's one in the example repo (`/examples/files/run-puppet.sh`):

```
#!/bin/bash
cd /etc/puppetlabs/code/environments/production && git pull
/opt/puppetlabs/bin/puppet apply manifests/
```

We will need to install this script on the node to be managed by Puppet, and create a cron job to run it regularly (I suggest every 15 minutes). Of course, we could do this work manually, but isn't this book partly about the advantages of automation? Very well, then: let's practice what we're preaching.

Writing a manifest to set up regular Puppet runs

In this section, we'll create the necessary Puppet manifests to install the `run-puppet` script on a node and run it regularly from cron:

1. Run the following commands to create the required directories in your Puppet repo:

   ```
   cd /home/ubuntu/puppet
   mkdir manifests files
   ```

2. Run the following command to copy the `run-puppet` script from the `examples/` directory:

   ```
   cp /examples/files/run-puppet.sh files/
   ```

3. Run the following command to copy the `run-puppet` manifest from the `examples/` directory:

   ```
   cp /ubuntu/examples/run-puppet.pp manifests/
   ```

4. Add and commit the files to Git with the following commands:

   ```
   git add manifests files
   git commit -m 'Add run-puppet script and cron job'
   git push origin master
   ```

Your Git repo now contains everything you need to automatically pull and apply changes on your managed nodes. In the next section, we'll see how to set up this process on a node.

> You might have noticed that every time you push files to your GitHub repo, Git prompts you for your username and password. If you want to avoid this, you can associate an SSH key with your GitHub account. Once you've done this, you'll be able to push without having to re-enter your credentials every time. For more information about using an SSH key with your GitHub account see this article:
> `https://help.github.com/articles/adding-a-new-ssh-key-to-your-github-account/`

Applying the run-puppet manifest

Having created and pushed the manifest necessary to set up automatic Puppet runs, we now need to pull and apply it on the target node.

In the cloned copy of your repo in `/etc/puppetlabs/code/environments/production`, run the following commands:

```
sudo git pull
sudo puppet apply manifests/
Notice: Compiled catalog for localhost in environment production in
0.08 seconds
Notice: /Stage[main]/Main/File[/usr/local/bin/run-puppet]/ensure:
defined content as '{md5}83a6903e69564bcecc8fd1a83b1a7beb'
Notice: /Stage[main]/Main/Cron[run-puppet]/ensure: created
Notice: Applied catalog in 0.07 seconds
```

You can see from Puppet's output that it has created the `/usr/local/bin/run-puppet` script and the `run-puppet` cron job. This will now run automatically every 15 minutes, pull any new changes from the Git repo, and apply the updated manifest.

The run-puppet script

The `run-puppet` script does the following two things in order to automatically update the target node:

1. Pull any changes from the Git server (`git pull`).
2. Apply the manifest (`puppet apply`).

Our Puppet manifest in `run-puppet.pp` deploys this script to the target node, using a `file` resource, and then sets up a cron job to run it every 15 minutes, using a `cron` resource. We haven't met the `cron` resource before, but we will cover it in more detail in *Chapter 4, Understanding Puppet resources*.

For now, just note that the `cron` resource has a name (`run-puppet`), which is just for the benefit of us humans, to remind us what it does, and it also has a `command` to run and `hour` and `minute` attributes to control when it runs. The value `*/15` tells `cron` to run the job every 15 minutes.

Testing automatic Puppet runs

To prove that the automatic Puppet run works, make a change to your manifest which creates a file (`/tmp/hello.txt`, for example). Commit and push this change to Git. Wait 15 minutes, and check your target node. The file should be present. If not, something is broken. To troubleshoot the problem, try running `sudo run-puppet` manually. If this works, check that the cron job is correctly installed by running `sudo crontab -l`. It should look something like the following:

```
# HEADER: This file was autogenerated at 2017-04-05 01:46:03 -0700 by
puppet.
# HEADER: While it can still be managed manually, it is definitely not
recommended.
# HEADER: Note particularly that the comments starting with 'Puppet
Name' should
# HEADER: not be deleted, as doing so could cause duplicate cron jobs.
# Puppet Name: run-puppet
*/15 * * * * /usr/local/bin/run-puppet
```

Managing multiple nodes

You now have a fully automated stand-alone Puppet infrastructure. Any change that you check in to your Git repo will be automatically applied to all nodes under Puppet management. To add more nodes to your infrastructure, follow these steps for each new node:

1. Install Puppet (not necessary if you're using the Vagrant box).
2. Clone your Git repo (as described in the *Cloning the repo* section).
3. Apply the manifest (as described in the *Applying the run-puppet manifest* section).

You might be wondering how to tell Puppet how to apply different manifests to different nodes. For example, you might be managing two nodes, one of which is a web server and the other a database server. Naturally, they will need different resources.

We'll learn more about nodes and how to control the application of resources to different nodes in *Chapter 8, Classes, roles, and profiles*, but first, we need to learn about Puppet's resources and how to use them. We'll do that in the next chapter.

Summary

In this chapter, we introduced the concepts of version control, and the essentials of Git in particular. We set up a new Git repo, created a GitHub account, pushed our code to it, and cloned it on a node. We wrote a shell script to automatically pull and apply changes from the GitHub repo on any node, and a Puppet manifest to install this script and run it regularly from `cron`.

In the next chapter, we'll explore the power of Puppet resources, going into more detail about the Puppet `file`, `package`, and `service` resources we've already encountered, and introducing three more important resource types: `user`, `cron`, and `exec`.

4

Understanding Puppet resources

> *Perplexity is the beginning of knowledge.*
>
> *—Khalil Gibran*

We've already met three important types of Puppet resources: `package`, `file`, and `service`. In this chapter, we'll learn more about these, plus other important resource types for managing users, groups, SSH keys, cron jobs, and arbitrary commands.

Files

We saw in *Chapter 2, Creating your first manifests* that Puppet can manage files on a node using the `file` resource, and we looked at an example which sets the contents of a file to a particular string using the `content` attribute. Here it is again (`file_hello.pp`):

```
file { '/tmp/hello.txt':
  content => "hello, world\n",
}
```

The path attribute

We've seen that every Puppet resource has a title (a quoted string followed by a colon). In the `file_hello` example, the title of the `file` resource is `'/tmp/hello.txt'`. It's easy to guess that Puppet is going to use this value as the path of the created file. In fact, `path` is one of the attributes you can specify for a `file`, but if you don't specify it, Puppet will use the title of the resource as the value of `path`.

Managing whole files

While it's useful to be able to set the contents of a file to a short text string, most files we're likely to want to manage will be too large to include directly in our Puppet manifests. Ideally, we would put a copy of the file in the Puppet repo, and have Puppet simply copy it to the desired place in the filesystem. The `source` attribute does exactly that (`file_source.pp`):

```
file { '/etc/motd':
  source => '/examples/files/motd.txt',
}
```

To try this example with your Vagrant box, run the following commands:

```
sudo puppet apply /examples/file_source.pp
cat /etc/motd
The best software in the world only sucks. The worst software is
significantly worse than that.
-Luke Kanies
```

(From now on, I won't give you explicit instructions on how to run the examples; just apply them in the same way using `sudo puppet apply` as shown here. All the examples in this book are in the `examples/` directory of the GitHub repo, and I'll give you the name of the appropriate file for each example, such as `file_source.pp`.)

[Why do we have to run `sudo puppet apply` instead of just `puppet apply`? Puppet has the permissions of the user who runs it, so if Puppet needs to modify a file owned by `root`, it must be run with `root`'s permissions (which is what `sudo` does). You will usually run Puppet as `root` because it needs those permissions to do things like installing packages, modifying config files owned by `root`, and so on.]

The value of the `source` attribute can be a path to a file on the node, as here, or an HTTP URL, as in the following example (`file_http.pp`):

```
file { '/tmp/README.md':
  source => 'https://raw.githubusercontent.com/puppetlabs/puppet/
master/README.md',
}
```

Although this is a handy feature, bear in mind that every time you add an external dependency like this to your Puppet manifest, you're adding a potential point of failure.

[Wherever you can, use a local copy of a file instead of having Puppet fetch it remotely every time. This particularly applies to software which needs to be built from a tarball downloaded from a website. If possible, download the tarball and serve it from a local webserver or file server. If this isn't practical, using a caching proxy server can help save time and bandwidth when you're building a large number of nodes.]

Ownership

On Unix-like systems, files are associated with an **owner**, a **group**, and a set of **permissions** to read, write, or execute the file. Since we normally run Puppet with the permissions of the `root` user (via `sudo`), the files Puppet manages will be owned by that user:

```
ls -l /etc/motd
-rw-r--r-- 1 root root 109 Aug 31 04:03 /etc/motd
```

Often, this is just fine, but if we need the file to belong to another user (for example, if that user needs to be able to write to the file), we can express this by setting the `owner` attribute (`file_owner.pp`):

```
file { '/etc/owned_by_ubuntu':
  ensure => present,
  owner  => 'ubuntu',
}
```

```
ls -l /etc/owned_by_ubuntu
-rw-r--r-- 1 ubuntu root 0 Aug 31 04:48 /etc/owned_by_ubuntu
```

You can see that Puppet has created the file and its owner has been set to `ubuntu`. You can also set the group ownership of the file using the `group` attribute (`file_group.pp`):

```
file { '/etc/owned_by_ubuntu':
  ensure => present,
  owner  => 'ubuntu',
  group  => 'ubuntu',
}
```

```
ls -l /etc/owned_by_ubuntu
-rw-r--r-- 1 ubuntu ubuntu 0 Aug 31 04:48 /etc/owned_by_ubuntu
```

Note that this time we didn't specify either a `content` or `source` attribute for the file, but simply `ensure => present`. In this case, Puppet will create a file of zero size.

Permissions

Files on Unix-like systems have an associated **mode** which determines access permissions for the file. It governs read, write, and execute permissions for the file's owner, any user in the file's group, and other users. Puppet supports setting permissions on files using the `mode` attribute. This takes an octal value (base 8, indicated by a leading 0 digit), with each digit representing a field of 3 binary bits: the permissions for owner, group, and other, respectively. In the following example, we use the `mode` attribute to set a mode of `0644` ("read and write for the owner, read-only for the group, and read-only for other users") on a file (`file_mode.pp`):

```
file { '/etc/owned_by_ubuntu':
  ensure => present,
  owner  => 'ubuntu',
  mode   => '0644',
}
```

This will be quite familiar to experienced system administrators, as the octal values for file permissions are exactly the same as those understood by the Unix `chmod` command. For more information, run the command `man chmod`.

Directories

Creating or managing permissions on a **directory** is a common task, and Puppet uses the `file` resource to do this too. If the value of the `ensure` attribute is `directory`, the file will be a directory (`file_directory.pp`):

```
file { '/etc/config_dir':
  ensure => directory,
}
```

As with regular files, you can use the `owner`, `group`, and `mode` attributes to control access to directories.

Trees of files

We've already seen that Puppet can copy a single file to the node, but what about a whole directory of files, possibly including subdirectories (known as a **file tree**)? The `recurse` attribute will take care of this (`file_tree.pp`):

```
file { '/etc/config_dir':
  source  => '/examples/files/config_dir',
  recurse => true,
}
```

```
ls /etc/config_dir/
1  2  3
```

When `recurse` is `true`, Puppet will copy all the files and directories (and their subdirectories) in the source directory (`/examples/files/config_dir/` in this example) to the target directory (`/etc/config_dir/`).

> If the target directory already exists and has files in it, Puppet will not interfere with them, but you can change this behavior using the `purge` attribute. If this is `true`, Puppet will delete any files and directories in the target directory which are not present in the source directory. Use this attribute with care.

Symbolic links

Another common requirement for managing files is to create or modify a **symbolic link** (known as a **symlink**, for short). You can have Puppet do this by setting `ensure => link` on the `file` resource and specifying the `target` attribute (`file_symlink.pp`):

```
file { '/etc/this_is_a_link':
  ensure => link,
  target => '/etc/motd',
}
```

```
ls -l /etc/this_is_a_link
lrwxrwxrwx 1 root root 9 Aug 31 05:05 /etc/this_is_a_link -> /etc/motd
```

Packages

We've already seen how to install a package using the `package` resource, and this is all you need to do with most packages. However, the `package` resource has a few extra features which may be useful.

Uninstalling packages

The `ensure` attribute normally takes the value `installed` in order to install a package, but if you specify `absent` instead, Puppet will **remove** the package if it happens to be installed. Otherwise, it will take no action. The following example will remove the `apparmor` package if it's installed (`package_remove.pp`):

```
package { 'apparmor':
  ensure => absent,
}
```

By default, when Puppet removes packages, it leaves in place any files managed by the package. To purge all the files associated with the package, use `purged` instead of `absent`.

Installing specific versions

If there are multiple versions of a package available to the system's package manager, specifying `ensure => installed` will cause Puppet to install the default version (usually the latest). But, if you need a specific version, you can specify that version string as the value of `ensure`, and Puppet will install that version (`package_version.pp`):

```
package { 'openssl':
  ensure => '1.0.2g-1ubuntu4.8',
}
```

It's a good idea to specify an exact version whenever you manage packages with Puppet, so that all the nodes will get the same version of a given package. Otherwise, if you use `ensure => installed`, they will just get whatever version was current at the time they were built, leading to a situation where different nodes have different package versions.

When a newer version of the package is released, and you decide it's time to upgrade to it, you can update the version string specified in the Puppet manifest and Puppet will upgrade the package everywhere.

Installing the latest version

On the other hand, if you specify `ensure => latest` for a package, Puppet will make sure that the latest available version is installed *every time the manifest is applied*. When a new version of the package becomes available, it will be installed automatically on the next Puppet run.

> This is not generally what you want when using a package repository that's not under your control (for example, the main Ubuntu repository). It means that packages will be upgraded at unexpected times, which may break your application (or at least result in unplanned downtime). A better strategy is to tell Puppet to install a specific version which you know works, and test upgrades in a controlled environment before rolling them out to production.

If you maintain your own package repository and control the release of new packages to it, `ensure => latest` can be a useful feature: Puppet will update a package as soon as you push a new version to the repo. If you are relying on upstream repositories, such as the Ubuntu repositories, it's better to manage the version number directly by specifying an explicit version as the value of `ensure`.

Installing Ruby gems

Although the `package` resource is most often used to install packages using the normal system package manager (in the case of Ubuntu, that's APT), it can install other kinds of packages as well. Library packages for the Ruby programming language are known as **gems**. Puppet can install Ruby gems for you using the `provider => gem` attribute (`package_gem.pp`):

```
package { 'ruby':
  ensure => installed,
}

package { 'puppet-lint':
  ensure   => installed,
  provider => gem,
}
```

`puppet-lint` is a Ruby gem and therefore we have to specify `provider => gem` for this package so that Puppet doesn't think it's a standard system package and try to install it via APT. Since the `gem` provider is not available unless Ruby is installed, we install the `ruby` package first, then the `puppet-lint` gem.

The `puppet-lint` tool, by the way, is a good thing to have installed. It will check your Puppet manifests for common style errors and make sure they comply with the official Puppet style guide. Try it now:

```
puppet-lint /examples/lint_test.pp
WARNING: indentation of => is not properly aligned (expected in column
11, but found it in column 10) on line 2
```

In this example, `puppet-lint` is warning you that the `=>` arrows are not lined up vertically, which the style guide says they should be:

```
file { '/tmp/lint.txt':
  ensure => file,
  content => "puppet-lint is your friend\n",
}
```

When `puppet-lint` produces no output, the file is free of lint errors.

Installing gems in Puppet's context

Puppet itself is written at least partly in Ruby, and makes use of several Ruby gems. To avoid any conflicts with the version of Ruby and gems which the node might need for other applications, Puppet packages its own version of Ruby and associated gems under the `/opt/puppetlabs/` directory. This means you can install (or remove) whichever system version of Ruby you like and Puppet will not be affected.

However, if you need to install a gem to extend Puppet's capabilities in some way, then doing it with a `package` resource and `provider => gem` won't work. That is, the gem will be installed, but only in the system Ruby context, and it won't be visible to Puppet.

Fortunately, the `puppet_gem` provider is available for exactly this purpose. When you use this provider, the gem will be installed in Puppet's context (and, naturally, won't be visible in the system context). The following example demonstrates how to use this provider (`package_puppet_gem.pp`):

```
package { 'r10k':
  ensure   => installed,
  provider => puppet_gem,
}
```

To see the gems installed in Puppet's context, use Puppet's own version of the `gem` command with the following path:

`/opt/puppetlabs/puppet/bin/gem list`

Using ensure_packages

To avoid potential package conflicts between different parts of your Puppet code or between your code and third-party modules, the Puppet standard library provides a useful wrapper for the `package` resource, called `ensure_packages()`. We'll cover this in detail in *Chapter 7, Mastering modules.*

Services

Although services are implemented in a number of varied and complicated ways at the operating system level, Puppet does a good job of abstracting away most of this with the `service` resource and exposing just the two attributes of services which you most commonly need to manage: whether they're running (`ensure`) and whether they start at boot time (`enable`). We covered the use of these in *Chapter 2, Creating your first manifests,* and most of the time, you won't need to know any more about `service` resources.

However, you'll occasionally encounter services which don't play well with Puppet, for a variety of reasons. Sometimes, Puppet is unable to detect that the service is already running and keeps trying to start it. Other times, Puppet may not be able to properly restart the service when a dependent resource changes. There are a few useful attributes for `service` resources which can help resolve these problems.

The hasstatus attribute

When a `service` resource has the attribute `ensure => running` attribute, Puppet needs to be able to check whether the service is, in fact, running. The way it does this depends on the underlying operating system. On Ubuntu 16 and later, for example, it runs `systemctl is-active SERVICE`. If the service is packaged to work with `systemd`, that should be just fine, but in many cases, particularly with older software, it may not respond properly.

If you find that Puppet keeps attempting to start the service on every Puppet run, even though the service is running, it may be that Puppet's default service status detection isn't working. In this case, you can specify the `hasstatus => false` attribute for the service (`service_hasstatus.pp`):

```
service { 'ntp':
  ensure    => running,
  enable    => true,
  hasstatus => false,
}
```

When hasstatus is false, Puppet knows not to try to check the service status using the default system service management command, and instead, will look in the process table for a running process which matches the name of the service. If it finds one, it will infer that the service is running and take no further action.

The pattern attribute

Sometimes, when using hasstatus => false, the service name as defined in Puppet doesn't actually appear in the process table, because the command that provides the service has a different name. If this is the case, you can tell Puppet exactly what to look for using the pattern attribute.

If hasstatus is false and pattern is specified, Puppet will search for the value of pattern in the process table to determine whether or not the service is running. To find the pattern you need, you can use the ps command to see the list of running processes:

```
ps ax
```

Find the process you're interested in and pick a string which will match only the name of that process. For example, if it's ntpd, you might specify the pattern attribute as ntpd (service_pattern.pp):

```
service { 'ntp':
  ensure    => running,
  enable    => true,
  hasstatus => false,
  pattern   => 'ntpd',
}
```

The hasrestart and restart attributes

When a service is notified (for example, if a file resource uses the notify attribute to tell the service its config file has changed, a common pattern which we looked at in *Chapter 2, Creating your first manifests*), Puppet's default behavior is to stop the service, then start it again. This usually works, but many services implement a restart command in their management scripts. If this is available, it's usually a good idea to use it: it may be faster or safer than stopping and starting the service. Some services take a while to shut down properly when stopped, for example, and Puppet may not wait long enough before trying to restart them, so that you end up with the service not running at all.

If you specify `hasrestart => true` for a service, then Puppet will try to send a `restart` command to it, using whatever service management command is appropriate for the current platform (`systemctl`, for example, on Ubuntu). The following example shows the use of `hasrestart` (`service_hasrestart.pp`):

```
service { 'ntp':
  ensure     => running,
  enable     => true,
  hasrestart => true,
}
```

To further complicate things, the default system service `restart` command may not work, or you may need to take certain special actions when the service is restarted (disabling monitoring notifications, for example). You can specify any `restart` command you like for the service using the `restart` attribute (`service_custom_restart.pp`):

```
service { 'ntp':
  ensure  => running,
  enable  => true,
  restart => '/bin/echo Restarting >>/tmp/debug.log && systemctl
restart ntp',
}
```

In this example, the `restart` command writes a message to a log file before restarting the service in the usual way, but it could, of course, do anything you need it to. Note that the `restart` command is only used when Puppet restarts the service (generally because it was notified by a change to some config file). It's not used when starting the service from a stopped state. If Puppet finds the service has stopped and needs to start it, it will use the normal system service start command.

In the extremely rare event that the service cannot be stopped or started using the default service management command, Puppet also provides the `stop` and `start` attributes so that you can specify custom commands to stop and start the service, just the same way as with the `restart` attribute. If you need to use either of these, though, it's probably safe to say that you're having a bad day.

Users

A user on Unix-like systems does not necessarily correspond to a human person who logs in and types commands, although it sometimes does. A user is simply a named entity that can own files and run commands with certain permissions and that may or may not have permission to read or modify other users' files. It's very common, for sound security reasons, to run each service on a system with its own user account. This simply means that the service runs with the identity and permissions of that user.

For example, a web server will often run as the `www-data` user, which exists solely to own files the web server needs to read and write. This limits the danger of a security breach via the web server, because the attacker would only have the `www-data` user's permissions, which are very limited, rather than the `root` user's, which can modify any aspect of the system. It is generally a bad idea to run services exposed to the public Internet as the `root` user. The service user should have only the minimum permissions it needs to operate the service.

Given this, an important part of system configuration involves creating and managing users, and Puppet's `user` resource provides a model for doing just that. Just as we saw with packages and services, the details of implementation and the commands used to manage users vary widely from one operating system to another, but Puppet provides an abstraction which hides those details behind a common set of attributes for users.

Creating users

The following example shows a typical `user` and `group` declaration in Puppet (`user.pp`):

```
group { 'devs':
  ensure => present,
  gid    => 3000,
}

user { 'hsing-hui':
  ensure => present,
  uid    => '3001',
  home   => '/home/hsing-hui',
  shell  => '/bin/bash',
  groups => ['devs'],
}
```

The user resource

The title of the resource is the username (login name) of the user; in this example, `hsing-hui`. The `ensure => present` attribute says that the user should exist on the system.

The `uid` attribute needs a little more explanation. On Unix-like systems, each user has an individual numerical id, known as the **uid**. The text name associated with the user is merely a convenience for those (mere humans, for example) who prefer strings to numbers. Access permissions are in fact based on the uid and not the username.

Why set the `uid` attribute? Often, when creating users manually, we don't specify a uid, so the system will assign one automatically. The problem with this is that if you create the same user (`hsing-hui`, for example) on three different nodes, you may end up with three different uids. This would be fine as long as you have never shared files between nodes, or copied data from one place to another. But in fact, this happens all the time, so it's important to make sure that a given user's uid is the same across all the nodes in your infrastructure. That's why we specify the `uid` attribute in the Puppet manifest.

The `home` attribute sets the user's home directory (this will be the current working directory when the user logs in, if she does log in, and also the default working directory for cron jobs that run as the user).

The `shell` attribute specifies the command-line shell to run when the user logs in interactively. For humans, this will generally be a user shell, such as `/bin/bash` or `/bin/sh`. For service users, such as `www-data`, the shell should be set to `/usr/sbin/nologin` (on Ubuntu systems), which does not allow interactive access, and prints a message saying `This account is currently not available`. All users who do not need to log in interactively should have the `nologin` shell.

If the user needs to be a member of certain groups, you can pass the `groups` attribute an array of the group names (just `devs` in this example).

Although Puppet supports a `password` attribute for `user` resources, I don't advise you to use it. Service users don't need passwords, and interactive users should be logging in with SSH keys. In fact, you should configure SSH to disable password logins altogether (set `PasswordAuthentication no` in `sshd_config`).

The group resource

The title of the resource is the name of the group (`devs`). You need not specify a `gid` attribute but, for the same reasons as the `uid` attribute, it's a good idea to do so.

Managing SSH keys

I like to have as few interactive logins as possible on production nodes, because it reduces the attack surface. Fortunately, with configuration management, it should rarely be necessary to actually log in to a node. The most common reasons for needing an interactive login are for system maintenance and troubleshooting, and for deployment. In both cases there should be a single account named for this specific purpose (for example, `admin` or `deploy`), and it should be configured with the SSH keys of any users or systems that need to log in to it.

Puppet provides the `ssh_authorized_key` resource to control the SSH keys associated with a user account. The following example shows how to use `ssh_authorized_key` to add an SSH key (mine, in this instance) to the `ubuntu` user on our Vagrant VM (`ssh_authorized_key.pp`):

```
ssh_authorized_key { 'john@bitfieldconsulting.com':
  user => 'ubuntu',
  type => 'ssh-rsa',
  key  => 'AAAAB3NzaC1yc2EAAAABIwAAAIEA3ATqENg+GWACa2
BzeqTdGnJhNoBer8x6pfWkzNzeM8Zx7/2Tf2pl7kHdbsiTXEUawq
zXZQtZzt/j3Oya+PZjcRpWNRzprSmd2UxEEPTqDw9LqY5S2B8og/
NyzWaIYPsKoatcgC7VgYHplcTbzEhGu8BsoEVBGYu3IRy5RkAcZik=',
}
```

The title of the resource is the SSH key comment, which reminds us who the key belongs to. The `user` attribute specifies the user account which this key should be authorized for. The `type` attribute identifies the SSH key type, usually `ssh-rsa` or `ssh-dss`. Finally, the `key` attribute sets the key itself. When this manifest is applied, it adds the following to the `ubuntu` user's `authorized_keys` file:

```
ssh-rsa AAAAB3NzaC1yc2EAAAABIwAAAIEA3ATqENg+GWACa2BzeqTdGnJhNoBer8x6pf
WkzNzeM8Zx7/2Tf2pl7kHdbsiTXEUawqzXZQtZzt/j3Oya+PZjcRpWNRzprSmd2UxEEPT
qDw9LqY5S2B8og/NyzWaIYPsKoatcgC7VgYHplcTbzEhGu8BsoEVBGYu3IRy5RkAcZik=
john@bitfieldconsulting.com
```

A user account can have multiple SSH keys associated with it, and anyone holding one of the corresponding private keys and its passphrase will be able to log in as that user.

Removing users

If you need to have Puppet remove user accounts (for example, as part of an employee leaving process), it's not enough to simply remove the `user` resource from the Puppet manifest. Puppet will ignore any users on the system that it doesn't know about, and it certainly will not remove anything it finds on the system that isn't mentioned in the Puppet manifest; that would be extremely undesirable (almost everything would be removed). So we need to retain the `user` declaration for a while, but set the `ensure` attribute to `absent` (`user_remove.pp`):

```
user { 'godot':
  ensure => absent,
}
```

Once Puppet has run everywhere, you can remove the `user` resource if you like, but it does no harm to simply leave it in place, and in fact, it's a good idea to do this, unless you can verify manually that the user has been deleted from every affected system.

> If you need to prevent a user logging in, but want to retain the account and any files owned by the user, for archival or compliance purposes, you can set their `shell` to `/usr/sbin/nologin`. You can also remove any `ssh_authorized_key` resources associated with their account, and set the `purge_ssh_keys` attribute to `true` on the `user` resource. This will remove any authorized keys for the user that are not managed by Puppet.

Cron resources

Cron is the mechanism on Unix-like systems which runs scheduled jobs, sometimes known as batch jobs, at specified times or intervals. For example, system housekeeping tasks, such as log rotation or checking for security updates, are run from cron. The details of what to run and when to run it are kept in a specially formatted file called `crontab` (short for **cron table**).

Puppet provides the `cron` resource for managing scheduled jobs, and we saw an example of this in the `run-puppet` manifest we developed in *Chapter 3, Managing your Puppet code with Git* (`run-puppet.pp`):

```
cron { 'run-puppet':
  command => '/usr/local/bin/run-puppet',
  hour    => '*',
  minute  => '*/15',
}
```

The title `run-puppet` identifies the cron job (Puppet writes a comment to the `crontab` file containing this name to distinguish it from other manually-configured cron jobs). The `command` attribute specifies the command for cron to run, and the `hour` and `minute` specify the time (`*/15` is a cron syntax, meaning "every 15 minutes").

> For more information about cron and the possible ways to specify the times of scheduled jobs, run the command `man 5 crontab`.

Attributes of the cron resource

The `cron` resource has a few other useful attributes which are shown in the following example (`cron.pp`):

```
cron { 'cron example':
  command     => '/bin/date +%F',
  user        => 'ubuntu',
  environment => ['MAILTO=admin@example.com', 'PATH=/bin'],
  hour        => '0',
  minute      => '0',
  weekday     => ['Saturday', 'Sunday'],
}
```

The `user` attribute specifies who should run the cron job (if none is specified, the job runs as `root`). If the `environment` attribute is given, it sets any environment variables the cron job might need. A common use for this is to email any output from the cron job to a specified email address, using the `MAILTO` variable.

As before, the `hour` and `minute` attributes set the time for the job to run, while you can use the `weekday` attribute to specify a particular day, or days, of the week. (The `monthday` attribute works the same way, and can take any range or array of values between 1-31 to specify the day of the month.)

> One important point about cron scheduling is that the default value for any schedule attribute is `*`, which means *all allowed values*. For example, if you do not specify an `hour` attribute, the cron job will be scheduled with an `hour` of `*`, meaning that it will run every hour. This is generally not what you want. If you do want it to run every hour, specify `hour => '*'` in your manifest, but otherwise, specify the particular hour it should run at. The same goes for `minute`. Accidentally leaving out the `minute` attribute and having a job run sixty times an hour can have amusing consequences, to say the least.

Randomizing cron jobs

If you run a cron job on many nodes, it's a good idea to make sure the job doesn't run everywhere at the same time. Puppet provides a built-in function `fqdn_rand()` to help with this; it provides a random number up to a specified maximum value, which will be different on each node, because the random number generator is seeded with the node's hostname.

If you have several such jobs to run, you can also supply a further seed value to the `fqdn_rand()` function, which can be any string and which will ensure that the value is different for each job (`fqdn_rand.pp`):

```
cron { 'run daily backup':
  command => '/usr/local/bin/backup',
  minute  => '0',
  hour    => fqdn_rand(24, 'run daily backup'),
}

cron { 'run daily backup sync':
  command => '/usr/local/bin/backup_sync',
  minute  => '0',
  hour    => fqdn_rand(24, 'run daily backup sync'),
}
```

Because we gave a different string as the second argument to `fqdn_rand` for each cron job, it will return a different random value for each `hour` attribute.

The range of values returned by `fqdn_rand()` includes 0, but does not include the maximum value you specify. So, in the previous example, the values for `hour` will be between 0 and 23, inclusive.

Removing cron jobs

Just as with `user` resources, or any type of resource, removing the resource declaration from your Puppet manifest does not remove the corresponding configuration from the node. In order to do that you need to specify `ensure => absent` on the resource.

Exec resources

While the other resource types we've seen so far (`file`, `package`, `service`, `user`, `ssh_authorized_key`, and `cron`) have modeled some concrete piece of state on the node, such as a file, the `exec` resource is a little different. An `exec` allows you to run any arbitrary command on the node. This might create or modify state, or it might not; anything you can run from the command line, you can run via an `exec` resource.

Automating manual interaction

The most common use for an `exec` resource is to simulate manual interaction on the command line. Some older software is not packaged for modern operating systems, and needs to be compiled and installed from source, which requires you to run certain commands. The authors of some software have also not realized, or don't care, that users may be trying to install their product automatically and have install scripts which prompt for user input. This can require the use of `exec` resources to work around the problem.

Attributes of the exec resource

The following example shows an `exec` resource for building and installing an imaginary piece of software (`exec.pp`):

```
exec { 'install-cat-picture-generator':
  cwd     => '/tmp/cat-picture-generator',
  command => '/tmp/cat-picture/generator/configure && /usr/bin/make
install',
  creates => '/usr/local/bin/cat-picture-generator',
}
```

The title of the resource can be anything you like, though, as usual with Puppet resources it must be unique. I tend to name `exec` resources after the problem they're trying to solve, as in this example.

The `cwd` attribute sets the working directory where the command will be run (**current working directory**). When installing software, this is generally the software source directory.

The `command` attribute gives the command to run. This must be the full path to the command, but you can chain several commands together using the shell `&&` operator. This executes the next command only if the previous one succeeded, so in the example, if the `configure` command completes successfully, Puppet will go on to run `make install`, otherwise, it will stop with an error.

If you apply this example, Puppet will give you an error like the following:

```
Error: /Stage[main]/Main/Exec[install-cat-picture-
generator]/returns: change from notrun to 0 failed:
Could not find command '/tmp/cat-picture/generator/
configure'
```

This is expected because the specified command does not, in fact, exist. In your own manifests, you may see this error if you give the wrong path to a command, or if the package that provides the command hasn't been installed yet.

The `creates` attribute specifies a file which should exist after the command has been run. If this file is present, Puppet will not run the command again. This is very useful because without a `creates` attribute, an `exec` resource will run every time Puppet runs, which is generally not what you want. The `creates` attribute tells Puppet, in effect, "Run the `exec` only if this file doesn't exist."

Let's see how this works, imagining that this `exec` is being run for the first time. We assume that the `/tmp/cat-picture/` directory exists and contains the source of the `cat-picture-generator` application.

1. Puppet checks the `creates` attribute and sees that the `/usr/local/bin/cat-picture-generator` file is not present; therefore, the `exec` resource must be run.
2. Puppet runs the `/tmp/cat-picture-generator/configure && /usr/bin/make install` command. As a side effect of these commands, the `/usr/local/bin/cat-picture-generator` file is created.
3. Next time Puppet runs, it again checks the `creates` attribute. This time `/usr/local/bin/cat-picture-generator` exists, so Puppet does nothing.

This `exec` resource will never be applied again so long as the file specified in the `creates` attribute exists. You can test this by deleting the file and applying Puppet again. The `exec` resource will be triggered and the file recreated.

> Make sure that your `exec` resources always include a `creates` attribute (or a similar control attribute, such as `onlyif` or `unless`, which we'll look at later in this chapter). Without this, the `exec` command will be run every time Puppet runs, which is almost certainly not what you want.

Note that building and installing software from source is not a recommended practice for production systems. It's better to build the software on a dedicated build server (perhaps using Puppet code similar to this example), create a system package for it, and then use Puppet to install that package on production nodes.

The user attribute

If you don't specify a `user` attribute for an `exec` resource, Puppet will run the command as the `root` user. This is often appropriate for installing system software or making changes to the system configuration, but if you need the command to run as a particular user, specify the `user` attribute, as in the following example (`exec_user.pp`):

```
exec { 'say-hello':
  command => '/bin/echo Hello, this is `whoami` >/tmp/hello-ubuntu.
txt',
  user    => 'ubuntu',
  creates => '/tmp/hello-ubuntu.txt',
}
```

This will run the specified command as the `ubuntu` user. The `whoami` command returns the name of the user running it, so when you apply this manifest, the file `/tmp/hello-ubuntu.txt` will be created with the following contents:

```
Hello, this is ubuntu
```

As with the earlier example, the `creates` attribute prevents Puppet from running this command more than once.

The onlyif and unless attributes

Suppose you only want an `exec` resource to be applied under certain conditions. For example, a command which processes incoming data files only needs to run if there are data files waiting to be processed. In this case, it's no good adding a `creates` attribute; we want the existence of a certain file to trigger the `exec`, not prevent it.

The `onlyif` attribute is a good way to solve this problem. It specifies a command for Puppet to run, and the exit status from this command determines whether or not the `exec` will be applied. On Unix-like systems, commands generally return an exit status of zero to indicate success and a non-zero value for failure. The following example shows how to use `onlyif` in this way (`exec_onlyif.pp`):

```
exec { 'process-incoming-cat-pictures':
  command => '/usr/local/bin/cat-picture-generator --import /tmp/
incoming/*',
  onlyif  => '/bin/ls /tmp/incoming/*',
}
```

The exact command isn't important here, but let's assume it's something that we would only want to run if there are any files in the `/tmp/incoming/` directory.

The onlyif attribute specifies the check command which Puppet should run first, to determine whether or not the exec resource needs to be applied. If there is nothing in the /tmp/incoming/ directory, then ls /tmp/incoming/* will return a non-zero exit status. Puppet interprets this as failure, so does not apply the exec resource.

On the other hand, if there are files in the /tmp/incoming/ directory, the ls command will return success. This tells Puppet the exec resource must be applied, so it proceeds to run the /usr/local/bin/cat-picture-generator command (and we can assume this command deletes the incoming files after processing).

You can think of the onlyif attribute as telling Puppet, "Run the exec resource *only if* this command succeeds."

The unless attribute is exactly the same as onlyif but with the opposite sense. If you specify a command to the unless attribute, the exec will always be run unless the command returns a zero exit status. You can think of unless as telling Puppet, "Run the exec resource *unless* this command succeeds."

When you apply your manifest, if you see an exec resource running every time which shouldn't be, check whether it specifies a creates, unless, or onlyif attribute. If it specifies the creates attribute, it may be looking for the wrong file; if the unless or onlyif command is specified, it may not be returning what you expect. You can see what command is being run and what output it generates by running sudo puppet apply with the -d (debug) flag:

```
sudo puppet apply -d exec_onlyif.pp
Debug: Exec[process-incoming-cat-pictures](provider=posix): Executing
check '/bin/ls /tmp/incoming/*'
Debug: Executing: '/bin/ls /tmp/incoming/*'
Debug: /Stage[main]/Main/Exec[process-incoming-cat-pictures]/onlyif: /
tmp/incoming/foo
```

The refreshonly attribute

It's quite common to use exec resources for one-off commands, such as rebuilding a database, or setting a system-tunable parameter. These generally only need to be triggered once, when a package is installed, or occasionally, when a config file is updated. If an exec resource needs to run only when some other Puppet resource is changed, we can use the refreshonly attribute to do this.

If `refreshonly` is `true`, the `exec` will never be applied unless another resource triggers it with `notify`. In the following example, Puppet manages the `/etc/aliases` file (which maps local usernames to email addresses), and a change to this file triggers the execution of the command `newaliases`, which rebuilds the system alias database (`exec_refreshonly.pp`):

```
file { '/etc/aliases':
  content => 'root: john@bitfieldconsulting.com',
  notify  => Exec['newaliases'],
}

exec { 'newaliases':
  command     => '/usr/bin/newaliases',
  refreshonly => true,
}
```

When this manifest is applied for the first time, the `/etc/aliases` resource causes a change to the file's contents, so Puppet sends a `notify` message to the `exec` resource. This causes the `newaliases` command to be run. If you apply the manifest again, you will see that the `aliases` file is not changed, so the `exec` is not run.

> While the `refreshonly` attribute is occasionally extremely useful, over-use of it can make your Puppet manifests hard to understand and debug, and it can also be rather fragile. Felix Frank makes this point in a blog post, *Friends Don't Let Friends Use Refreshonly*:
>
> "With the `exec` resource type considered the last ditch, its `refreshonly` parameter should be seen as especially outrageous. To make an `exec` resource fit into Puppet's model better, you should use [the `creates`, `onlyif`, or `unless`] parameters instead." Refer to:
>
> `http://ffrank.github.io/misc/2015/05/26/friends-don't-let-friends-use-refreshonly/`

Note that you don't need to use the `refreshonly` attribute in order to make the `exec` resource notifiable by other resources. Any resource can notify an `exec` resource in order to make it run; however, if you don't want it to run *unless* it's notified, use `refreshonly`.

> By the way, if you actually want to manage email aliases on a node, use Puppet's built-in `mailalias` resource. The previous example is just to demonstrate the use of `refreshonly`.

The logoutput attribute

When Puppet runs shell commands via an `exec` resource, the output is normally hidden from us. However, if the command doesn't seem to be working properly, it can be very useful to see what output it produced, as this usually tells us why it didn't work.

The `logoutput` attribute determines whether Puppet will log the output of the `exec` command along with the usual informative Puppet output. It can take three values: `true`, `false`, or `on_failure`.

If `logoutput` is set to `on_failure` (which is the default), Puppet will only log command output when the command fails (that is, returns a non-zero exit status). If you never want to see command output, set it to `false`.

Sometimes, however, the command returns a successful exit status but does not appear to do anything. Setting `logoutput` to `true` will force Puppet to log the command output regardless of exit status, which should help you figure out what's going on.

The timeout attribute

Sometimes, commands can take a long time to run, or never terminate at all. By default, Puppet allows an `exec` command to run for 300 seconds, at which point Puppet will terminate it if it has not finished. If you need to allow a little longer for the command to complete, you can use the `timeout` attribute to set this. The value is the maximum execution time for the command in seconds.

Setting a `timeout` value of `0` disables the automatic timeout altogether and allows the command to run forever. This should be the last resort, as a command which blocks or hangs could stop Puppet's automatic runs altogether if no timeout is set. To find a suitable value for `timeout`, try running the command a few times and choose a value which is perhaps twice as long as a typical run. This should avoid failures caused by slow network conditions, for example, but not block Puppet from running altogether.

How not to misuse exec resources

The `exec` resource can do anything to the system that you could do from the command line. As you can imagine, such a powerful tool can be misused. In theory, Puppet is a declarative language: the manifest specifies the way things should be, and it is up to Puppet to take the necessary actions to make them so. Manifests are therefore what computer scientists call **idempotent**: the system is always in the same state after the catalog has been applied, and however many times you apply it, it will always be in that state.

The exec resource rather spoils this theoretical picture, by allowing Puppet manifests to have side-effects. Since your exec command can do anything, it could, for example, create a new 1 GB file on disk with a random name, and since this will happen every time Puppet runs, you could rapidly run out of disk space. It's best to avoid commands with side-effects like this. In general, there's no way to know from within Puppet exactly what changes to a system were caused by an exec resource.

Commands run via exec are also sometimes used to bypass Puppet's existing resources. For example, if the user resource doesn't do quite what you want for some reason, you could create a user by running the adduser command directly from an exec. This is also a bad idea, since by doing this you lose the declarative and cross-platform nature of Puppet's built-in resources. exec resources potentially change the state of the node in a way that's invisible to Puppet's catalog.

> In general, if you need to manage a concrete aspect of system state which isn't supported by Puppet's built-in resource types, you should think about creating a custom resource type and provider to do what you want. This extends Puppet to add a new resource type, which you can then use to model the state of that resource in your manifests. Creating custom types and providers is an advanced topic and not covered in this book, but if you want to know more, consult the Puppet documentation:
>
> https://docs.puppet.com/guides/custom_types.html

You should also think twice before running complex commands via exec, especially commands which use loops or conditionals. It's a better idea to put any complicated logic in a shell script (or, even better, in a real programming language), which you can then deploy and run with Puppet (avoiding, as we've said, unnecessary side-effects).

> As a matter of good Puppet style, every exec resource should have at least one of creates, onlyif, unless, or refreshonly specified, to stop it from being applied on every Puppet run. If you find yourself using exec just to run a command every time Puppet runs, make it a cron job instead.

Summary

We've explored Puppet's `file` resource in detail, covering file sources, ownership, permissions, directories, symbolic links, and file trees. We've learned how to manage packages by installing specific versions, or the latest version, and how to uninstall packages. We've covered Ruby gems, both in the system context and Puppet's internal context. Along the way, we met the very useful `puppet-lint` tool.

We have looked at `service` resources, including the `hasstatus`, `pattern`, `hasrestart`, `restart`, `stop`, and `start` attributes. We've learned how to create users and groups, manage home directories, shells, UIDs, and SSH authorized keys. We saw how to schedule, manage, and remove cron jobs.

Finally, we've learned all about the powerful `exec` resource, including how to run arbitrary commands, and how to run commands only under certain conditions, or only if a specific file is not present. We've seen how to use the `refreshonly` attribute to trigger an `exec` resource when other resources are updated, and we've explored the useful `logoutput` and `timeout` attributes of `exec` resources.

In the next chapter, we'll find out how to represent data and variables in Puppet manifests, including strings, numbers, Booleans, arrays, and hashes. We'll learn how to use variables and conditional expressions to determine which resources are applied, and we'll also learn about Puppet's `facts` hash and how to use it to get information about the system.

5

Variables, expressions, and facts

It is impossible to begin to learn that which one thinks one already knows.

—Epictetus

In this chapter, you will learn about Puppet variables and data types, expressions, and conditional statements. You will also learn how Puppet manifests can get data about the node using Facter, find out which are the most important standard facts, and see how to create your own external facts. Finally, you will use Puppet's `each` function to iterate over arrays and hashes, including Facter data.

Introducing variables

A **variable** in Puppet is simply a way of giving a name to a particular value, which we could then use wherever we would use the literal value (`variable_string.pp`):

```
$php_package = 'php7.0-cli'

package { $php_package:
  ensure => installed,
}
```

The dollar sign (`$`) tells Puppet that what follows is a variable name. Variable names must begin with a lowercase letter or an underscore, though the rest of the name can also contain uppercase letters or numbers.

A variable can contain different types of data; one such type is a **String** (like `php7.0-cli`), but Puppet variables can also contain **Number** or **Boolean** values (`true` or `false`). Here are a few examples (`variable_simple.pp`):

```
$my_name = 'Zaphod Beeblebrox'
$answer = 42
$scheduled_for_demolition = true
```

Using Booleans

Strings and numbers are straightforward, but Puppet also has a special data type to represent true or false values, which we call **Boolean** values, after the logician George Boole. We have already encountered some Boolean values in Puppet resource attributes (`service.pp`):

```
service { 'sshd':
  ensure => running,
  enable => true,
}
```

The only allowed values for Boolean variables are the literal values `true` and `false`, but Boolean variables can also hold the values of conditional expressions (expressions whose value is `true` or `false`), which we'll explore later in this chapter.

You might be wondering what type the value `running` is in the previous example. It's actually a string, but a special, unquoted kind of string called a **bare word**. Although it would be exactly the same to Puppet if you used a normal quoted string `'running'` here, it's considered good style to use bare words for attribute values which can only be one of a small number of words (for example, the `ensure` attribute on services can only take the values `running` or `stopped`). By contrast, `true` is not a bare word but a Boolean value, and it is not interchangeable with the string `'true'`. Always use the unquoted literal values `true` or `false` for Boolean values.

Interpolating variables in strings

It's no good being able to store something in a variable if you can't get it out again, and one of the most common ways to use a variable's value is to **interpolate** it in a string. When you do this, Puppet inserts the current value of the variable into the contents of the string, replacing the name of the variable. String interpolation looks like this (`string_interpolation.pp`):

```
$my_name = 'John'
notice("Hello, ${my_name}! It's great to meet you!")
```

When you apply this manifest, the following output is printed:

```
Notice: Scope(Class[main]): Hello, John! It's great to meet you!
```

To interpolate (that is, to insert the value of) a variable in a string, prefix its name with a `$` character and surround it with curly braces (`{}`). This tells Puppet to replace the variable's name with its value in the string.

We sneaked a new Puppet function, `notice()`, into the previous example. It has no effect on the system, but it prints out the value of its argument. This can be very useful for troubleshooting problems or finding out what the value of a variable is at a given point in your manifest.

Creating arrays

A variable can also hold more than one value. An **Array** is an ordered sequence of values, each of which can be of any type. The following example creates an array of **Integer** values (`variable_array.pp`):

```
$heights = [193, 120, 181, 164, 172]

$first_height = $heights[0]
```

You can refer to any individual element of an array by giving its index number in square brackets, where the first element is index `[0]`, the second is `[1]`, and so on. (If you find this confusing, you're not alone, but it may help to think of the index as representing an offset from the beginning of the array. Naturally, then, the offset of the first element is 0.)

Declaring arrays of resources

You already know that in Puppet resource declarations, the title of the resource is usually a string, such as the path to a file or the name of a package. You might as well ask, "What happens if you supply an array of strings as the title of a resource instead of a single string? Does Puppet create multiple resources, one for each element in the array?" Let's try an experiment where we do exactly that with an array of package names and see what happens (`resource_array.pp`):

```
$dependencies = [
  'php7.0-cgi',
  'php7.0-cli',
  'php7.0-common',
  'php7.0-gd',
  'php7.0-json',
  'php7.0-mcrypt',
  'php7.0-mysql',
  'php7.0-soap',
]

package { $dependencies:
  ensure => installed,
}
```

If our intuition is right, applying the previous manifest should give us a package resource for each package listed in the `$dependencies` array, and each one should be installed. Here's what happens when the manifest is applied:

```
sudo apt-get update
sudo puppet apply /examples/resource_array.pp
Notice: Compiled catalog for ubuntu-xenial in environment production
in 0.68 seconds
Notice: /Stage[main]/Main/Package[php7.0-cgi]/ensure: created
Notice: /Stage[main]/Main/Package[php7.0-cli]/ensure: created
Notice: /Stage[main]/Main/Package[php7.0-common]/ensure: created
Notice: /Stage[main]/Main/Package[php7.0-gd]/ensure: created
Notice: /Stage[main]/Main/Package[php7.0-json]/ensure: created
Notice: /Stage[main]/Main/Package[php7.0-mcrypt]/ensure: created
```

```
Notice: /Stage[main]/Main/Package[php7.0-mysql]/ensure: created
Notice: /Stage[main]/Main/Package[php7.0-soap]/ensure: created
Notice: Applied catalog in 56.98 seconds
```

Giving an array of strings as the title of a resource results in Puppet creating multiple resources, all identical except for the title. You can do this not just with packages, but also with files, users, or, in fact, any type of resource. We'll see some more sophisticated ways of creating resources from data in *Chapter 6, Managing data with Hiera*.

Why did we run `sudo apt-get update` before applying the manifest? This is the Ubuntu command to update the system's local package catalog from the upstream servers. It's always a good idea to run this before installing any package to make sure you're installing the latest version. In your production Puppet code, of course, you can run this via an `exec` resource.

Understanding hashes

A **hash**, also known as a dictionary in some programming languages, is like an array, but instead of just being a sequence of values, each value has a name (`variable_hash.pp`):

```
$heights = {
  'john'    => 193,
  'rabiah'  => 120,
  'abigail' => 181,
  'melina'  => 164,
  'sumiko'  => 172,
}

notice("John's height is ${heights['john']}cm.")
```

The name for each value is known as the **key**. In the previous example, the keys of this hash are `john`, `rabiah`, `abigail`, `melina`, and `sumiko`. To look up the value of a given key, you put the key in square brackets after the hash name: `$heights['john']`.

Puppet style note

Did you spot the trailing comma on the last hash key-value pair and the last element of the array in the previous example? Although the comma isn't strictly required, it's good style to add one. The reason is that it's very common to want to add another item to an array or hash, and if your last item already has a trailing comma, you won't have to remember to add one when extending the list.

Setting resource attributes from a hash

You might have noticed that a hash looks a lot like the attributes of a resource: it's a one-to-one mapping between names and values. Wouldn't it be convenient if, when declaring resources, we could just specify a hash containing all the attributes and their values? As it happens, you can do just that (`hash_attributes.pp`):

```
$attributes = {
  'owner' => 'ubuntu',
  'group' => 'ubuntu',
  'mode'  => '0644',
}

file { '/tmp/test':
  ensure => present,
  *      => $attributes,
}
```

The `*` character, cheerfully named the **attribute splat operator**, tells Puppet to treat the specified hash as a list of attribute-value pairs to apply to the resource. This is exactly equivalent to specifying the same attributes directly, as in the following example:

```
file { '/tmp/test':
  ensure => present,
  owner  => 'vagrant',
  group  => 'vagrant',
  mode   => '0644',
}
```

Introducing expressions

Variables are not the only things in Puppet that have a value. Expressions also have a value. The simplest expressions are just literal values:

```
42
true
'Oh no, not again.'
```

You can combine numeric values with arithmetic operators, such as `+`, `-`, `*`, and `/`, to create **arithmetic expressions**, which have a numeric value, and you can use these to have Puppet do calculations (`expression_numeric.pp`):

```
$value = (17 * 8) + (12 / 4) - 1
notice($value)
```

The most useful expressions, though, are which that evaluate to `true` or `false`, known as **Boolean expressions**. The following is a set of examples of Boolean expressions, all of which evaluate to `true` (`expression_boolean.pp`):

```
notice(9 < 10)
notice(11 > 10)
notice(10 >= 10)
notice(10 <= 10)
notice('foo' == 'foo')
notice('foo' in 'foobar')
notice('foo' in ['foo', 'bar'])
notice('foo' in { 'foo' => 'bar' })
notice('foo' =~ /oo/)
notice('foo' =~ String)
notice(1 != 2)
```

Meeting Puppet's comparison operators

All the operators in the Boolean expressions shown in the previous example are known as **comparison operators**, because they compare two values. The result is either `true` or `false`. These are the comparison operators Puppet provides:

- `==` and `!=` (equal, not equal)
- `>`, `>=`, `<`, and `<=` (greater than, greater than or equal to, less than, less than or equal to)
- `A in B` (`A` is a substring of `B`, `A` is an element of the array `B`, or `A` is a key of the hash `B`)
- `A =~ B` (`A` is matched by the regular expression `B`, or `A` is a value of data type `B`. For example, the expression `'hello' =~ String` is `true`, because the value `'hello'` is of type String.)

Introducing regular expressions

The `=~` operator tries to match a given value against a **regular expression**. A regular expression (*regular* in the sense of constituting a pattern or a rule) is a special kind of expression which specifies a set of strings. For example, the regular expression `/a+/` describes the set of all strings that contain one or more consecutive `as`: `a`, `aa`, `aaa`, and so on, as well as all strings which contain such a sequence among other characters. The slash characters `//` delimit a regular expression in Puppet.

When we say a regular expression **matches** a value, we mean the value is one of the set of strings specified by the regular expression. The regular expression `/a+/` would match the string `aaa` or the string `Aaaaargh!`, for example.

The following example shows some regular expressions that match the string `foo` (`regex.pp`):

```
$candidate = 'foo'
notice($candidate =~ /foo/) # literal
notice($candidate =~ /f/)   # substring
notice($candidate =~ /f.*/) # f followed by zero or more characters
notice($candidate =~ /f.o/) # f, any character, o
notice($candidate =~ /fo+/) # f followed by one or more 'o's
notice($candidate =~ /[fgh]oo/) # f, g, or h followed by 'oo'
```

Regular expressions are more-or-less a standard language for expressing string patterns. It's a complicated and powerful language, which really deserves a book of its own (and there are several), but suffice it to say for now that Puppet's regular expression syntax is the same as that used in the Ruby language. You can read more about it in the Ruby documentation at:

`http://ruby-doc.org/core/Regexp.html`

Using conditional expressions

Boolean expressions, like those in the previous example, are useful because we can use them to make choices in the Puppet manifest. We can apply certain resources only if a given condition is met, or we can assign an attribute one value or another, depending on whether some expression is true. An expression used in this way is called a **conditional expression**.

Making decisions with if statements

The most common use of a conditional expression is in an `if` statement. The following example shows how to use `if` to decide whether to apply a resource (`if.pp`):

```
$install_perl = true
if $install_perl {
  package { 'perl':
    ensure => installed,
  }
} else {
  package { 'perl':
    ensure => absent,
  }
}
```

You can see that the value of the Boolean variable `$install_perl` governs whether or not the `perl` package is installed. If `$install_perl` is `true`, Puppet will apply the following resource:

```
package { 'perl':
  ensure => installed,
}
```

If, on the other hand, `$install_perl` is `false`, the resource applied will be:

```
package { 'perl':
  ensure => absent,
}
```

You can use `if` statements to control the application of any number of resources or, indeed, any part of your Puppet manifest. You can leave out the `else` clause if you like; in that case, when the value of the conditional expression is `false`, Puppet will do nothing.

Choosing options with case statements

The `if` statement allows you to take a yes/no decision based on the value of a Boolean expression. But if you need to make a choice among more than two options, you can use a `case` statement instead (`case.pp`):

```
$webserver = 'nginx'
case $webserver {
  'nginx': {
    notice("Looks like you're using Nginx! Good choice!")
  }
  'apache': {
    notice("Ah, you're an Apache fan, eh?")
  }
  'IIS': {
    notice('Well, somebody has to.')
  }
  default: {
    notice("I'm not sure which webserver you're using!")
  }
}
```

In a `case` statement, Puppet compares the value of the expression to each of the cases listed in order. If it finds a match, the corresponding resources are applied. The special case called `default` always matches, and you can use it to make sure that Puppet will do the right thing even if none of the other cases match.

Finding out facts

It's very common for Puppet manifests to need to know something about the system they're running on, for example, its hostname, IP address, or operating system version. Puppet's built-in mechanism for getting system information is called **Facter**, and each piece of information provided by Facter is known as a **fact**.

Using the facts hash

You can access Facter facts in your manifest using the **facts hash**. This is a Puppet variable called `$facts` which is available everywhere in the manifest, and to get a particular fact, you supply the name of the fact you want as the key (`facts_hash.pp`):

```
notice($facts['kernel'])
```

On the Vagrant box, or any Linux system, this will return the value `Linux`.

In older versions of Puppet, each fact was a distinct global variable, like this:

```
notice($::kernel)
```

You will still see this style of fact reference in some Puppet code, though it is now deprecated and will eventually stop working, so you should always use the `$facts` hash instead.

Running the facter command

You can also use the `facter` command to see the value of particular facts, or just see what facts are available. For example, running `facter os` on the command line will show you the hash of available OS-related facts:

```
facter os
{
  architecture => "amd64",
  distro => {
    codename => "xenial",
    description => "Ubuntu 16.04 LTS",
    id => "Ubuntu",
    release => {
      full => "16.04",
      major => "16.04"
    }
  },
  family => "Debian",
  hardware => "x86_64",
  name => "Ubuntu",
```

```
    release => {
      full => "16.04",
      major => "16.04"
    },
    selinux => {
      enabled => false
    }
  }
```

You can also use the `puppet facts` command to see what facts will be available to Puppet manifests. This will also include any custom facts defined by third-party Puppet modules (see *Chapter 7, Mastering modules*, for more information about this).

Accessing hashes of facts

As in the previous example, many facts actually return a hash of values, rather than a single value. The value of the `$facts['os']` fact is a hash with the keys `architecture`, `distro`, `family`, `hardware`, `name`, `release`, and `selinux`. Some of those are also hashes; it's hashes all the way down!

As you know, to access a particular value in a hash, you specify the key name in square brackets. To access a value inside a hash, you add another key name in square brackets after the first, as in the following example (`facts_architecture.pp`):

```
notice($facts['os']['architecture'])
```

You can keep on appending more keys to get more and more specific information (`facts_distro_codename.pp`):

```
notice($facts['os']['distro']['codename'])
```

Key fact

The operating system major release is a very handy fact and one you'll probably use often:

```
$facts['os']['release']['major']
```

Referencing facts in expressions

Just as with ordinary variables or values, you can use facts in expressions, including conditional expressions (`fact_if.pp`):

```
if $facts['os']['selinux']['enabled'] {
  notice('SELinux is enabled')
} else {
  notice('SELinux is disabled')
}
```

Although conditional expressions based on facts can be useful, an even better way of making decisions based on facts in your manifests is to use Hiera, which we'll cover in the next chapter. For example, if you find yourself writing an `if` or `case` statement which chooses different resources depending on the operating system version, consider using a Hiera query instead.

Using memory facts

Another useful set of facts is that relating to the **system memory**. You can find out the total physical memory available, and the amount of memory currently used, as well as the same figures for swap memory.

One common use for this is to configure applications dynamically based on the amount of system memory. For example, the MySQL parameter `innodb_buffer_pool_size` specifies the amount of memory allocated to database query cache and indexes, and it should generally be set as high as possible ("*as large a value as practical, leaving enough memory for other processes on the node to run without excessive paging*", according to the documentation). So you might decide to set this to three-quarters of total memory (for example), using a fact and an arithmetic expression, as in the following snippet (`fact_memory.pp`):

```
$buffer_pool = $facts['memory']['system']['total_bytes'] * 3/4
notice("innodb_buffer_pool_size=${buffer_pool}")
```

Key fact

The total system memory fact will help you calculate configuration parameters which vary as a fraction of memory:

```
$facts['memory']['system']['total_bytes']
```

Discovering networking facts

Most applications use the network, so you'll find Facter's network-related facts very useful for anything to do with network configuration. The most commonly used facts are the system hostname, fully qualified domain name (FQDN), and IP address (`fact_networking.pp`):

```
notice("My hostname is ${facts['hostname']}")
notice("My FQDN is ${facts['fqdn']}")
notice("My IP is ${facts['networking']['ip']}")
```

> **Key fact**
>
> The system hostname is something you'll need to refer to often in your manifests:
>
> ```
> $facts['hostname']
> ```

Providing external facts

While the built-in facts available to Puppet provide a lot of important information, you can make the `$facts` hash even more useful by extending it with your own facts, known as **external facts**. For example, if nodes are located in different cloud providers, each of which requires a slightly different networking setup, you could create a custom fact called `cloud` to document this. You can then use this fact in manifests to make decisions.

Puppet looks for external facts in the `/opt/puppetlabs/facter/facts.d/` directory. Try creating a file in that directory called `facts.txt` with the following contents (`fact_external.txt`):

```
cloud=aws
```

A quick way to do this is to run the following command:

```
sudo cp /examples/fact_external.txt /opt/puppetlabs/facter/facts.d
```

The `cloud` fact is now available in your manifests. You can check that the fact is working by running the following command:

```
sudo facter cloud
aws
```

To use the fact in your manifest, query the `$facts` hash just as you would for a built-in fact (`fact_cloud.pp`):

```
case $facts['cloud'] {
  'aws': {
    notice('This is an AWS cloud node ')
  }
```

```
    'gcp': {
      notice('This is a Google cloud node')
    }
    default: {
      notice("I'm not sure which cloud I'm in!")
    }
  }
```

You can put as many facts in a single text file as you like, or you can have each fact in a separate file: it doesn't make any difference. Puppet will read all the files in the `facts.d/` directory and extract all the `key=value` pairs from each one.

Text files work well for simple facts (those that return a single value). If your external facts need to return structured data (arrays or hashes, for example), you can use a YAML or JSON file instead to do this. We'll be learning more about YAML in the next chapter, but for now, if you need to build structured external facts, consult the Puppet documentation for details.

It's common to set up external facts like this at build time, perhaps as part of an automated bootstrap script (see *Chapter 12, Putting it all together*, for more about the bootstrap process).

Creating executable facts

External facts are not limited to static text files. They can also be the output of scripts or programs. For example, you could write a script that calls a web service to get some data, and the result would be the value of the fact. These are known as **executable facts**.

Executable facts live in the same directory as other external facts (`/opt/puppetlabs/facter/facts.d/`), but they are distinguished by having the execute bit set on their files (recall that files on Unix-like systems each have a set of bits indicating their read, write, and execute permissions) and they also can't be named with `.txt`, `.yaml`, or `.json` extensions. Let's build an executable fact which simply returns the current date, as an example:

1. Run the following command to copy the executable fact example into the external fact directory:

   ```
   sudo cp /examples/date.sh /opt/puppetlabs/facter/facts.d
   ```

2. Set the execute bit on the file with the following command:

   ```
   sudo chmod a+x /opt/puppetlabs/facter/facts.d/date.sh
   ```

3. Now test the fact:

   ```
   sudo facter date
   2017-04-12
   ```

Here is the script which generates this output (`date.sh`):

```
#!/bin/bash
echo "date=`date +%F`"
```

Note that the script has to output `date=` before the actual date value. This is because Facter expects executable facts to output a list of `key=value` pairs (just one such pair, in this case). The `key` is the name of the fact (`date`), and the `value` is whatever is returned by `` `date +%F` `` (the current date in ISO 8601 format). You should use ISO 8601 format (`YYYY-MM-DD`) whenever you need to represent dates, by the way, because it's not only the international standard date format, but it is also unambiguous and sorts alphabetically.

As you can see, executable facts are quite powerful because they can return any information which can be generated by a program (the program could make network requests or database queries, for example). However, you should use executable facts with care, as Puppet has to evaluate *all* external facts on the node every time it runs, which means running every script in `/opt/puppetlabs/facter/facts.d`.

> If you don't need the information from an executable fact to be regenerated every time Puppet runs, consider running the script from a cron job at longer intervals and having it write output to a static text file in the facts directory instead.

Iterating over arrays

Iteration (doing something repeatedly) is a useful technique in your Puppet manifests to avoid lots of duplicated code. For example, consider the following manifest, which creates several files with identical properties (`iteration_simple.pp`):

```
file { '/usr/local/bin/task1':
  content => "echo I am task1\n",
  mode    => '0755',
}

file { '/usr/local/bin/task2':
  content => "echo I am task2\n",
  mode    => '0755',
}

file { '/usr/local/bin/task3':
  content => "echo I am task3\n",
  mode    => '0755',
}
```

You can see that each of these resources is identical, except for the task number: task1, task2, and task3. Clearly, this is a lot of typing and should you later decide to change the properties of these scripts (for example, moving them to a different directory), you'll have to find and change each one in the manifest. For three resources, this is already annoying, but for thirty or a hundred resources it's completely impractical. We need a better solution.

Using the each function

Puppet provides the each function to help with just this kind of situation. The each function takes an array and applies a block of Puppet code to each element of the array. Here's the same example we saw previously, only this time using an array and the each function (iteration_each.pp):

```
$tasks = ['task1', 'task2', 'task3']
$tasks.each | $task | {
  file { "/usr/local/bin/${task}":
    content => "echo I am ${task}\n",
    mode    => '0755',
  }
}
```

Now this looks more like a computer program! We have a **loop**, created by the each function. The loop goes round and round, creating a new file resource for each element of the $tasks array. Let's look at a schematic version of an each loop:

```
ARRAY.each | ELEMENT | {
  BLOCK
}
```

The following list describes the components of the each loop:

- ARRAY can be any Puppet array variable or literal value (it could even be a call to Hiera that returns an array). In the previous example, we used $tasks as the array.
- ELEMENT is the name of a variable which will hold, each time round the loop, the value of the current element in the array. In the previous example, we decided to name this variable $task, although we could have called it anything.
- BLOCK is a section of Puppet code. This could consist of a function call, resource declarations, include statements, conditional statements: anything which you can put in a Puppet manifest, you can also put inside a loop block. In the previous example, the only thing in the block was the file resource, which creates /usr/local/bin/$task.

Iterating over hashes

The `each` function works not only on arrays, but also on hashes. When iterating over a hash, the loop takes two `ELEMENT` parameters: the first is the hash key, and the second is the value. The following example shows how to use `each` to iterate over a hash resulting from a Facter query (`iteration_hash.pp`):

```
$nics = $facts['networking']['interfaces']
$nics.each | String $interface, Hash $attributes | {
  notice("Interface ${interface} has IP ${attributes['ip']}")
}
```

The list of interfaces returned by `$facts['networking']['interfaces']` is a hash, where the key is the name of the interface (for example, `lo0` for the local loopback interfaces) and the value is a hash of the interface's attributes (including the IP address, netmask, and so on). Applying the manifest in the previous example gives this result (on my Vagrant box):

```
sudo puppet apply /examples/iteration_hash.pp
Notice: Scope(Class[main]): Interface enp0s3 has IP 10.0.2.15
Notice: Scope(Class[main]): Interface lo has IP 127.0.0.1
```

Summary

In this chapter, we've gained an understanding of how Puppet's variable and data type system works, including the basic data types: Strings, Numbers, Booleans, Arrays, and Hashes. We've seen how to interpolate variables in strings and how to quickly create sets of similar resources using an array of resource names. We've learned how to set common attributes for resources using a hash of attribute-value pairs and the attribute splat operator.

We've seen how to use variables and values in expressions, including arithmetic expressions, and explored the range of Puppet's comparison operators to generate Boolean expressions. We've used conditional expressions to build `if…else` and `case` statements and had a brief introduction to regular expressions.

We've learned how Puppet's Facter subsystem supplies information about the node via the facts hash and how to use facts in our own manifests and in expressions. We've pointed out some key facts, including the operating system release, the system memory capacity, and the system hostname. We've seen how to create custom external facts, such as a `cloud` fact, and how to dynamically generate fact information using executable facts.

Finally, we've learned about iteration in Puppet using the `each` function and how to create multiple resources based on data from arrays or hashes, including Facter queries.

In the next chapter, we'll stay with the topic of data and explore Puppet's powerful Hiera database. We'll see what problems Hiera solves, look at how to set up and query Hiera, how to write data sources, how to create Puppet resources directly from Hiera data, and also how to use Hiera encryption to manage secret data.

6
Managing data with Hiera

What you don't know can't hurt me.

—Edward S. Marshall

In this chapter, you will learn why it's useful to separate your data and code. You will see how to set up Puppet's built-in Hiera mechanism, how to use it to store and query configuration data, including encrypted secrets such as passwords, and how to use Hiera data to create Puppet resources.

Why Hiera?

What do we mean by **configuration data**? There will be lots of pieces of information in your manifests which we can regard as configuration data: for example, the values of all your resource attributes. Look at the following example:

```
package { 'puppet-agent':
  ensure => '5.2.0-1xenial',
}
```

The preceding manifest declares that version `5.2.0-1xenial` of the `puppet-agent` package should be installed. But what happens when a new version of Puppet is released? When you want to upgrade to it, you'll have to find this code, possibly deep in multiple levels of directories, and edit it to change the desired version number.

Data needs to be maintained

Multiply this by all the packages managed throughout your manifest, and there is there's already a problem. But this is just one piece of data that needs to be maintained, and there are many more: the times of cron jobs, the email addresses for reports to be sent to, the URLs of files to fetch from the web, the parameters for monitoring checks, the amount of memory to configure for the database server, and so on. If these values are embedded in code in hundreds of manifest files, you're setting up trouble for the future.

How can you make your config data easy to find and maintain?

Settings depend on nodes

Mixing data with code makes it harder to find and edit that data. But there's another problem. What if you have two nodes to manage with Puppet, and there's a config value which needs to be different on each of them? For example, they might both have a cron job to run the backup, but the job needs to run at a different time on each node.

How can you use different values for different nodes, without having lots of complicated logic in your manifest?

Operating systems differ

What if you have some nodes running Ubuntu 16, and some on Ubuntu 18? As you'll know if you've ever had to upgrade the operating system on a node, things change from one version to the next. For example, the name of the database server package might have changed from `mysql-server` to `mariadb-server`.

How can you find the right value to use in your manifest depending on what operating system the node is running?

The Hiera way

What we want is a kind of central database in Puppet where we can look up configuration settings. The data should be stored separately from Puppet code, and make it easy to find and edit values. It should be possible to look up values with a simple function call in Puppet code or templates. Further, we need to be able to specify different values depending on things like the hostname of the node, the operating system, or potentially anything else. We would also like to be able to enforce a particular data type for values, such as String or Boolean. The database should do all of this work for us, and just return the appropriate value to the manifest where it's needed.

Fortunately, Hiera does exactly this. Hiera lets you store your config data in simple text files (actually, YAML, JSON, or HOCON files, which use popular structured text formats), and it looks like the following example:

```
---
  test: 'This is a test'
  consul_node: true
  apache_worker_factor: 100
  apparmor_enabled: true
  ...
```

In your manifest, you query the database using the `lookup()` function, as in the following example (`lookup.pp`):

```
file { lookup('backup_path', String):
  ensure => directory,
}
```

The arguments to `lookup` are the name of the Hiera key you want to retrieve (for example `backup_path`), and the expected data type (for example `String`).

Setting up Hiera

Hiera needs to know one or two things before you can start using it, which are specified in the Hiera configuration file, named `hiera.yaml` (not to be confused this with Hiera data files, which are also YAML files, and we'll find about those later in this chapter.) Each Puppet environment has its own local Hiera config file, located at the root of the environment directory (for example, for the `production` environment, the local Hiera config file would be `/etc/puppetlabs/code/environments/production/hiera.yaml`).

Hiera can also use a global config file located at `/etc/puppetlabs/puppet/hiera.yaml`, which takes precedence over the per-environment file, but the Puppet documentation recommends you only use this config layer for certain exceptional purposes, such as temporary overrides; all your normal Hiera data and configuration should live at the environment layer.

The following example shows a minimal `hiera.yaml` file (`hiera_minimal.config.yaml`):

```
---
version: 5

defaults:
  datadir: data
  data_hash: yaml_data

hierarchy:
  - name: "Common defaults"
    path: "common.yaml"
```

YAML files begin with three dashes and a newline (`---`). This is part of the YAML format, not a Hiera feature; it's the syntax indicating the start of a new YAML document.

The most important setting in the `defaults` section is `datadir`. This tells Hiera in which directory to look for its data files. Conventionally, this is in a `data/` subdirectory of the Puppet manifest directory, but you can change this if you need to.

Large organizations may find it useful to manage Hiera data files separately to Puppet code, perhaps in a separate Git repo (for example, you might want to give certain people permission to edit Hiera data, but not Puppet manifests).

The `hierarchy` section is also interesting. This tells Hiera which files to read for its data and in which order. In the example only `Common defaults` is defined, telling Hiera to look for data in a file called `common.yaml`. We'll see later in this chapter what else you can do with the `hierarchy` section.

Adding Hiera data to your Puppet repo

Your Vagrant VM is already set up with a suitable Hiera config and the sample data file, in the `/etc/puppetlabs/code/environments/pbg` directory. Try it now:

Run the following commands:

```
sudo puppet lookup --environment pbg test
--- This is a test
```

We haven't seen the `--environment` switch before, so it's time to briefly introduce Puppet environments. A Puppet **environment** is a directory containing a Hiera config file, Hiera data, a set of Puppet manifests—in other words, a complete, self-contained Puppet setup. Each environment lives in a named directory under `/etc/puppetlabs/code/environments`. The default environment is `production`, but you can use any environment you like by giving the `--environment` switch to the `puppet lookup` command. In the example, we are telling Puppet to use the `/etc/puppetlabs/code/environments/pbg` directory.

When you come to add Hiera data to your own Puppet environment, you can use the example `hiera.yaml` and data files as a starting point.

Troubleshooting Hiera

If you don't get the result `This is a test`, your Hiera setup is not working properly. If you see the warning `Config file not found, using Hiera defaults`, check that your Vagrant box has an `/etc/puppetlabs/code/environments/pbg` directory. If not, destroy and re-provision your Vagrant box with:

```
vagrant destroy
scripts/start_vagrant.sh
```

If you see an error like the following, it generally indicates a problem with the Hiera data file syntax:

```
Error: Evaluation Error: Error while evaluating a Function Call,
(/etc/puppetlabs/code/environments/pbg/hiera.yaml): did not find
expected key while parsing a block mapping at line 11 column 5  at
line 1:8 on node ubuntu-xenial
```

If this is the case, check the syntax of your Hiera data files.

Querying Hiera

In Puppet manifests, you can use the `lookup()` function to query Hiera for the specified key (you can think of Hiera as a key-value database, where the keys are strings, and values can be any type).

In general, you can use a call to `lookup()` anywhere in your Puppet manifests you might otherwise use a literal value. The following code shows some examples of this (`lookup2.pp`):

```
notice("Apache is set to use ${lookup('apache_worker_factor',
Integer)} workers")

unless lookup('apparmor_enabled', Boolean) {
  exec { 'apt-get -y remove apparmor': }
}

notice('dns_allow_query enabled: ', lookup('dns_allow_query',
Boolean))
```

To apply this manifest in the example environment, run the following command:

```
sudo puppet apply --environment pbg /examples/lookup2.pp
Notice: Scope(Class[main]): Apache is set to use 100 workers
Notice: Scope(Class[main]): dns_allow_query enabled:  true
```

Typed lookups

As we've seen, `lookup()` takes a second parameter which specifies the expected type of the value to be retrieved. Although this is optional, you should always specify it, to help catch errors. If you accidentally look up the wrong key, or mistype the value in the data file, you'll get an error like this:

```
Error: Evaluation Error: Error while evaluating a Function Call,
Found value has wrong type, expects a Boolean value, got String at /
examples/lookup_type.pp:1:8 on node ubuntu-xenial
```

Types of Hiera data

As we've seen, Hiera data is stored in text files, structured using the format called **YAML Ain't Markup Language**, which is a common way of organizing data. Here's another snippet from our sample Hiera data file, which you'll find at `/etc/puppetlabs/code/environments/pbg/data/common.yaml` on the VM:

```
syslog_server: '10.170.81.32'
monitor_ips:
```

```
    - '10.179.203.46'
    - '212.100.235.160'
    - '10.181.120.77'
    - '94.236.56.148'
  cobbler_config:
    manage_dhcp: true
    pxe_just_once: true
```

There are actually three different kinds of Hiera data structures present: **single values**, **arrays**, and **hashes**. We'll examine these in detail in a moment.

Single values

Most Hiera data consists of a key associated with a single value, as in the previous example:

```
syslog_server: '10.170.81.32'
```

The value can be any legal Puppet value, such as a String, as in this case, or it can be an Integer:

```
apache_worker_factor: 100
```

Boolean values

You should specify Boolean values in Hiera as either `true` or `false`, without surrounding quotes. However, Hiera is fairly liberal in what it interprets as Boolean values: any of `true`, `on`, or `yes` (with or without quotes) are interpreted as a true value, and `false`, `off`, or `no` are interpreted as a false value. For clarity, though, stick to the following format:

```
consul_node: true
```

When you use `lookup()` to return a Boolean value in your Puppet code, you can use it as the conditional expression in, for example, an `if` statement:

```
if lookup('is_production', Boolean) {
  ...
```

Arrays

Usefully, Hiera can also store an array of values associated with a single key:

```
monitor_ips:
  - '10.179.203.46'
  - '212.100.235.160'
  - '10.181.120.77'
  - '94.236.56.148'
```

The key (`monitor_ips`) is followed by a list of values, each on its own line and preceded by a hyphen (`-`). When you call `lookup('monitor_ips', Array)` in your code, the values will be returned as a Puppet array.

Hashes

As we saw in *Chapter 5, Variables, expressions, and facts*, a hash (also called a **dictionary** in some programming languages) is like an array where each value has an identifying name (called the **key**), as in the following example:

```
cobbler_config:
  manage_dhcp: true
  pxe_just_once: true
```

Each key-value pair in the hash is listed, indented, on its own line. The `cobbler_config` hash has two keys, `manage_dhcp` and `pxe_just_once`. The value associated with each of those keys is `true`.

When you call `lookup('cobbler_config', Hash)` in a manifest, the data will be returned as a Puppet hash, and you can reference individual values in it using the normal Puppet hash syntax, as we saw in *Chapter 5, Variables, expressions, and facts* (`lookup_hash.pp`):

```
$cobbler_config = lookup('cobbler_config', Hash)
$manage_dhcp = $cobbler_config['manage_dhcp']
$pxe_just_once = $cobbler_config['pxe_just_once']
if $pxe_just_once {
  notice('pxe_just_once is enabled')
} else {
  notice('pxe_just_once is disabled')
}
```

Since it's very common for Hiera data to be a hash of hashes, you can retrieve values from several levels down in a hash by using the following "dot notation" (`lookup_hash_dot.pp`):

```
$web_root = lookup('cms_parameters.static.web_root', String)
notice("web_root is ${web_root}")
```

Interpolation in Hiera data

Hiera data is not restricted to literal values; it can also include the value of Facter facts or Puppet variables, as in the following example:

```
backup_path: "/backup/%{facts.hostname}"
```

Anything within the %{} delimiters inside a quoted string is evaluated and interpolated by Hiera. Here, we're using the dot notation to reference a value inside the $facts hash.

Using lookup()

Helpfully, you can also interpolate Hiera data in Hiera data, by using the lookup() function as part of the value. This can save you repeating the same value many times, and can make your data more readable, as in the following example (also from hiera_sample.yaml):

```
ips:
  home: '130.190.0.1'
  office1: '74.12.203.14'
  office2: '95.170.0.75'
firewall_allow_list:
  - "%{lookup('ips.home')}"
  - "%{lookup('ips.office1')}"
  - "%{lookup('ips.office2')}"
```

This is much more readable than simply listing a set of IP addresses with no indication of what they represent, and it prevents you accidentally introducing errors by updating a value in one place but not another. Use Hiera interpolation to make your data self-documenting.

Using alias()

When you use the lookup() function in a Hiera string value, the result is always a string. This is fine if you're working with string data, or if you want to interpolate a Hiera value into a string containing other text. However, if you're working with arrays, hashes, or Boolean values, you need to use the alias() function instead. This lets you re-use any Hiera data structure within Hiera, just by referencing its name:

```
firewall_allow_list:
  - "%{lookup('ips.home')}"
  - "%{lookup('ips.office1')}"
  - "%{lookup('ips.office2')}"
vpn_allow_list: "%{alias('firewall_allow_list')}"
```

Don't be fooled by the surrounding quotes: it may look as though vpn_allow_list will be a string value, but because we are using alias(), it will actually be an array, just like the value it is aliasing (firewall_allow_list).

Using literal()

Because the percent character (`%`) tells Hiera to interpolate a value, you might be wondering how to specify a literal percent sign in data. For example, Apache uses the percent sign in its configuration to refer to variable names like `%{HTTP_HOST}`. To write values like these in Hiera data, we need to use the `literal()` function, which exists only to refer to a literal percent character. For example, to write the value `%{HTTP_HOST}` as Hiera data, we would need to write:

```
%{literal('%')}{HTTP_HOST}
```

You can see a more complicated example in the sample Hiera data file:

```
force_www_rewrite:
  comment: "Force WWW"
  rewrite_cond: "%{literal('%')}{HTTP_HOST} !^www\\. [NC]"
  rewrite_rule: "^(.*)$ https://www.%{literal('%')}{HTTP_
HOST}%{literal('%')}{REQUEST_URI} [R=301,L]"
```

The hierarchy

So far, we've only used a single Hiera data source (`common.yaml`). Actually, you can have as many data sources as you like. Each usually corresponds to a YAML file, and they are listed in the `hierarchy` section of the `hiera.yaml` file, with the highest-priority source first and the lowest last:

```
hierarchy:
  ...
  - name: "Host-specific data"
    path: "nodes/%{facts.hostname}.yaml"
  - name: "OS release-specific data"
    path: "os/%{facts.os.release.major}.yaml"
  - name: "OS distro-specific data"
    path: "os/%{facts.os.distro.codename}.yaml"
  - name: "Common defaults"
    path: "common.yaml"
```

In general, though, you should keep as much data as possible in the `common.yaml` file, simply because it's easier to find and maintain data if it's in one place, rather than scattered through several files.

For example, if you have some Hiera data which is only used on the `monitor` node, you might be tempted to put it in a `nodes/monitor.yaml` file. But, unless it has to override some settings in `common.yaml`, you'll just be making it harder to find and update. Put everything in `common.yaml` that you can, and reserve other data sources only for overrides to common values.

Dealing with multiple values

You may be wondering what happens if the same key is listed in more than one Hiera data source. For example, imagine the first source contains the following:

```
consul_node: false
```

Also, assume that `common.yaml` contains:

```
consul_node: true
```

What happens when you call `lookup('consul_node', Boolean)` with this data? There are two different values for `consul_node` in two different files, so which one does Hiera return?

The answer is that Hiera searches data sources in the order they are listed in the `hierarchy` section; that is to say, in priority order. It returns the first value found, so if there are multiple values, only the value from the first—that is, highest-priority—data source will be returned (that's the "hierarchy" part).

Merge behaviors

We said in the previous section that if there is more than one value matching the specified key, the first matching data source takes priority over the others. This is the default behavior, and this is what you'll usually want. However, sometimes you may want `lookup()` to return the union of all the matching values found, throughout the hierarchy. Hiera allows you to specify which of these strategies it should use when multiple values match your lookup.

This is called a **merge behavior**, and you can specify which merge behavior you want as the third argument to `lookup()`, after the key and data type (`lookup_merge.pp`):

```
notice(lookup('firewall_allow_list', Array, 'unique'))
```

The default merge behavior is called `first`, and it returns only one value, the first found. By contrast, the `unique` merge behavior returns all the values found, as a flattened array, with duplicates removed (hence `unique`).

If you are looking up hash data, you can use the `hash` merge behavior to return a merged hash containing all the keys and values from all matching hashes found. If Hiera finds two hash keys with the same name, only the value of the first will be returned. This is known as a **shallow merge**. If you want a deep merge (that is, one where matching hashes will be merged at all levels, instead of just the top level) use the `deep` merge behavior.

If this all sounds a bit complicated, don't worry. The default merge behavior is probably what you want most of the time, and if you should happen to need one of the other behaviors instead, you can read more about it in the Puppet documentation.

Data sources based on facts

The hierarchy mechanism lets you set common default values for all situations (usually in `common.yaml`), but override them in specific circumstances. For example, you can set a data source in the hierarchy based on the value of a Puppet fact, such as the hostname:

```
- name: "Host-specific data"
  path: "nodes/%{facts.hostname}.yaml"
```

Hiera will look up the value of the specified fact and search for a data file with that name in the `nodes/` directory. In the previous example, if the node's hostname is `web1`, Hiera will look for the data file `nodes/web1.yaml` in the Hiera data directory. If this file exists and contains the specified Hiera key, the `web1` node will receive that value for its lookup, while other nodes will get the default value from `common`.

Note that you can organize your Hiera data files in subdirectories under the main `data/` directory if you like, such as `data/nodes/`.

Another useful fact to reference in the hierarchy is the operating system major version or codename. This is very useful when you need your manifest to work on more than one release of the operating system. If you have more than a handful of nodes, migrating to the latest OS release is usually a gradual process, upgrading one node at a time. If something has changed from one version to the next that affects your Puppet manifest, you can use the `os.distro.codename` fact to select the appropriate Hiera data, as in the following example:

```
- name: "OS-specific data"
  path: "os/%{facts.os.distro.codename}.yaml"
```

Alternatively, you can use the `os.release.major` fact:

```
- name: "OS-specific data"
  path: "os/%{facts.os.release.major}.yaml"
```

For example, if your node is running Ubuntu 16.04 Xenial, Hiera will look for a data file named `os/xenial.yaml` (if you're using `os.distro.codename`) or `os/16.04.yaml` (if you're using `os.release.major`) in the Hiera data directory.

For more information about facts in Puppet, see *Chapter 5, Variables, expressions, and facts*.

What belongs in Hiera?

What data should you put in Hiera, and what should be in your Puppet manifests? A good rule of thumb about when to separate data and code is to ask yourself what might **change** in the future. For example, the exact version of a package is a good candidate for Hiera data, because it's quite likely you'll need to update it in the future.

Another characteristic of data that belongs in Hiera is that it's **specific** to your site or company. If you take your Puppet manifest and give it to someone else in another company or organization, and she has to modify any values in the code to make it work at her site, then those values should probably be in Hiera. This makes it much easier to share and re-use code; all you have to do is edit some values in Hiera.

If the same data is needed in **more than one place** in your manifests, it's also a good idea for that data to be stored in Hiera. Otherwise, you have to either repeat the data, which makes it harder to maintain, or use a global variable, which is bad style in any programming language, and especially so in Puppet.

If you have to change a data value when you apply your manifests on a different **operating system**, that's also a candidate for Hiera data. As we've seen in this chapter, you can use the hierarchy to select the correct value based on facts, such as the operating system or version.

One other kind of data that belongs in Hiera is parameter values for classes and modules; we'll see more about that in *Chapter 7, Mastering modules*.

Creating resources with Hiera data

When we started working with Puppet, we created resources directly in the manifest using literal attribute values. In this chapter, we've seen how to use Hiera data to fill in the title and attributes of resources in the manifest. We can now take this idea one step further and create resources **directly from Hiera** queries. The advantage of this method is that we can create any number of resources of any type, based purely on data.

Building resources from Hiera arrays

In *Chapter 5, Variables, expressions, and facts*, we learned how to use Puppet's `each` function to iterate over an array or hash, creating resources as we go. Let's apply this technique to some Hiera data. In our first example, we'll create some user resources from a Hiera array.

Run the following command:

```
sudo puppet apply --environment pbg /examples/hiera_users.pp
Notice: /Stage[main]/Main/User[katy]/ensure: created
Notice: /Stage[main]/Main/User[lark]/ensure: created
Notice: /Stage[main]/Main/User[bridget]/ensure: created
Notice: /Stage[main]/Main/User[hsing-hui]/ensure: created
Notice: /Stage[main]/Main/User[charles]/ensure: created
```

Here's the data we're using (from the `/etc/puppetlabs/code/environments/pbg/data/common.yaml` file):

```
users:
  - 'katy'
  - 'lark'
  - 'bridget'
  - 'hsing-hui'
  - 'charles'
```

And here's the code which reads it and creates the corresponding user instances (`hiera_users.pp`):

```
lookup('users', Array[String]).each | String $username | {
  user { $username:
    ensure => present,
  }
}
```

Combining Hiera data with resource iteration is a powerful idea. This short manifest could manage all the users in your infrastructure, without you ever having to edit the Puppet code to make changes. To add new users, you need only edit the Hiera data.

Building resources from Hiera hashes

Of course, real life is never quite as simple as a programming language example. If you were really managing users with Hiera data in this way, you'd need to include more data than just their names: you'd need to be able to manage shells, UIDs, and so on, and you'd also need to be able to remove the users if necessary. To do that, we will need to add some structure to the Hiera data.

Run the following command:

```
sudo puppet apply --environment pbg /examples/hiera_users2.pp
Notice: Compiled catalog for ubuntu-xenial in environment pbg in 0.05
seconds
Notice: /Stage[main]/Main/User[katy]/uid: uid changed 1001 to 1900
Notice: /Stage[main]/Main/User[katy]/shell: shell changed '' to '/bin/
bash'
Notice: /Stage[main]/Main/User[lark]/uid: uid changed 1002 to 1901
Notice: /Stage[main]/Main/User[lark]/shell: shell changed '' to '/bin/
sh'
Notice: /Stage[main]/Main/User[bridget]/uid: uid changed 1003 to 1902
Notice: /Stage[main]/Main/User[bridget]/shell: shell changed '' to '/
bin/bash'
Notice: /Stage[main]/Main/User[hsing-hui]/uid: uid changed 1004 to
1903
Notice: /Stage[main]/Main/User[hsing-hui]/shell: shell changed '' to
'/bin/sh'
Notice: /Stage[main]/Main/User[charles]/uid: uid changed 1005 to 1904
Notice: /Stage[main]/Main/User[charles]/shell: shell changed '' to '/
bin/bash'
Notice: Applied catalog in 0.17 seconds
```

The first difference from the previous example is that instead of the data being a simple array, it's a hash of hashes:

```
users2:
  'katy':
    ensure: present
    uid: 1900
    shell: '/bin/bash'
  'lark':
    ensure: present
    uid: 1901
    shell: '/bin/sh'
  'bridget':
    ensure: present
    uid: 1902
    shell: '/bin/bash'
  'hsing-hui':
    ensure: present
    uid: 1903
    shell: '/bin/sh'
  'charles':
    ensure: present
    uid: 1904
    shell: '/bin/bash'
```

Here's the code which processes that data (`hiera_users2.pp`):

```
lookup('users2', Hash, 'hash').each | String $username, Hash $attrs |
{
  user { $username:
    * => $attrs,
  }
}
```

Each of the keys in the `users2` hash is a username, and each value is a hash of user attributes such as `uid` and `shell`.

When we call `each` on this hash, we specify two parameters to the loop instead of one:

```
| String $username, Hash $attrs |
```

As we saw in *Chapter 5, Variables, expressions, and facts*, when iterating over a hash, these two parameters receive the hash key and its value, respectively.

Inside the loop, we create a user resource for each element of the hash:

```
user { $username:
  * => $attrs,
}
```

You may recall from the previous chapter that the `*` operator (the attribute splat operator) tells Puppet to treat `$attrs` as a hash of attribute-value pairs. So the first time round the loop, with user `katy`, Puppet will create a user resource equivalent to the following manifest:

```
user { 'katy':
  ensure => present,
  uid    => 1900,
  shell  => '/bin/bash',
}
```

Every time we go round the loop with the next element of `users`, Puppet will create another user resource with the specified attributes.

The advantages of managing resources with Hiera data

The previous example makes it easy to manage users across your network without having to edit Puppet code: if you want to remove a user, for example, you would simply change her `ensure` attribute in the Hiera data to `absent`. Although each of the users happens to have the same set of attributes specified, this isn't essential; you could add any attribute supported by the Puppet `user` resource to any user in the data. Also, if there's an attribute whose value is always the same for all users, you need not list it in the Hiera data for every user. You can add it as a literal attribute value of the `user` resource inside the loop, and thus every user will have it.

This makes it easier to add and update users on a routine basis, but there are other advantages too: for example, you could write a simple web application which allowed HR staff to add or edit users using a browser interface, and it would only need to output a YAML file with the required data. This is much easier and more robust than trying to generate Puppet code automatically. Even better, you could pull user data from an LDAP or **Active Directory** (**AD**) server and put it into Hiera YAML format for input into this manifest.

This is a very powerful and flexible technique, and of course you can use it to manage any kind of Puppet resource: files, packages, Apache virtual hosts, MySQL databases—anything you can do with a resource you can do with Hiera data and `each`. You can also use Hiera's override mechanism to create different sets of resources for different nodes, roles, or operating systems.

However, you shouldn't over-use this technique. Creating resources from Hiera data adds a layer of abstraction which makes it harder to understand the code for anyone trying to read or maintain it. With Hiera, it can also be difficult to work out from inspection exactly what data the node will get in a given set of circumstances. Keep your hierarchy as simple as possible, and reserve the data-driven resources trick for situations where you have a large and variable number of resources which you need to update frequently. In *Chapter 11, Orchestrating cloud resources*, we'll see how to use the same technique to manage cloud instances, for example.

Managing secret data

Puppet often needs to know your secrets; for example, passwords, private keys, and other credentials need to be configured on the node, and Puppet must have access to this information. The problem is how to make sure that no-one else does. If you are checking this data into a Git repo, it will be available to anybody who has access to the repo, and if it's a public GitHub repo, everybody in the world can see it.

Clearly, it's essential to be able to encrypt secret data in such a way that Puppet can decrypt it on individual nodes where it's needed, but it's indecipherable to anybody who does not have the key. The popular GnuPG encryption tool is a good choice for this. It lets you encrypt data using a public key which can be distributed widely, but only someone with the corresponding private key can decrypt the information.

Hiera has a pluggable **backend** system which allows it to support various different ways of storing data. One such backend is called `hiera-eyaml-gpg`, which allows Hiera to use a GnuPG-encrypted data store. Rather than encrypting a whole data file, `hiera-eyaml-gpg` lets you mix encrypted and plaintext data in the same YAML file. That way, even someone who doesn't have the private key can still edit and update the plaintext values in Hiera data files, although the encrypted data values will be unreadable to them.

Setting up GnuPG

First, we'll need to install GnuPG and create a key pair for use with Hiera. The following instructions will help you do this:

1. Run the following command:

   ```
   sudo apt-get install gnupg rng-tools
   ```

2. Once GnuPG is installed, run the following command to generate a new key pair:

   ```
   gpg --gen-key
   ```

3. When prompted, select the RSA and RSA key type:

   ```
   Please select what kind of key you want:
      (1) RSA and RSA (default)
      (2) DSA and Elgamal
      (3) DSA (sign only)
      (4) RSA (sign only)
   Your selection? 1
   ```

4. Select a 2,048 bit key size:

   ```
   RSA keys may be between 1024 and 4096 bits long.
   What keysize do you want? (2048) 2048
   ```

5. Enter `0` for the key expiry time:

   ```
   Key is valid for? (0) 0
   Key does not expire at all
   Is this correct? (y/N) y
   ```

6. When prompted for a real name, email address, and comment for the key, enter whatever is appropriate for your site:

```
Real name: Puppet
Email address: puppet@cat-pictures.com
Comment:
You selected this USER-ID:
    "Puppet <puppet@cat-pictures.com>"

Change (N)ame, (C)omment, (E)mail or (O)kay/(Q)uit? o
```

7. When prompted for a passphrase, just hit *Enter* (the key can't have a passphrase, because Puppet won't be able to supply it).

It may take a few moments to generate the key, but once this is complete, GnuPG will print out the key fingerprint and details (yours will look different):

```
pub   2048R/40486112 2016-09-30
      Key fingerprint = 6758 6CEE D221 7AA0 8369  FF3A FEC1 0055 4048
6112
uid                  Puppet <puppet@cat-pictures.com>
sub   2048R/472954EB 2016-09-30
```

This key is now stored in your GnuPG keyring, and Hiera will be able to use it to encrypt and decrypt your secret data on this node. We'll see later in the chapter how to distribute this key to other nodes managed by Puppet.

Adding an encrypted Hiera source

A Hiera source using GPG-encrypted data needs a couple of extra parameters. Here's the relevant section from the example `hiera.yaml` file:

```
- name: "Secret data (encrypted)"
  lookup_key: eyaml_lookup_key
  path: "secret.eyaml"
  options:
    gpg_gnupghome: '/home/ubuntu/.gnupg'
```

As with normal data sources, we a have `name` and a `path` to the data file, but we also need to specify the `lookup_key` function, which in this case is `eyaml_lookup_key`, and set `options['gpg_gnupghome']` to point to the GnuPG directory, where the decryption key lives.

Creating an encrypted secret

You're now ready to add some secret data to your Hiera store.

1. Create a new empty Hiera data file with the following commands:

```
cd /etc/puppetlabs/code/environments/pbg
sudo touch data/secret.eyaml
```

2. Run the following command to edit the data file using the `eyaml` editor (which automatically encrypts the data for you when you save it). Instead of `puppet@cat-pictures.com`, use the email address that you entered when you created your GPG key.

```
sudo /opt/puppetlabs/puppet/bin/eyaml edit --gpg-always-trust
--gpg-recipients=puppet@cat-pictures.com data/secret.eyaml
```

3. If the system prompts you to select your default editor, choose the editor you prefer. If you're familiar with Vim, I recommend you choose that, but otherwise, you will probably find `nano` the easiest option. (You should learn Vim, but that's a subject for another book.)
4. Your selected editor will be started with the following text already inserted in the file:

```
#| This is eyaml edit mode. This text (lines starting with #| at
the top of the
#| file) will be removed when you save and exit.
#|  - To edit encrypted values, change the content of the
DEC(<num>)::PKCS7[]!
#|     block (or DEC(<num>)::GPG[]!).
#|     WARNING: DO NOT change the number in the parentheses.
#|  - To add a new encrypted value copy and paste a new block from
the
#|     appropriate example below. Note that:
#|      * the text to encrypt goes in the square brackets
#|      * ensure you include the exclamation mark when you copy and
paste
#|      * you must not include a number when adding a new block
#|     e.g. DEC::PKCS7[]! -or- DEC::GPG[]!
```

5. Enter the following text below the commented message, exactly as shown, including the beginning three hyphens:

```
---
  test_secret: DEC::GPG[This is a test secret]!
```

6. Save the file and exit the editor.

7. Run the following command to test that Puppet can read and decrypt your secret:

```
sudo puppet lookup --environment pbg test_secret
--- This is a test secret
```

How Hiera decrypts secrets

To prove to yourself that the secret data is actually encrypted, run the following command to see what it looks like in the data file on disk:

```
cat data/secret.eyaml
---
  test_secret: ENC[GPG,hQEMA4+8DyxHKVTrAQf/QQPL4zD2kkU7T+FhaEdptu68RA
w2m2KAXGujjnQPXoONrbh1QjtzZiJBlhqOP+7JwvzejED0NXNMkmWTGfCrOBvQlZS0U9V
rgsyq5mACPHyeLqFbdeOjNEIR7gLP99aykAmbO2mRqfXvns+cZgaTUEPXOPyipY5Q6w6/
KeBEvekTIZ6ME9Oketj+1/zyDz4qWH+0nLwdD9L279d7hnokpts2tp+gpCUc0/qKsTXpdT
RPE2R0kg9Bl84OP3fFlTSTgcT+pS8Dfa1/ZzALfHmULcC3hckG9ZSR+0cd6MyJzucwiJC
reIfR/cDfqpsENNM6PNkTAHEHrAqPrSDXilg1KtJSAfZ9rS8KtRyhoSsk+XyrxIRH/S1Qg
1dgFb8VqJzWjFl6GBJZemy7z+xjoWHyznbABVwp0KXNGgn/0idxfhz1mTo2/49POFiVF4M
Bo/6/EEU4cw==]
```

Of course, the actual ciphertext will be different for you, since you're using a different encryption key. The point is, though, the message is completely scrambled. GnuPG's encryption algorithms are extremely strong; even using every computer on Earth simultaneously, it would take (on average) many times the current age of the Universe to unscramble data encrypted with a 2,048-bit key. (Or, to put it a different way, the chances of decrypting the data within a reasonable amount of time are many billions to one.)

When you reference a Hiera key such as `test_secret` in your manifest, what happens next? Hiera consults its list of data sources configured in `hiera.yaml`. The first source in the hierarchy is `secret.eyaml`, which contains the key we're interested in (`test_secret`). Here's the value:

```
ENC[GPG,hQEMA4 ... EEU4cw==]
```

The `ENC` tells Hiera that this is an encrypted value, and the `GPG` identifies which type of encryption is being used (`hiera-eyaml` supports several encryption methods, of which GPG is one). Hiera calls the GPG subsystem to process the encrypted data, and GPG searches the keyring to find the appropriate decryption key. Assuming it finds the key, GPG decrypts the data and passes the result back to Hiera, which returns it to Puppet, and the result is the plaintext:

```
This is a test secret
```

The beauty of the system is that all of this complexity is hidden from you; all you have to do is call the function `lookup('test_secret', String)` in your manifest, and you get the answer.

Editing or adding encrypted secrets

If the secret data is stored in encrypted form, you might be wondering how to edit it when you want to change the secret value. Fortunately, there's a way to do this. Recall that when you first entered the secret data, you used the following command:

```
sudo /opt/puppetlabs/puppet/bin/eyaml edit --gpg-always-trust --gpg-recipients=puppet@cat-pictures.com data/secret.eyaml
```

If you run the same command again, you'll find that you're looking at your original plaintext (along with some explanatory comments):

```
---
  test_secret: DEC(1)::GPG[This is a test secret]!
```

You can edit the `This is a test secret` string (make sure to leave everything else exactly as it is, including the `DEC::GPG[]!` delimiters). When you save the file and close the editor, the data will be re-encrypted using your key, if it has changed.

Don't remove the `(1)` in parentheses after `DEC`; it tells Hiera that this is an existing secret, not a new one. As you add more secrets to this file, they will be identified with increasing numbers.

For convenience of editing, I suggest you make a shell script, called something like `/usr/local/bin/eyaml_edit`, which runs the `eyaml edit` command. There's an example on your Vagrant box, at `/examples/eyaml_edit.sh`, which you can copy to `/usr/local/bin` and edit (as before, substitute the `gpg-recipients` email address with the one associated with your GPG key):

```
#!/bin/bash
/opt/puppetlabs/puppet/bin/eyaml edit --gpg-always-trust --gpg-recipients=puppet@cat-pictures.com /etc/puppetlabs/code/environments/pbg/data/secret.eyaml
```

Now, whenever you need to edit your secret data, you can simply run the following command:

```
sudo eyaml_edit
```

To add a new secret, add a line like this:

```
  new_secret: DEC::GPG[Somebody wake up Hicks]!
```

When you save and quit the editor, the newly-encrypted secret will be stored in the data file.

Distributing the decryption key

Now that your Puppet manifests use encrypted Hiera data, you'll need to make sure that each node running Puppet has a copy of the decryption key. Export the key to a text file using the following command (use your key's email address, of course):

```
sudo sh -c 'gpg --export-secret-key -a puppet@cat-pictures.com >key.
txt'
```

Copy the `key.txt` file to any nodes which need the key, and run the following command to import it:

```
sudo gpg --import key.txt
sudo rm key.txt
```

Make sure that you delete all copies of the text file once you have imported the key.

Important note

Because all Puppet nodes have a copy of the decryption key, this method only protects your secret data from someone who does not have access to the nodes. It is still considerably better than putting secret data in your manifests in plaintext, but it has the disadvantage that someone with access to a node can decrypt, modify, and re-encrypt the secret data. For improved security you should use a secrets management system where the node does not have the key, and Puppet has read-only access to secrets. Some options here include Vault, from Hashicorp, and Summon, from Conjur.

Summary

In this chapter we've outlined some of the problems with maintaining configuration data in Puppet manifests, and introduced Hiera as a powerful solution. We've seen how to configure Puppet to use the Hiera data store, and how to query Hiera keys in Puppet manifests using `lookup()`.

We've looked at how to write Hiera data sources, including string, array, and hash data structures, and how to interpolate values into Hiera strings using `lookup()`, including Puppet facts and other Hiera data, and how to duplicate Hiera data structures using `alias()`. We've learned how Hiera's hierarchy works, and how to configure it using the `hiera.yaml` file.

We've seen how our example Puppet infrastructure is configured to use Hiera data, and demonstrated the process by looking up a data value in a Puppet manifest. In case of problems, we also looked at some common Hiera errors, and we've discussed rules of thumb about when to put data into Hiera.

We've explored using Hiera data to create resources, using an `each` loop over an array or hash. Finally, we've covered using encrypted data with Hiera, using the `hiera-eyaml-gpg` backend, and we've seen how to create a GnuPG key and use it to encrypt a secret value, and retrieve it again via Puppet. We've explored the process Hiera uses to find and decrypt secret data, developed a simple script to make it easy to edit encrypted data files, and outlined a basic way to distribute the decryption key to multiple nodes.

In the next chapter, we'll look at how to find and use public modules from Puppet Forge; how to use public modules to manage software including Apache, MySQL, and archive files; how to use the `r10k` tool to deploy and manage third-party modules; and how to write and structure your own modules.

7
Mastering modules

> *There are no big problems, there are just a lot of little problems.*
>
> *—Henry Ford*

In this chapter you'll learn about Puppet Forge, the public repository for Puppet modules, and you'll see how to install and use third-party modules from Puppet Forge, using the `r10k` module management tool. You'll see examples of how to use three important Forge modules: `puppetlabs/apache`, `puppetlabs/mysql`, and `puppet/archive`. You'll be introduced to some useful functions provided by `puppetlabs/stdlib`, the Puppet standard library. Finally, working through a complete example, you'll learn how to develop your own Puppet module from scratch, how to add appropriate metadata for your module, and how to upload it to Puppet Forge.

Using Puppet Forge modules

Although you could write your own manifests for everything you want to manage, you can save yourself a lot of time and effort by using public Puppet modules wherever possible. A **module** in Puppet is a self-contained unit of shareable, reusable code, usually designed to manage one particular service or piece of software, such as the Apache web server.

What is the Puppet Forge?

The **Puppet Forge** is a public repository of Puppet modules, many of them officially supported and maintained by Puppet and all of which you can download and use.
You can browse the Forge at the following URL:

`https://forge.puppet.com/`

One of the advantages of using a well-established tool like Puppet is that there are a large number of mature public modules available, which cover the most common software you're likely to need. For example, here is a small selection of the things you can manage with public modules from Puppet Forge:

- MySQL/PostgreSQL/SQL Server
- Apache/Nginx
- Java/Tomcat/PHP/Ruby/Rails
- HAProxy
- Amazon AWS
- Docker
- Jenkins
- Elasticsearch/Redis/Cassandra
- Git repos
- Firewalls (via iptables)

Finding the module you need

The Puppet Forge home page has a search bar at the top. Type what you're looking for into this box, and the website will show you all the modules which match your search keywords. Often, there will be more than one result, so how do you decide which module to use?

The best choice is a **Puppet Supported** module, if one is available. These are officially supported and maintained by Puppet, and you can be confident that supported modules will work with a wide range of operating systems and Puppet versions. Supported modules are indicated by a yellow **SUPPORTED** flag in search results, or you can browse the list of all supported modules at the following URL:

`https://forge.puppet.com/modules?endorsements=supported`

The next best option is a **Puppet Approved** module. While not officially supported, these modules are recommended by Puppet and have been checked to make sure they follow best practices and meet certain quality standards. Approved modules are indicated by a green **APPROVED** flag in search results, or you can browse the list of all approved modules at the following URL:

`https://forge.puppet.com/modules?endorsements=approved`

Assuming that a Puppet-Supported or Puppet-Approved module is not available, another useful way to choose modules is by looking at the number of downloads. Selecting the **Most Downloads** tab on the Puppet Forge search results page will sort the results by downloads, with the most popular modules first. The most-downloaded modules are not necessarily the best, of course, but they're usually a good place to start.

It's also worth checking the latest release date for modules. If the module you're looking at hasn't been updated in over a year, it may be better to go with a more actively-maintained module, if one is available. Clicking on the **Latest release** tab will sort search results by the most recently updated.

You can also filter search results by operating system support and Puppet version compatibility; this can be very useful for finding a module that works with your system.

Having chosen the module you want, it's time to add it to your Puppet infrastructure.

Using r10k

In the past, many people used to download Puppet Forge modules directly and check a copy of them into their codebase, effectively forking the module repo (and some still do this). There are many drawbacks to this approach. One is that your codebase becomes cluttered with code that is not yours, and this can make it difficult to search for the code you want. Another is that it's difficult to test your code with different versions of public modules, without creating your own Git branches, redownloading the modules, and so on. You also won't get future bug fixes and improvements from the Puppet Forge modules unless you manually update your copies. In many cases, you will need to make small changes or fixes to the modules to use them in your environment, and your version of the module will then diverge from the upstream version, storing up maintenance problems for the future.

A much better approach to module management, therefore, is to use the `r10k` tool, which eliminates these problems. Instead of downloading the modules you need directly and adding them to your codebase, `r10k` installs your required modules on each Puppet-managed node, using a special text file called a **Puppetfile**. `r10k` will manage the contents of your `modules/` directory, based entirely on the Puppetfile metadata. The module code is never checked into your codebase, but always downloaded from the Puppet Forge when requested. So you can stay up to date with the latest releases if you want, or pin each module to a specified version which you know works with your manifest.

`r10k` is the de facto standard module manager for Puppet deployments, and we'll be using it to manage modules throughout the rest of this book.

In this example, we'll use `r10k` to install the `puppetlabs/stdlib` module. The Puppetfile in the example repo contains a list of all the modules we'll use in this book. Here it is (we'll look more closely at the syntax in a moment):

```
forge 'http://forge.puppetlabs.com'

mod 'garethr/docker', '5.3.0'
mod 'puppet/archive', '1.3.0'
mod 'puppet/staging', '2.2.0'
mod 'puppetlabs/apache', '2.0.0'
mod 'puppetlabs/apt', '3.0.0'
mod 'puppetlabs/aws', '2.0.0'
mod 'puppetlabs/concat', '4.0.1'
mod 'puppetlabs/docker_platform', '2.2.1'
mod 'puppetlabs/mysql', '3.11.0'
mod 'puppetlabs/stdlib', '4.17.1'
mod 'stahnma/epel', '1.2.2'

mod 'pbg_ntp',
  :git => 'https://github.com/bitfield/pbg_ntp.git',
  :tag => '0.1.4'
```

Follow these steps:

1. Run the following commands to clear out your `modules/` directory, if there's anything in it (make sure you have backed up anything here you want to keep):

   ```
   cd /etc/puppetlabs/code/environments/pbg
   sudo rm -rf modules/
   ```

2. Run the following command to have `r10k` process the example Puppetfile here and install your requested modules:

   ```
   sudo r10k puppetfile install --verbose
   ```

r10k downloads all the modules listed in the Puppetfile into the modules/ directory. All modules in this directory will be automatically loaded by Puppet and available for use in your manifests. To test that the stdlib module is correctly installed, run the following command:

```
sudo puppet apply --environment pbg -e "notice(upcase('hello'))"
Notice: Scope(Class[main]): HELLO
```

The upcase function, which converts its string argument to uppercase, is part of the stdlib module. If this doesn't work, then stdlib has not been properly installed. As in previous examples, we're using the --environment pbg switch to tell Puppet to look for code, modules, and data in the /etc/puppetlabs/code/environments/pbg directory.

Understanding the Puppetfile

The example Puppetfile begins with the following:

```
forge 'http://forge.puppetlabs.com'
```

The forge statement specifies the repository where modules should be retrieved from.

There follows a group of lines beginning with mod:

```
mod 'garethr/docker', '5.3.0'
mod 'puppet/archive', '1.3.0'
mod 'puppet/staging', '2.2.0'
...
```

The mod statement specifies the name of the module (puppetlabs/stdlib) and the specific version of the module to install (4.17.0).

Managing dependencies with generate-puppetfile

r10k does not automatically manage dependencies between modules. For example, the puppetlabs/apache module depends on having both puppetlabs/stdlib and puppetlabs/concat installed. r10k will not automatically install these for you unless you specify them, so you also need to include them in your Puppetfile.

However, you can use the generate-puppetfile tool to find out what dependencies you need so that you can add them to your Puppetfile.

1. Run the following command to install the generate-puppetfile gem:

   ```
   sudo gem install generate-puppetfile
   ```

2. Run the following command to generate the Puppetfile for a list of specified modules (list all the modules you need on the command line, separated by spaces):

```
generate-puppetfile puppetlabs/docker_platform
Installing modules. This may take a few minutes.
Your Puppetfile has been generated. Copy and paste between the
markers:
=============================================
forge 'http://forge.puppetlabs.com'

# Modules discovered by generate-puppetfile
mod 'garethr/docker', '5.3.0'
mod 'puppetlabs/apt', '3.0.0'
mod 'puppetlabs/docker_platform', '2.2.1'
mod 'puppetlabs/stdlib', '4.17.1'
mod 'stahnma/epel', '1.2.2'
=============================================
```

3. Run the following command to generate a list of updated versions and dependencies for an existing Puppetfile:

```
generate-puppetfile -p /etc/puppetlabs/code/environments/pbg/
Puppetfile
```

This is an extremely useful tool both for finding dependencies you need to specify in your Puppetfile and for keeping your Puppetfile up to date with the latest versions of all the modules you use.

Using modules in your manifests

Now that we know how to find and install public Puppet modules, let's see how to use them. We'll work through a few examples, using the `puppetlabs/mysql` module to set up a MySQL server and database, using the `puppetlabs/apache` module to set up an Apache website, and using `puppet/archive` to download and unpack a compressed archive. After you've tried out these examples, you should feel quite confident in your ability to find an appropriate Puppet module, add it to your `Puppetfile`, and deploy it with `r10k`.

Using puppetlabs/mysql

Follow these steps to run the `puppetlabs/mysql` example:

1. If you've previously followed the steps in the *Using r10k* section, the required module will already be installed. If not, run the following commands to install it:

```
cd /etc/puppetlabs/code/environments/pbg
sudo r10k puppetfile install
```

2. Run the following command to apply the manifest:

```
sudo puppet apply --environment=pbg /examples/module_mysql.pp
Notice: Compiled catalog for ubuntu-xenial in environment pbg in
0.89 seconds
Notice: /Stage[main]/Mysql::Server::Config/File[/etc/mysql]/
ensure: created
Notice: /Stage[main]/Mysql::Server::Config/File[/etc/mysql/
conf.d]/ensure: created
Notice: /Stage[main]/Mysql::Server::Config/File[mysql-config-
file]/ensure: defined content as '{md5}44e7aa974ab98260d7d013a2087
f1c77'
Notice: /Stage[main]/Mysql::Server::Install/Package[mysql-server]/
ensure: created
Notice: /Stage[main]/Mysql::Server::Root_password/Mysql_
user[root@localhost]/password_hash: password_hash changed '' to
'*F4AF2E5D85456A908E0F552F0366375B06267295'
Notice: /Stage[main]/Mysql::Server::Root_password/File[/root/.
my.cnf]/ensure: defined content as '{md5}4d59f37fc8a385c9c50f8bb32
86b7c85'
Notice: /Stage[main]/Mysql::Client::Install/Package[mysql_client]/
ensure: created
Notice: /Stage[main]/Main/Mysql::Db[cat_pictures]/Mysql_
database[cat_pictures]/ensure: created
Notice: /Stage[main]/Main/Mysql::Db[cat_pictures]/Mysql_
user[greebo@localhost]/ensure: created
Notice: /Stage[main]/Main/Mysql::Db[cat_pictures]/Mysql_
grant[greebo@localhost/cat_pictures.*]/ensure: created
Notice: Applied catalog in 79.85 seconds
```

Let's take a look at the example manifest (`module_mysql.pp`). The first part installs the MySQL server itself, by including the class `mysql::server`:

```
# Install MySQL and set up an example database
include mysql::server
```

The `mysql::server` class accepts a number of parameters, most of which we needn't worry about for now, but we would like to set a couple of them for this example. Although you can set the values for class parameters directly in your Puppet manifest code, just as you would for resource attributes, I'll show you a better way to do it: using Hiera's automatic parameter lookup mechanism.

We mentioned briefly in *Chapter 6, Managing data with Hiera*, that Hiera can supply values for class and module parameters, but how does it work, exactly? When you include a class x which takes a parameter y, Puppet automatically searches Hiera for any keys matching the name x::y. If it finds one, it uses that value for the parameter. Just as with any other Hiera data, you can use the hierarchy to set different values for different nodes, roles, or operating systems.

In this example, our parameters are set in the example Hiera data file (/etc/puppetlabs/code/environments/pbg/data/common.yaml):

```
mysql::server::root_password: 'hairline-quotient-inside-tableful'
mysql::server::remove_default_accounts: true
```

The root_password parameter, as you'd expect, sets the password for the MySQL root user. We also enable remove_default_accounts, which is a security feature. MySQL ships with various default user accounts for testing purposes, which should be turned off in production. This parameter disables these default accounts.

Note that although we've specified the password in plain text for the purposes of clarity, in your production manifests, this should be encrypted, just as with any other credentials or secret data (see *Chapter 6, Managing data with Hiera*).

Next comes a resource declaration:

```
mysql::db { 'cat_pictures':
  user     => 'greebo',
  password => 'tabby',
  host     => 'localhost',
  grant    => ['SELECT', 'UPDATE'],
}
```

As you can see, this looks just like the built-in resources we've used before, such as the file and package resources. In effect, the mysql module has added a new resource type to Puppet: mysql::db. This resource models a specific MySQL database: cat_pictures in our example.

The title of the resource is the name of the database, in this case, cat_pictures. There follows a list of attributes. The user, password, and host attributes specify that the user greebo should be allowed to connect to the database from localhost using the password tabby. The grant attribute specifies the MySQL privileges that the user should have: SELECT and UPDATE on the database.

When this manifest is applied, Puppet will create the `cat_pictures` database and set up the `greebo` user account to access it. This is a very common pattern for Puppet manifests which manage an application: usually, the application needs some sort of database to store its state, and user credentials to access it. The `mysql` module lets you configure this very easily.

So we can now see the general principles of using a Puppet Forge module:

- We add the module and its dependencies to our `Puppetfile` and deploy it using `r10k`
- We `include` the class in our manifest, supplying any required parameters as Hiera data
- Optionally, we add one or more resource declarations of a custom resource type defined by the module (in this case, a MySQL database)

Almost all Puppet modules work in a similar way. In the next section, we'll look at some key modules which you're likely to need in the course of managing servers with Puppet.

Using puppetlabs/apache

Most applications have a web interface of some kind, which usually requires a web server, and the venerable Apache remains a popular choice. The `puppetlabs/apache` module not only installs and configures Apache, but also allows you to manage virtual hosts (individual websites, such as the frontend for your application).

Here's an example manifest which uses the `apache` module to create a simple virtual host serving an image file (`module_apache.pp`):

```
include apache

apache::vhost { 'cat-pictures.com':
  port          => '80',
  docroot       => '/var/www/cat-pictures',
  docroot_owner => 'www-data',
  docroot_group => 'www-data',
}

file { '/var/www/cat-pictures/index.html':
  content => "<img
    src='http://bitfieldconsulting.com/files/happycat.jpg'>",
  owner   => 'www-data',
  group   => 'www-data',
}
```

Follow these steps to apply the manifest:

1. If you've previously followed the steps in the *Using r10k* section, the required module will already be installed. If not, run the following commands to install it:

   ```
   cd /etc/puppetlabs/code/environments/pbg
   sudo r10k puppetfile install
   ```

2. Run the following command to apply the manifest:

   ```
   sudo puppet apply --environment=pbg /examples/module_apache.pp
   ```

3. To test the new website, point your browser to (for Vagrant users; if you're not using the Vagrant box, browse to port `80` on the server you're managing with Puppet) `http://localhost:8080/`

You should see a picture of a happy cat:

Let's go through the manifest and see how it works in detail.

1. It starts with the `include` declaration which actually installs Apache on the server (`module_apache.pp`):

   ```
   include apache
   ```

2. There are many parameters you could set for the `apache` class, but in this example, we only need to set one, and as with the other examples, we set it using Hiera data in the example Hiera file:

   ```
   apache::default_vhost: false
   ```

   This disables the default **Apache 2 Test Page** virtual host.

3. Next comes a resource declaration for an `apache::vhost` resource, which creates an Apache virtual host or website.

```
apache::vhost { 'cat-pictures.com':
  port          => '80',
  docroot       => '/var/www/cat-pictures',
  docroot_owner => 'www-data',
  docroot_group => 'www-data',
}
```

   The title of the resource is the domain name which the virtual host will respond to (`cat-pictures.com`). The `port` tells Apache which port to listen on for requests. The `docroot` identifies the pathname of the directory where Apache will find the website files on the server. Finally, the `docroot_owner` and `docroot_group` attributes specify the user and group which should own the `docroot/` directory.

4. Finally, we create an `index.html` file to add some content to the website, in this case, an image of a happy cat.

```
file { '/var/www/cat-pictures/index.html':
  content => "<img
    src='http://bitfieldconsulting.com/files/happycat.jpg'>",
  owner   => 'www-data',
  group   => 'www-data',
}
```

Note that port `80` on the Vagrant box is mapped to port `8080` on your local machine, so browsing to `http://localhost:8080` is the equivalent of browsing directly to port `80` on the Vagrant box. If for some reason you need to change this port mapping, edit your `Vagrantfile` (in the Puppet Beginner's Guide repo) and look for the following line:

```
config.vm.network "forwarded_port", guest: 80, host:
8080
```

Change these settings as required and run the following command on your local machine in the PBG repo directory:

```
vagrant reload
```

Using puppet/archive

While installing software from packages is a common task, you'll also occasionally need to install software from archive files, such as a tarball (a `.tar.gz` file) or ZIP file. The `puppet/archive` module is a great help for this, as it provides an easy way to download archive files from the Internet, and it can also unpack them for you.

In the following example, we'll use the `puppet/archive` module to download and unpack the latest version of the popular WordPress blogging software. Follow these steps to apply the manifest:

1. If you've previously followed the steps in the *Using r10k* section, the required module will already be installed. If not, run the following commands to install it:

   ```
   cd /etc/puppetlabs/code/environments/pbg
   sudo r10k puppetfile install
   ```

2. Run the following command to apply the manifest:

   ```
   sudo puppet apply --environment=pbg /examples/module_archive.pp
   Notice: Compiled catalog for ubuntu-xenial in environment
   production in 2.50 seconds
   Notice: /Stage[main]/Main/Archive[/tmp/wordpress.tar.gz]/ensure:
   download archive from https://wordpress.org/latest.tar.gz to /tmp/
   wordpress.tar.gz and extracted in /var/www with cleanup
   ```

Unlike the previous modules in this chapter, there's nothing to install with `archive`, so we don't need to include the class itself. All you need to do is declare an `archive` resource. Let's look at the example in detail to see how it works (`module_archive.pp`):

```
archive { '/tmp/wordpress.tar.gz':
  ensure       => present,
  extract      => true,
  extract_path => '/var/www',
  source       => 'https://wordpress.org/latest.tar.gz',
  creates      => '/var/www/wordpress',
  cleanup      => true,
}
```

1. The title gives the path to where you want the archive file to be downloaded (`/tmp/wordpress.tar.gz`). Assuming you don't need to keep the archive file after it's been unpacked, it's usually a good idea to put it in `/tmp`.
2. The `extract` attribute determines whether or not Puppet should unpack the archive; this should usually be set to `true`.

3. The `extract_path` attribute specifies where to unpack the contents of the archive. In this case, it makes sense to extract it to a subdirectory of `/var/www/`, but this will vary depending on the nature of the archive. If the archive file contains software which will be compiled and installed, for example, it may be a good idea to unpack it in `/tmp/`, so that the files will be automatically cleaned up after the next reboot.
4. The `source` attribute tells Puppet where to download the archive from, usually (as in this example) a web URL.
5. The `creates` attribute works exactly the same way as `creates` on an `exec` resource, which we looked at in *Chapter 4, Understanding Puppet resources*. It specifies a file which unpacking the archive will create. If this file exists, Puppet knows the archive has already been unpacked, so it does not need to unpack it again.
6. The `cleanup` attribute tells Puppet whether or not to delete the archive file once it has been unpacked. Usually, this will be set to `true`, unless you need to keep the archive around or unless you don't need to unpack it in the first place.

> Once the file has been deleted by `cleanup`, Puppet won't redownload the archive file `/tmp/wordpress.tar.gz` the next time you apply the manifest, even though it has `ensure => present`. The `creates` clause tells Puppet that the archive has already been downloaded and extracted.

Exploring the standard library

One of the oldest-established Puppet Forge modules is `puppetlabs/stdlib`, the official Puppet standard library. We looked at this briefly earlier in the chapter when we used it as an example of installing a module with `r10k`, but let's look more closely now and see what the standard library provides and where you might use it.

Rather than managing some specific software or file format, the standard library aims to provide a set of functions and resources which could be useful in any piece of Puppet code. Consequently, well-written Forge modules use the facilities of the standard library rather than implementing their own utility functions which do the same thing.

You should do the same in your own Puppet code: when you need a particular piece of functionality, check the standard library first to see if it solves your problem rather than implementing it yourself.

Before trying the examples in this section, make sure the `stdlib` module is installed by following these steps: If you've previously followed the steps in the *Using r10k* section, the required module will already be installed. If not, run the following commands to install it:

```
cd /etc/puppetlabs/code/environments/pbg
sudo r10k puppetfile install
```

Safely installing packages with ensure_packages

As you know, you can install a package using the `package` resource, like this (`package.pp`):

```
package { 'cowsay':
  ensure => installed,
}
```

But what happens if you also install the same package in another class in a different part of your manifest? Puppet will refuse to run, with an error like this:

```
Error: Evaluation Error: Error while evaluating a Resource Statement,
Duplicate declaration: Package[cowsay] is already declared in file /
examples/package.pp:1; cannot redeclare at /examples/package.pp:4 at /
examples/package.pp:4:1 on node ubuntu-xenial
```

If both of your classes really require the package, then you have a problem. You could create a class which simply declares the package, and then include that in both classes, but that is a lot of overhead for a single package. Worse, if the duplicate declaration is in a third-party module, it may not be possible, or advisable, to change that code.

What we need is a way to declare a package which will not cause a conflict if that package is also declared somewhere else. The standard library provides this facility in the `ensure_packages()` function. Call `ensure_packages()` with an array of package names, and they will be installed if they are not already declared elsewhere (`package_ensure.pp`):

```
ensure_packages(['cowsay'])
```

To apply this example, run the following command:

```
sudo puppet apply --environment=pbg /examples/package_ensure.pp
```

You can try all the remaining examples in this chapter in the same way. Make sure you supply the `--environment=pbg` switch to `puppet apply`, as the necessary modules are only installed in the `pbg` environment.

If you need to pass additional attributes to the package resource, you can supply them in a hash as the second argument to ensure_packages(), like this (package_ensure_params.pp):

```
ensure_packages(['cowsay'],
  {
    'ensure' => 'latest',
  }
)
```

Why is this better than using the package resource directly? When you declare the same package resource in more than one place, Puppet will give an error message and refuse to run. If the package is declared by ensure_packages(), however, Puppet will run successfully.

Since it provides a safe way to install packages without resource conflicts, you should always use ensure_packages() instead of the built-in package resource. It is certainly essential if you're writing modules for public release, but I recommend you use it in all your code. We'll use it to manage packages throughout the rest of this book.

Modifying files in place with file_line

Often, when managing configuration with Puppet, we would like to change or add a particular line to a file, without incurring the overhead of managing the whole file with Puppet. Sometimes it may not be possible to manage the whole file in any case, as another Puppet class or another application may be managing it. We could write an exec resource to modify the file for us, but the standard library provides a resource type for exactly this purpose: file_line.

Here's an example of using the file_line resource to add a single line to a system config file (file_line.pp):

```
file_line { 'set ulimits':
  path => '/etc/security/limits.conf',
  line => 'www-data         -       nofile          32768',
}
```

If there is a possibility that some other Puppet class or application may need to modify the target file, use file_line instead of managing the file directly. This ensures that your class won't conflict with any other attempts to control the file.

You can also use `file_line` to find and modify an existing line, using the `match` attribute (`file_line_match.pp`):

```
file_line { 'adjust ulimits':
  path  => '/etc/security/limits.conf',
  line  => 'www-data          -       nofile          9999',
  match => '^www-data .* nofile',
}
```

The value of `match` is a regular expression, and if Puppet finds a line in the file which matches this expression, it will replace it with the value of `line`. (If you need to potentially change multiple lines, set the `multiple` attribute to `true` or Puppet will complain when more than one line matches the expression.)

You can also use `file_line` to delete a line in a file if it is present (`file_line_absent.pp`):

```
file_line { 'remove dash from valid shells':
  ensure            => absent,
  path              => '/etc/shells',
  match             => '^/bin/dash',
  match_for_absence => true,
}
```

Note that when using `ensure => absent`, you also need to set the `match_for_absence` attribute to `true` if you want Puppet to actually delete matching lines.

Introducing some other useful functions

The `grep()` function will search an array for a regular expression and return all matching elements (`grep.pp`):

```
$values = ['foo', 'bar', 'baz']
notice(grep($values, 'ba.*'))

# Result: ['bar', 'baz']
```

The `member()` and `has_key()` functions return `true` if a given value is in the specified array or hash, respectively (`member_has_key.pp`):

```
$values = [
  'foo',
  'bar',
  'baz',
]
```

```
notice(member($values, 'foo'))

# Result: true

$valuehash = {
  'a' => 1,
  'b' => 2,
  'c' => 3,
}
notice(has_key($valuehash, 'b'))

# Result: true
```

The `empty()` function returns `true` if its argument is an empty string, array, or hash (`empty.pp`):

```
notice(empty(''))

# Result: true

notice(empty([]))

# Result: true

notice(empty({}))

# Result: true
```

The `join()` function joins together the elements of a supplied array into a string, using a given separator character or string (`join.pp`):

```
$values = ['1', '2', '3']
notice(join($values, '... '))

# Result: '1... 2... 3'
```

The `pick()` function is a neat way to provide a default value when a variable happens to be empty. It takes any number of arguments and returns the first argument which is not undefined or empty (`pick.pp`):

```
$remote_host = ''
notice(pick($remote_host, 'localhost'))

# Result: 'localhost'
```

Sometimes you need to parse structured data in your Puppet code which comes from an outside source. If that data is in YAML format, you can use the `loadyaml()` function to read and parse it into a native Puppet data structure (`loadyaml.pp`):

```
$db_config = loadyaml('/examples/files/database.yml')
notice($db_config['development']['database'])

# Result: 'dev_db'
```

The `dirname()` function is very useful if you have a string path to a file or directory and you want to reference its parent directory, for example to declare it as a Puppet resource (`dirname.pp`):

```
$file = '/var/www/vhosts/mysite'
notice(dirname($file))

# Result: '/var/www/vhosts'
```

The pry debugger

When a Puppet manifest doesn't do quite what you expect, troubleshooting the problem can be difficult. Printing out the values of variables and data structures with `notice()` can help as can running `puppet apply -d` to see detailed debug output, but if all else fails, you can use the standard library's `pry()` method to enter an interactive debugger session (`pry.pp`):

```
pry()
```

With the `pry` gem installed in Puppet's context, you can call `pry()` at any point in your code. When you apply the manifest, Puppet will start an interactive Pry shell at the point where the `pry()` function is called. You can then run the `catalog` command to inspect Puppet's catalog, which contains all the resources currently declared in your manifest:

```
sudo puppet apply --environment=pbg /examples/pry_install.pp
sudo puppet apply --environment=pbg /examples/pry.pp
...
[1] pry(#<Puppet::Parser::Scope>)> catalog
=> #<Puppet::Resource::Catalog:0x00000001bbcf78
...
 @resource_table={["Stage", "main"]=>Stage[main]{}, ["Class",
"Settings"]=>Class[Settings]{}, ["Class", "main"]=>Class[main]{}},
 @resources=[["Stage", "main"], ["Class", "Settings"], ["Class",
"main"]],
...
```

Once you've finished inspecting the catalog, type `exit` to quit the debugger and continue applying your Puppet manifest.

Writing your own modules

As we've seen, a Puppet module is a way of grouping together a set of related code and resources that performs some particular task, like managing the Apache web server or dealing with archive files. But how do you actually create a module? In this section, we'll develop a module of our own to manage the NTP service, familiar to most system administrators as the easiest way to keep server clocks synchronized with the Internet time standard. (Of course, it's not necessary to write your own module for this because a perfectly good one exists on Puppet Forge. But we'll do so anyway, for learning purposes.)

Creating a repo for your module

If we're going to use our new module alongside others that we've installed from Puppet Forge, then we should create a new Git repo just for our module. Then we can add its details to our Puppetfile and have `r10k` install it for us.

If you've already worked through *Chapter 3, Managing your Puppet code with Git*, you'll have created a GitHub account. If not, go to that chapter and follow the instructions in the *Creating a GitHub account and project* section before continuing:

1. Log in to your GitHub account and click the **Start a project** button.
2. On the **Create a new repository** screen, enter a suitable name for your repo (I'm using `pbg_ntp` for the Puppet Beginner's Guide's NTP module).
3. Check the **Initialize this repository with a README** box.
4. Click **Create repository**.
5. GitHub will take you to the project page for the new repository. Click the **Clone or download** button. If you're using GitHub with an SSH key, as we discussed in *Chapter 3, Managing your Puppet code with Git*, copy the **Clone with SSH** link. Otherwise, click **Use HTTPS** and copy the **Clone with HTTPS** link.
6. On your own computer, or wherever you develop Puppet code, run the following command to clone the new repo (use the GitHub URL you copied in the previous step instead of this one):

   ```
   git clone https://github.com/bitfield/pbg_ntp.git
   ```

When the clone operation completes successfully, you're ready to get started with creating your new module.

Writing the module code

As you'll see if you look inside the Puppet Forge modules you've already installed, modules have a standard directory structure. This is so that Puppet can automatically find the manifest files, templates, and other components within the module. Although complex modules have many subdirectories, the only ones we will be concerned with in this example are manifests and files. In this section, we'll create the necessary subdirectories, write the code to manage NTP, and add a config file which the code will install.

All the code and files for this module are available in the GitHub repo at the following URL:

https://github.com/bitfield/pbg_ntp

1. Run the following commands to create the `manifests` and `files` subdirectories:

```
cd pbg_ntp
mkdir manifests
mkdir files
```

2. Create the file `manifests/init.pp` with the following contents:

```
# Manage NTP
class pbg_ntp {
  ensure_packages(['ntp'])

  file { '/etc/ntp.conf':
    source  => 'puppet:///modules/pbg_ntp/ntp.conf',
    notify  => Service['ntp'],
    require => Package['ntp'],
  }

  service { 'ntp':
    ensure => running,
    enable => true,
  }
}
```

3. Create the file `files/ntp.conf` with the following contents:

```
driftfile /var/lib/ntp/ntp.drift

pool 0.ubuntu.pool.ntp.org iburst
pool 1.ubuntu.pool.ntp.org iburst
pool 2.ubuntu.pool.ntp.org iburst
pool 3.ubuntu.pool.ntp.org iburst
```

```
pool ntp.ubuntu.com

restrict -4 default kod notrap nomodify nopeer noquery limited
restrict -6 default kod notrap nomodify nopeer noquery limited
restrict 127.0.0.1
restrict ::1
```

4. Run the following commands to add, commit, and push your changes to GitHub (you'll need to enter your GitHub username and password if you're not using an SSH key):

```
git add manifests/ files/
git commit -m 'Add module manifest and config file'
[master f45dc50] Add module manifest and config file
 2 files changed, 29 insertions(+)
 create mode 100644 files/ntp.conf
 create mode 100644 manifests/init.pp
git push origin master
```

Notice that the `source` attribute for the `ntp.conf` file looks like the following:

```
puppet:///modules/pbg_ntp/ntp.conf
```

We haven't seen this kind of file source before, and it's generally only used within module code. The `puppet://` prefix indicates that the file comes from within the Puppet repo, and the path `/modules/pbg_ntp/` tells Puppet to look within the `pbg_ntp` module for it. Although the `ntp.conf` file is actually in the directory `modules/pbg_ntp/files/`, we don't need to specify the `files` part: that's assumed, because this is a `file` resource. (It's not just you: this confuses everybody.)

Rather than installing the `ntp` package via a `package` resource, we use `ensure_packages()` from the standard library, as described earlier in this chapter.

Creating and validating the module metadata

Every Puppet module should have a file in its top-level directory named `metadata.json`, which contains helpful information about the module that can be used by module management tools, including Puppet Forge.

Create the file `metadata.json` with the following contents (use your own name and GitHub URLs):

```
{
  "name": "pbg_ntp",
  "version": "0.1.1",
  "author": "John Arundel",
  "summary": "Example module to manage NTP",
```

```
    "license": "Apache-2.0",
    "source": "https://github.com/bitfield/pbg_ntp.git",
    "project_page": "https://github.com/bitfield/pbg_ntp",
    "tags": ["ntp"],
    "dependencies": [
      {"name":"puppetlabs/stdlib",
        "version_requirement":">= 4.17.0 < 5.0.0"}
    ],
    "operatingsystem_support": [
      {
        "operatingsystem": "Ubuntu",
        "operatingsystemrelease": [ "16.04" ]
      }
    ]
  }
```

Most of these are fairly self-explanatory. `tags` is an array of strings which will help people find your module if it is listed on Puppet Forge, and it's usual to tag your module with the name of the software or service it manages (in this case, `ntp`).

If your module relies on other Puppet modules, which is very likely (for example, this module relies on `puppetlabs/stdlib` for the `ensure_packages()` function) you use the `dependencies` metadata to record this. You should list each module used by your module along with the earliest and latest versions of that module which will work with your module. (If the currently-released version works, specify the next major release as the latest version. For example, if your module works with `stdlib` version 4.17.0 and that's the latest version available, specify 5.0.0 as the highest compatible version.)

Finally, the `operatingsystem_support` metadata lets you specify which operating systems and versions your module works with. This is very helpful for people searching for a Puppet module which will work with their operating system. If you know your module works with Ubuntu 16.04, as the example module does, you can list that in the `operatingsystem_support` section. The more operating systems your module can support, the better, so if possible, test your module on other operating systems and list them in the metadata once you know they work.

For full details on module metadata and how to use it, see the Puppet documentation:

`https://docs.puppet.com/puppet/latest/reference/modules_metadata.html`

It's important to get the metadata for your module right, and there's a little tool that can help you with this, called `metadata-json-lint`.

1. Run the following commands to install `metadata-json-lint` and check your metadata:

   ```
   sudo gem install metadata-json-lint
   metadata-json-lint metadata.json
   ```

2. If `metadata-json-lint` produces no output, your metadata is valid and you can go on to the next steps. If you see error messages, fix the problem before continuing.
3. Run the following commands to add, commit, and push your metadata file to GitHub:

   ```
   git add metadata.json
   git commit -m 'Add metadata.json'
   git push origin master
   ```

Tagging your module

Just like when you use third-party Puppet Forge modules, it's important to be able to specify in your Puppetfile the exact version of your module to be installed. You can do this by using Git tags to attach a version tag to a specific commit in your module repo. As you develop the module further and make new releases, you can add a new tag for each release.

For the first release of your module, which according to the metadata is version 0.1.1, run the following commands to create and push the release tag:

```
git tag -a 0.1.1 -m 'Release 0.1.1'
git push origin 0.1.1
```

Installing your module

We can use `r10k` to install our new module, just as we did with the Puppet Forge modules, with one small difference. Since our module isn't on the Puppet Forge (yet), just specifying the name of the module in our Puppetfile isn't enough; we need to supply the Git URL so that `r10k` can clone the module from GitHub.

1. Add the following `mod` statement to your Puppetfile (using your GitHub URL instead of mine):

   ```
   mod 'pbg_ntp',
     :git => 'https://github.com/bitfield/pbg_ntp.git',
     :tag => '0.1.1'
   ```

2. Because the module also requires `puppetlabs/stdlib`, add this `mod` statement too:

   ```
   mod 'puppetlabs/stdlib', '4.17.0'
   ```

3. Now install the module in the normal way with `r10k`:

   ```
   sudo r10k puppetfile install --verbose
   ```

`r10k` can install a module from any Git repo you have access to; all you have to do is add the `:git` and `:tag` parameters to the `mod` statement in your Puppetfile.

Applying your module

Now that you've created, uploaded, and installed your module, we can use it in a manifest:

```
sudo puppet apply --environment=pbg -e 'include pbg_ntp'
```

If you're using the Vagrant box or a recent version of Ubuntu, your server will most likely be running NTP already, so the only change you'll see Puppet apply will be the `ntp.conf` file. Nonetheless, it confirms that your module works.

More complex modules

Of course, the module we've developed is a very trivial example. However, it demonstrates the essential requirements of a Puppet module. As you become a more advanced Puppet coder, you will be creating and maintaining much more complicated modules, similar to those you download and use from Puppet Forge.

Real-world modules often feature one or more of the following components:

- Multiple manifest files and subdirectories
- Parameters (which may be supplied directly or looked up from Hiera data)
- Custom facts and custom resource types and providers
- Example code showing how to use the module
- Specs and tests which developers can use to validate their changes
- Dependencies on other modules (which must be declared in the module metadata)
- Support for multiple operating systems

You can find more detailed information about modules and advanced features of modules in the Puppet documentation:

`https://docs.puppet.com/puppet/latest/reference/modules_fundamentals.html`

Uploading modules to Puppet Forge

It's very easy to upload a module to the Puppet Forge: all you need to do is sign up for an account, use the `puppet module build` command to create an archive file of your module, and upload it via the Puppet Forge website.

Before deciding to write a module in the first place, though, you should check whether there is already a module on the Puppet Forge which does what you need. There are over 4,500 modules available at the time of writing, so it's quite likely that you'll be able to use an existing Puppet Forge module instead of writing your own. Contributing a new module when there is already one available just makes it more difficult for users to choose which module they should use. For example, there are currently 150 modules which manage the Nginx web server. Surely this is at least 149 too many, so only submit a new module if you've made sure that there are no similar modules already on the Puppet Forge.

If there is a module which covers the software you want to manage, but it doesn't support your operating system or version, consider improving this module instead of starting a new one. Contact the module author to see whether and how you can help improve their module and extend support to your operating system. Similarly, if you find bugs in a module or want to make improvements to it, open an issue (if there is an issue tracker associated with the module), fork the GitHub repo (if it's versioned on GitHub), or contact the author to find out how you can help. The vast majority of Puppet Forge modules are written and maintained by volunteers, so your support and contributions benefit the entire Puppet community.

If you don't want to fork or contribute to an existing module, consider writing a small wrapper module which extends or overrides the existing module, rather than creating a new module from scratch.

If you do decide to write and publish your own module, use facilities from the standard library wherever possible, such as `ensure_packages()`. This will give your module the best chance of being compatible with other Forge modules.

If you want to contribute more to the Puppet module community, consider joining the Vox Pupuli group, which maintains over a hundred open source Puppet modules:

`https://voxpupuli.org/`

Summary

In this chapter, we've gained an understanding of Puppet modules, including an introduction to the Puppet Forge module repository. We've seen how to search for the modules we need and how to evaluate the results, including **Puppet Approved** and **Puppet Supported** modules, operating system support, and download count.

We've looked at using the `r10k` tool to download and manage Puppet modules in your infrastructure and how to specify the modules and versions you need in your Puppetfile. We've worked through detailed examples of using three important Forge modules: `puppetlabs/apache`, `puppetlabs/mysql`, and `puppet/archive`.

Introducing the standard library for Puppet, we've covered the use of `ensure_packages()` to avoid package conflicts between modules, the `file_line` resource, which provides line-level editing for config files, and a host of useful functions for manipulating data, as well as looking at the Pry debugger.

To fully understand how modules work, we've developed a simple module from scratch to manage the NTP service, hosted in its own Git repository and managed via a Puppetfile and `r10k`. We've seen what metadata modules require and how to create it and validate it using `metadata-json-lint`.

Finally, we've looked at some of the features of more sophisticated modules, discussed uploading modules to the Puppet Forge, and outlined some considerations to bear in mind when you're deciding whether to start a new module or extend and improve an existing one.

In the next chapter, we'll look at how to organize your Puppet code into classes, how to pass parameters to your classes, how to create defined resource types, and how to structure your manifests using roles, profiles, and how to include classes on a node using Hiera data.

8

Classes, roles, and profiles

Our life is frittered away by detail. Simplify, simplify!

—Henry David Thoreau

In this chapter you will explore the details of Puppet classes, the distinction between defining a class and including the class, how to supply parameters to classes, and how to declare classes with parameters and specify appropriate data types for them. You'll learn how to create defined resource types, and how they differ from classes. You'll also see how to organize your Puppet code using the concepts of nodes, roles, and profiles.

Classes

We've come across the **class** concept a few times so far in this book, without really explaining it. Let's explore a little further now and see how to use this key Puppet language building block.

The class keyword

You may have noticed that in the code for our example NTP module in *Chapter 7, Mastering modules* (in the *Writing the module code* section), we used the `class` keyword:

```
class pbg_ntp {
  ...
}
```

If you're wondering what the `class` keyword does, the surprising answer is nothing at all. Nothing, that is, except inform Puppet that the resources it contains should be grouped together and given a name (`pbg_ntp`), and that these resources should not be applied yet.

You can then use this name elsewhere to tell Puppet to apply all the resources in the class together. We declared our example module by using the `include` keyword:

```
include ntp
```

The following example shows a class **definition**, which makes the class available to Puppet, but does not (yet) apply any of its contained resources:

```
class CLASS_NAME {
  ...
}
```

The following example shows a **declaration** of the `CLASS_NAME` class. A declaration tells Puppet to apply all the resources in that class (and the class must have already been defined):

```
include CLASS_NAME
```

You may recall from *Chapter 7, Mastering modules*, that we used Hiera's automatic parameter lookup mechanism to supply parameters to classes. We'll find out more about this shortly, but first, how do we write a class that accepts parameters?

Declaring parameters to classes

If all a class does is group together related resources, that's still useful, but a class becomes much more powerful if we can use **parameters**. Parameters are just like resource attributes: they let you pass data to the class to change how it's applied.

The following example shows how to define a class that takes parameters. It's a simplified version of the `pbg_ntp` class we developed for our NTP module (`class_params.pp`):

```
# Manage NTP
class pbg_ntp_params (
  String $version = 'installed',
) {
  ensure_packages(['ntp'],
    {
      'ensure' => $version,
    }
  )
}
```

The important part to look at is in parentheses after the start of the class definition. This specifies the parameters that the class accepts:

```
String $version = 'installed',
```

`String` tells Puppet that we expect this value to be a String, and it will raise an error if we try to pass it anything else, such as an Integer. `$version` is the name of the parameter. Finally, the `'installed'` part specifies a **default value** for the parameter. If someone declares this class without supplying the `pbg_ntp_params::version` parameter, Puppet will fill it in automatically using this default value.

If you don't supply a default value for a parameter, that makes the parameter **mandatory**, so Puppet will not let you declare the class without supplying a value for that parameter.

When you declare this class, you do it in exactly the same way that we did previously with the Puppet Forge modules, using the `include` keyword and the name of the class:

```
include pbg_ntp_params
```

There are no mandatory parameters for this class, so you need not supply any, but if you do, add a value like the following to your Hiera data, and Puppet will look it up automatically when the class is included:

```
pbg_ntp_params::version: 'latest'
```

Classes can take more than one parameter, of course, and the following (contrived) example shows how to declare multiple parameters of various types (`class_params2.pp`):

```
# Manage NTP
class pbg_ntp_params2 (
  Boolean $start_at_boot,
  String[1] $version                        = 'installed',
  Enum['running', 'stopped'] $service_state = 'running',
```

```
) {
  ensure_packages(['ntp'],
    {
      'ensure' => $version,
    }
  )

  service { 'ntp':
    ensure => $service_state,
    enable => $start_at_boot,
  }
}
```

To pass parameters to this class, add Hiera data like the following:

```
pbg_ntp_params2::start_at_boot: true
pbg_ntp_params2::version: 'latest'
pbg_ntp_params2::service_state: 'running'
```

Let's look closely at the parameter list:

```
Boolean $start_at_boot,
String[1] $version                         = 'installed',
Enum['running', 'stopped'] $service_state = 'running',
```

The first parameter is of `Boolean` type and named `$start_at_boot`. There's no default value, so this parameter is mandatory. Mandatory parameters must be declared first, before any optional parameters (that is, parameters with a default value).

The `$version` parameter we saw in the previous example, but now it's a `String[1]` instead of a `String`. What's the difference? A `String[1]` is a String with at least one character. This means that you can't pass the empty string to such a parameter, for example. It's a good idea to specify a minimum length for String parameters, if appropriate, to catch the case where an empty string is accidentally passed to the class.

The final parameter, `$service_state` is of a new type, `Enum`, which we haven't come across before. With an **Enum parameter**, we can specify exactly the list of allowed values it can take.

If your class expects a String parameter which can only take one of a handful of values, you can list them all in an `Enum` parameter declaration, and Puppet will not allow any value to be passed to that parameter unless it is in that list. In our example, if you try to declare the `pbg_ntp_params2` class and pass the value `bogus` to the `$service_state` parameter, you'll get this error:

```
Error: Evaluation Error: Error while evaluating a Resource Statement,
Class[Pbg_ntp_params2]: parameter 'service_state' expects a match for
Enum['running', 'stopped'], got String at /examples/class_params2.
pp:22:1 on node ubuntu-xenial
```

Just like any other parameter, an `Enum` parameter can take a default value, as it does in our example.

Automatic parameter lookup from Hiera data

We've seen in this chapter, and the previous one that we can use Hiera data to pass parameters to classes. If we include a class named `ntp`, which accepts a parameter `version`, and a key exists in Hiera named `ntp::version`, its value will be passed to the `ntp` class as the value of `version`. For example, if the Hiera data looks like the following:

```
ntp::version: 'latest'
```

Puppet will automatically find this value and pass it to the `ntp` class when it's declared.

In general, Puppet determines parameter values in the following order of priority, highest first:

1. Literal parameters specified in a class declaration (you may see older code which does this)
2. Automatic parameter lookup from Hiera (the key must be named `CLASS_NAME::PARAMETER_NAME`)
3. Default values specified in a class definition

Parameter data types

You should always specify types for your class parameters, as it makes it easier to catch errors where the wrong parameters or values are being supplied to the class. If you're using a String parameter, for example, if possible, make it an Enum parameter with an exact list of the values your class accepts. If you can't restrict it to a set of allowed values, specify a minimum length with `String[x]`. (If you need to specify a maximum length too, the syntax is `String[min, max]`.)

Available data types

So far in this chapter, we've encountered the data types String, Enum, and Boolean. Here are the others:

- Integer (whole numbers)
- Float (floating-point numbers, which have optional decimal fractions)
- Numeric (matches either integers or floats)
- Array
- Hash
- Regexp
- Undef (matches a variable or parameter which hasn't been assigned a value)
- Type (data type of literal values which represent Puppet data types, such as String, Integer, and Array)

There are also *abstract* data types, which are more general:

- Optional (matches a value which may be undefined, or not supplied)
- Pattern (matches Strings which conform to a specified regular expression)
- Scalar (matches Numeric, String, Boolean, or Regexp values, but not Array, Hash, or Undef)
- Data (matches Scalar values, but also Array, Hash, and Undef)
- Collection (matches Array or Hash)
- Variant (matches one of a specified list of data types)
- Any (matches any data type)

In general, you should use as specific a data type as possible. For example, if you know that a parameter will always be an integer number, use `Integer`. If it needs to accept floating-point values as well, use `Numeric`. If it could be a String as well as a Number, use `Scalar`.

Content type parameters

Types which represent a collection of values, such as `Array` and `Hash` (or their parent type, `Collection`) can also take a parameter indicating the type of values they contain. For example, `Array[Integer]` matches an array of Integer values.

If you declare a content type parameter to a collection, then all the values in that collection must match the declared type. If you don't specify a content type, the default is `Data`, which matches (almost) any type of value. The content type parameter can itself take parameters: `Array[Integer[1]]` declares an array of positive Integers.

Hash takes two content type parameters, the first indicating the data type of its keys, the second the data type of its values. `Hash[String, Integer]` declares a hash whose keys are Strings, each of which is associated with an Integer value (this would match, for example, the hash `{'eggs' => 61}`).

Range parameters

Most types can also accept parameters in square brackets, which make the type declaration more specific. For example, we've already seen that `String` can take a pair of parameters indicating the minimum and maximum length of the string.

Most types can take **range parameters**: `Integer[0]` matches any Integer greater than or equal to zero, while `Float[1.0, 2.0]` matches any Float between 1.0 and 2.0 inclusive.

If either range parameter is the special value `default`, the default minimum or maximum value for the type will be used. For example, `Integer[default, 100]` matches any Integer less than or equal to 100.

For arrays and hashes, the range parameters specify the minimum and maximum number of elements or keys: `Array[Any, 16]` specifies an array of no less than 16 elements of `Any` type. `Hash[Any, Any, 5, 5]` specifies a hash containing exactly five key-value pairs.

You can specify both range and content type parameters at once: `Array[String, 1, 10]` matches an array of between one and ten strings. `Hash[String, Hash, 1]` specifies a hash with String keys and Hash values, containing at least one key-value pair with String keys and values of type Hash.

Flexible data types

If you don't know exactly what type the values may be, you can use one of Puppet's more flexible **abstract types**, such as `Variant`, which specifies a list of allowed types. For example, `Variant[String, Integer]` allows its value to be either a String or an Integer.

Similarly, `Array[Variant[Enum['true', 'false'], Boolean]]` declares an array of values which can be either the String values `'true'` or `'false'` or the Boolean values `true` and `false`.

The `Optional` type is very useful when a value may be undefined. For example, `Optional[String]` specifies a String parameter which may or may not be passed to the class. Normally, if a parameter is declared without a default value, Puppet will give an error when it is not supplied. If it is declared `Optional`, however, it may be omitted, or set to `Undef` (meaning that the identifier is defined, but has no value).

The `Pattern` type allows you to specify a regular expression. All Strings matching that regular expression will be allowed values for the parameter. For example, `Pattern[/a/]` will match any String which contains the lowercase letter a. In fact, you can specify as many regular expressions as you like. `Pattern[/a/, /[0-9]/]` matches any String which contains the letter `a`, or any string which contains a digit.

Defined resource types

Whereas a class lets you group together related resources, a **defined resource type** lets you create new kinds of resources and declare as many instances of them as you like. A defined resource type definition looks a lot like a class (`defined_resource_type.pp`):

```
# Manage user and SSH key together
define user_with_key(
  Enum[
    'ssh-dss',
    'dsa',
    'ssh-rsa',
    'rsa',
    'ecdsa-sha2-nistp256',
    'ecdsa-sha2-nistp384',
    'ecdsa-sha2-nistp521',
    'ssh-ed25519',
    'ed25519'
  ] $key_type,
  String $key,
) {
  user { $title:
    ensure     => present,
    managehome => true,
  }

  file { "/home/${title}/.ssh":
    ensure => directory,
    owner  => $title,
    group  => $title,
    mode   => '0700',
  }

  ssh_authorized_key { $title:
    user => $title,
    type => $key_type,
    key  => $key,
  }
}
```

You can see that instead of the `class` keyword, we use the `define` keyword. This tells Puppet that we are creating a defined resource type instead of a class. The type is called `user_with_key`, and once it's defined, we can declare as many instances of it as we want, just like any other Puppet resource:

```
user_with_key { 'john':
  key_type => 'ssh-rsa',
  key      => 'AAAA...AcZik=',
}
```

When we do this, Puppet applies all the resources inside `user_with_key`: a user, a `.ssh` directory for that user, and an `ssh_authorized_key` for the user, containing the specified key.

Wait, we seem to be referring to a parameter called `$title` in the example code. Where does that come from? `$title` is a special parameter which is always available in classes and defined resource types, and its value is the title of this particular declaration of the class or type. In the example, that's `john`, because we gave the declaration of `user_with_key` the title `john`.

So what's the difference between defined resource types and classes? They look pretty much the same. They seem to act the same. Why would you use one rather than the other? The most important difference is that you can only have **one declaration** of a given class on a given node, whereas you can have as many different instances of a defined resource type as you like. The only restriction is that, like all Puppet resources, the title of each instance of the defined resource type must be unique.

Recall our example `ntp` class, which installs and runs the NTP daemon. Usually, you would only want one NTP service per node. There's very little point in running two. So we declare the class once, which is all we need.

Contrast this with the `user_with_key` defined resource type. It's quite likely that you'll want more than one `user_with_key` on a given node, perhaps several. In this case, a defined resource type is the right choice.

Defined resource types are ideal in modules when you want to make a resource available to users of the module. For example, in the `puppetlabs/apache` module, the `apache::vhost` resource is a defined resource type, provided by the `apache` class. You can think of a defined resource type as being a wrapper for a collection of multiple resources.

Remember this rule of thumb when deciding whether to create a class or a defined resource type: if it's reasonable to have more than one instance on a given node, it should be a defined resource type, but if there will only ever be one instance, it should be a class.

Type aliases

It's straightforward to define new **type aliases**, using the `type` keyword (`type_alias.pp`):

```
type ServiceState = Enum['running', 'stopped']

define myservice(ServiceState $state) {
  service { $name:
    ensure => $state,
  }
}

myservice { 'ntp':
  state => 'running',
}
```

Creating a type alias can be very useful when you want to ensure, for example, that parameter values match a complex pattern, which would be tiresome to duplicate. You can define the pattern in one place and declare multiple parameters of that type (`type_alias_pattern.pp`):

```
type IPAddress = Pattern[/\A([0-9]|[1-9][0-9]|1[0-9]{2}|2[0-4][0-
9]|25[0-5])(\.([0-9]|[1-9][0-9]|1[0-9]{2}|2[0-4][0-9]|25[0-5])){3}\z/]

define socket_server(
  IPAddress $listen_address,
  IPAddress $public_address,
) {
  # ...
}

socket_server { 'myserver':
  listen_address => '0.0.0.0',
  public_address => $facts['networking']['ip'],
}
```

When creating a type alias in a module, it should be in a file named after the type in the `types` subdirectory of the module. For example, a type named `IPAddress` should be defined in the file `types/ipaddress.pp`.

Managing classes with Hiera

In *Chapter 3, Managing your Puppet code with Git*, we saw how to set up your Puppet repo on multiple nodes and auto-apply the manifest using a cron job and the `run-puppet` script. The `run-puppet` script runs the following commands:

```
cd /etc/puppetlabs/code/environments/production && git pull
/opt/puppetlabs/bin/puppet apply manifests/
```

You can see that everything in the `manifests/` directory will be applied on every node. Clearly, Puppet is much more useful when we can apply different manifests on each node; some nodes will be web servers, others database servers, and so on. In fact, we would like to include some classes on all nodes, for general administration, such as managing user accounts, and other classes only on specific nodes. So how do we do that?

Using include with lookup()

Previously, when including classes in our manifest, we've used the `include` keyword with a literal class name, as in the following example:

```
include postgresql
include apache
```

However, `include` can also be used as a function, which takes an array of class names to include:

```
include(['postgresql', 'apache'])
```

We already know that we can use Hiera to return different values for a query based on the node name (or anything else defined in the hierarchy), so let's define a suitable array in Hiera data, as in the following example:

```
classes:
- postgresql
- apache
```

Now we can simply use `lookup()` to get this Hiera value, and pass the result to the `include()` function:

```
include(lookup('classes'), Array[String], 'unique')
```

In effect, this is your entire Puppet manifest. Every node will apply this manifest, and thus include the classes assigned to it by the Hiera data. Since the top-level manifest file is traditionally named `site.pp`, you can put this `include` line in `manifests/site.pp`, and the `papply` or `run-puppet` scripts will apply it because they apply everything in the `manifests/` directory.

Common and per-node classes

We can specify a set of classes in `common.yaml` which will be applied to all nodes: things such as user accounts, SSH and `sudoers` config, time zone, NTP setup, and so on. The complete example repo outlined in *Chapter 12, Putting it all together* has a typical set of such classes defined in `common.yaml`.

However, some classes will only be needed on particular nodes. Add these to the per-node Hiera data file. For example, our `pbg` environment on the Vagrant box contains the following in `hiera.yaml`:

```
- name: "Host-specific data"
  path: "nodes/%{facts.hostname}.yaml"
```

So per-node data for a node named `node1` will live in the `nodes/node1.yaml` file under the `data/` directory.

Let's see a complete example. Suppose your `common.yaml` file contains the following:

```
classes:
- postgresql
- apache
```

And suppose your per-node file (`nodes/node1.yaml`) also contains:

```
classes:
- tomcat
- my_app
```

Now, what happens when you apply the following manifest in `manifests/site.pp` on `node1`?

```
include(lookup('classes'), Array[String], 'unique')
```

Which classes will be applied? You may recall from *Chapter 6, Managing data with Hiera* that the `unique` merge strategy finds all values for the given key throughout the hierarchy, merges them together, and returns them as a flattened array, with duplicates removed. So the result of this `lookup()` call will be the following array:

```
[apache, postgresql, tomcat, my_app]
```

This is the complete list of classes that Puppet will apply to the node. Of course, you can add classes at any other level of the hierarchy, if you need to, but you will probably find the common and per-node levels to be the most useful for including classes.

Naturally, even though some nodes may include the same classes as others, they may need different configuration values for the classes. You can use Hiera in the same way to supply different parameters for the included classes, as described in the *Automatic parameter lookup from Hiera data* section earlier in this chapter.

Roles and profiles

Now that we know how to include different sets of classes on a given node, depending on the job the node is supposed to do, let's think more about how to name those classes in the most helpful way. For example, consider the following list of included classes for a certain node:

```
classes:
- postgresql
- apache
- java
- tomcat
- my_app
```

The class names give some clues as to what this node might be doing. It looks like it's probably an app server running a Java app named `my_app` served by Tomcat behind Apache, and backed by a PostgreSQL database. That's a good start, but we can do even better than this, and we'll see how in the next section.

Roles

To make it obvious that the node is an app server, why don't we create a class called `role::app_server`, which exists only to encapsulate the node's included classes? That class definition might look like this (`role_app_server.pp`):

```
# Be an app server
class role::app_server {
  include postgresql
  include apache
  include java
  include tomcat
  include my_app
}
```

We call this idea a **role class**. A role class could simply be a module in its own right, or to make it clear that this is a role class, we could organize it into a special `role` module. If you keep all your role classes in a single module, then they will all be named `role::something`, depending on the role they implement.

> It's important to note that role classes are not special to Puppet in any way. They're just ordinary classes; we call them role classes only to remind ourselves that they are for expressing the roles assigned to a particular node.

The value of `classes` in Hiera is now reduced to just the following:

```
classes:
- role::app_server
```

Looking at the Hiera data, it's now very easy to see what the node's job is—what its *role* is—and all app servers now just need to include `role::app_server`. When or if the list of classes required for app servers changes, you don't need to find and update the Hiera `classes` value for every app server; you just need to edit the `role::app_server` class.

Profiles

We can tidy up our manifest quite a bit by adopting the rule of thumb that, apart from common configuration in `common.yaml`, **nodes should only include role classes**. This makes the Hiera data more self-documenting, and our role classes are all neatly organized in the `role` module, each of them encapsulating all the functionality required for that role. It's a big improvement. But can we do even better?

Let's look at a role class such as `role::app_server`. It contains lots of lines including modules, like the following:

```
include tomcat
```

If all you need to do is include a module and have the parameters automatically looked up from Hiera data, then there's no problem. This is the kind of simple, encouraging, unrealistic example you'll see in product documentation or on a conference slide.

Real-life Puppet code is often more complicated, however, with logic and conditionals and special cases, and extra resources that need to be added, and so forth. We don't want to duplicate all this code when we use Tomcat as part of another role (for example, serving another Tomcat-based app). How can we neatly encapsulate it at the right level of abstraction and avoid duplication?

We could, of course, create a custom module for each app, which hides away all that messy support code. However, it's a big overhead to create a new module just for a few lines of code, so it seems like there should be a niche for a small layer of code which bridges the gap between roles and modules.

We call this a **profile class**. A profile encapsulates some specific piece of software or functionality which is required for a role. In our example, the `app_server` role requires several pieces of software: PostgreSQL, Tomcat, Apache, and so on. Each of these can now have its own profile.

Let's rewrite the `app_server` role to include profiles, instead of modules (`role_app_server_profiles.pp`):

```
# Be an app server
class role::app_server {
  include profile::postgresql
  include profile::apache
  include profile::java
  include profile::tomcat
  include profile::my_app
}
```

What would be in these profile classes? The `profile::tomcat` class, for example, would set up the specific configuration of Tomcat required, along with any app-specific or site-specific resources required, such as firewall rules, `logrotate` config, file and directory permissions, and so on. The profile wraps the module, configures it, and provides everything the module does not, in order to support this particular application or site.

The `profile::tomcat` class might look something like the following example, adapted from a real production manifest (`profile_tomcat.pp`):

```
# Site-specific Tomcat configuration
class profile::tomcat {
  tomcat::install { '/usr/share/tomcat7':
    install_from_source => false,
    package_ensure      => present,
    package_name        => ['libtomcat7-java','tomcat7-
common','tomcat7'],
  }

  exec { 'reload-tomcat':
    command     => '/usr/sbin/service tomcat7 restart',
    refreshonly => true,
  }
```

```
  lookup('tomcat_allowed_ips', Array[String[7]]).each |String $source_
ip| {
    firewall { "100 Tomcat access from ${source_ip}":
      proto  => 'tcp',
      dport  => '8080',
      source => $source_ip,
      action => 'accept',
    }
  }

  file { '/usr/share/tomcat7/logs':
    ensure  => directory,
    owner   => 'tomcat7',
    require => Tomcat::Install['/usr/share/tomcat7'],
  }

  file { '/etc/logrotate.d/tomcat7':
    source => 'puppet:///site-modules/profile/tomcat/tomcat7.
logrotate',
  }
}
```

The exact contents of this class don't really matter here, but the point you should take away is that this kind of site-specific 'glue' code, wrapping third-party modules and connecting them with particular applications, should live in a profile class.

In general, a profile class should include everything needed to make that particular software component or service work, including other profiles if necessary. For example, every profile which requires a specific configuration of Java should include that Java profile. You can include a profile from multiple other profiles without any conflicts.

Using profile classes in this way both makes your role classes neater, tidier, and easier to maintain, but it also allows you to reuse the profiles for different roles. The `app_server` role includes these profiles, and other roles can include them as well. This way, our code is organized to reduce duplication and encourage re-use. The second rule of thumb is, **roles should only include profiles**.

If you're still confused about the exact distinction between roles and profiles, don't worry: you're in good company. Let's try and define them as succinctly as possible:

- **Roles** identify a particular function for a node, such as being an app server or a database server. A role exists to document what a node is for. Roles should only include profiles, but they can include any number of profiles.

- **Profiles** identify a particular piece of software or functionality which contributes to a role; for example, the `tomcat` profile is required for the `app_server` role. Profiles generally install and configure a specific software component or service, its associated business logic, and any other Puppet resources needed. Profiles are the 'glue layer' which sits between roles and modules.

It's possible that your manifest may be so simple that you can organize it using only roles or only profiles. That's fine, but when things start getting more complex and you find yourself duplicating code, consider refactoring it to use the roles-and-profiles pattern in the way we've seen here.

Summary

In this chapter, we've looked at a range of different ways of organizing your Puppet code. We've covered classes in detail, explaining how to define them using the `class` keyword to define a new class, using the `include` keyword to declare the class, and using Hiera's automatic parameter lookup mechanism to supply parameters for included classes.

Declaring parameters involves specifying the allowable data types for parameters, and we've had a brief overview of Puppet's data types, including scalars, collections, content types and range parameters, abstract types, flexible types, and introduced creating your own type aliases. We've also introduced the defined resource type, and explained the difference between defined resource types and classes, and when you would use one or the other.

We've also looked at how to use the `classes` array in Hiera to include common classes on all nodes, and other classes only on particular nodes. We've introduced the idea of the role class, which encapsulates everything needed for a node to fulfil a particular role, such as an app server.

Finally, we've seen how to use profile classes to configure and support a particular software package or service, and how to compose several profile classes into a single role class. Between them, roles and profiles bridge the gap between the Hiera `classes` array, at the top level, and modules and configuration data (at the lowest level). We can summarize the rules by saying that *nodes should only include roles, and roles should only include profiles.*

In the next chapter we'll look at using Puppet to create files using templates, iteration, and Hiera data.

9

Managing files with templates

Simplicity does not precede complexity, but follows it.

—Alan Perlis

In this chapter, we'll learn about an important and powerful feature of Puppet: the **template**. We'll see how to use a simple template to interpolate the values of Puppet variables, facts, and Hiera data into a file, and we'll also introduce more complex templates using iteration and conditional statements to generate dynamic configuration files.

What are templates?

In previous chapters, we've used Puppet to manage the **contents of files** on the node by various means, including setting the contents to a literal string using the `content` attribute, and copying a file from a Puppet module using the `source` attribute. While these methods are very useful, they are limited in one respect: they can only use **static text**, rather than building the contents of the file dynamically, based on Puppet data.

The dynamic data problem

To see why this is a problem, consider a common Puppet file management task such as a backup script. There are a number of site- and node-specific things the backup script needs to know: the local directories to back up, the destination to copy them to, and any credentials needed to access the backup storage. While we could insert these into the script as literal values, this is rather inflexible. We might have to maintain several versions of the script, each identical to the others except for a backup location, for example. This is clearly less than satisfactory.

Consider a configuration file for an application where some of the settings depend on specific information about the node: the available memory, perhaps. Obviously, we don't want to have to maintain multiple versions of an almost identical config file, each containing a suitable value for all the different sizes of memory we may come across. We have a way of obtaining that information directly in Puppet, as we've seen in *Chapter 5, Variables, expressions, and facts*, and we also have a flexible, powerful database for configuration data, as we saw in *Chapter 6, Managing data with Hiera*. The question is how we can insert this data dynamically into text files.

Puppet template syntax

Puppet's **template** mechanism is one way to achieve this. A template is simply an ordinary text file, containing special placeholder markers which Puppet will replace with the relevant data values. The following example shows what these markers look like (`aws_credentials.epp`):

```
aws_access_key_id = <%= $aws_access_key %>
```

Everything outside the `<%=` and `%>` delimiters is literal text and will be rendered as-is by Puppet.

The text inside the delimiters, however, is interpreted as a Puppet expression (in this case, just the variable `$aws_access_key`), which will be evaluated when the template is compiled, and the result will be interpolated into the text.

For example, if the variable `$aws_access_key` has the value `AKIAIAF7V6N2PTOIZVA2`, then when the template is processed by Puppet the resulting output text will look like the following:

```
aws_access_key_id = AKIAIAF7V6N2PTOIZVA2
```

You can have as many of these delimited expressions (called **tags**) in the template as you like, and they will all be evaluated and interpolated when the template is used.

Puppet's template mechanism is called **EPP** (for **Embedded Puppet**), and template files have the extension `.epp`.

Using templates in your manifests

Since the end result of a template is a file, you won't be surprised that we use Puppet's `file` resource to work with templates. In fact, we use an attribute of the `file` resource that you've seen before: the `content` attribute.

Referencing template files

Recall from *Chapter 2, Creating your first manifests*, that you can use the `content` attribute to set a file's contents to a literal string:

```
file { '/tmp/hello.txt':
  content => "hello, world\n",
}
```

And, of course, you can interpolate the value of Puppet expressions into that string:

```
file { "/usr/local/bin/${task}":
  content => "echo I am ${task}\n",
  mode    => '0755',
}
```

So far, so familiar, but we can take one further step and replace the literal string with a call to the `epp()` function (`file_epp.pp`):

```
file { '/usr/local/bin/backup':
  content => epp('/examples/backup.sh.epp',
    {
      'data_dir' => '/examples',
    }
  ),
  mode    => '0755',
}
```

Puppet will compile the template file referenced by backup.sh.epp, replacing any tags with the value of their expressions, and the resulting text will be written to the file /usr/local/bin/backup. The template file might look something like the following (backup.sh.epp):

```
<%- | String $data_dir | -%>
#!/bin/bash
mkdir -p /backup
tar cvzf /backup/backup.tar.gz <%= $data_dir %>
```

You can use the epp() function anywhere a string is expected, but it's most common to use it to manage a file, as shown in the example.

To reference a template file from within a module (for example, in our NTP module from *Chapter 7, Mastering modules*), put the file in the modules/pbg_ntp/templates/ directory, and prefix the filename with pbg_ntp/, as in the following example:

```
file { '/etc/ntp.conf':
  content => epp('pbg_ntp/ntp.conf.epp'),
}
```

> **Remember**
>
> Don't include templates/ as part of the path. Puppet knows it's a template, so it will automatically look in the templates/ directory of the named module.

Inline templates

Your template text need not be in a separate file: if it's a short template, you can put it in a literal string in your Puppet manifest and use the inline_epp() function to compile it (file_inline_epp.pp):

```
$web_root = '/var/www'
$backup_dir = '/backup/www'

file { '/usr/local/bin/backup':
  content => inline_epp('rsync -a <%= $web_root %>/ <%= $backup_dir
%>/'),
  mode    => '0755',
}
```

Note that we used a **single-quoted string** to specify the inline template text. If we'd used a double-quoted string, Puppet would have interpolated the values of $web_root and $backup_dir *before* processing the template, which is not what we want.

In general, though, it's better and more readable to use a separate template file for all but the simplest templates.

Template tags

The tag we've been using in the examples so far in this chapter is known as an **expression-printing tag**:

```
<%= $aws_access_key %>
```

Puppet expects the contents of this tag to have a value, which will then be inserted into the template in place of the tag.

A **non-printing tag** is very similar, but will not generate any output. It has no = sign in the opening delimiter:

```
<% notice("This has no effect on the template output") %>
```

You can also use a **comment tag** to add text which will be removed when Puppet compiles the template:

```
<%# This is a comment, and it will not appear in the output of the
template %>
```

Computations in templates

So far, we've simply interpolated the value of a variable into our template, but we can do more. Template tags can contain any valid Puppet expression.

It's very common for certain values in config files to be **computed** from other values, such as the amount of physical memory on the node. We saw an example of this in *Chapter 5, Variables, expressions, and facts*, where we computed a config value based on the value of `$facts['memory']['system']['total_bytes']`.

Naturally, whatever we can do in Puppet code, we can also do in a template, so here's the same computation in template form (`template_compute.epp`):

```
innodb_buffer_pool_size=<%= $facts['memory']['system']['total_bytes']
* 3/4 %>
```

The generated output (on my Vagrant box) is as follows:

```
sudo puppet epp render --environment pbg /examples/template_compute.
epp
innodb_buffer_pool_size=780257280
```

You're not restricted to numerical computations; you can do anything a Puppet expression can do, including string manipulation, array and hash lookups, fact references, function calls, and so on.

Conditional statements in templates

You might not be very impressed with templates so far, pointing out that you can already interpolate the values of Puppet expressions in strings, and hence files, without using a template. That said, templates allow you to interpolate data into much bigger files than it would be practical or desirable to create with a literal string in your Puppet manifest.

Templates also allow you to do something else very useful: **include or exclude sections of text** based on the result of some Puppet conditional expression.

We've already met conditional statements in manifests in *Chapter 5, Variables, expressions, and facts*, where we used them to conditionally include sets of Puppet resources (`if.pp`):

```
if $install_perl {
  ...
} else {
  ...
}
```

Since the content of template tags is just Puppet code, you can use an `if` statement in a template too. Here's a similar example to the previous one, but this time controlling inclusion of a block of configuration in a template (`template_if.epp`):

```
<% if $ssl_enabled { -%>
  ## SSL directives
  SSLEngine on
  SSLCertificateFile      "<%= $ssl_cert %>"
  SSLCertificateKeyFile   "<%= $ssl_key %>"
  ...
<% } -%>
```

This looks a little more complicated, but it's actually exactly the same logic as in the previous example. We have an `if` statement which tests the value of a Boolean variable, `$ssl_enabled`, and depending on the result, the following block is either included or excluded.

You can see that the `if` statement and the closing } are enclosed in non-printing tags, so they generate no output themselves, and as Puppet compiles the template, it will execute the Puppet code within the tags and that will determine the output. If `$ssl_enabled` is true, the file generated by the template will contain the following:

```
## SSL directives
SSLEngine on
SSLCertificateFile      "<%= $ssl_cert %>"
SSLCertificateKeyFile   "<%= $ssl_key %>"
...
```

Otherwise, this part of the template will be omitted. This is a very useful way of conditionally including blocks in a configuration file.

Just as with `if` statements in manifest files, you can also use `else` to include an alternative block instead, if the conditional statement is false.

Notice that the closing tags in the previous example had an extra leading hyphen: `-%>`.

When you use this syntax, Puppet suppresses any trailing whitespace and linebreak after the tag. It's common to use this syntax with non-printing template tags, because otherwise you'd end up with empty lines in the output.

Iteration in templates

If we can generate parts of a file from Puppet expressions, and also include or exclude parts of the file depending on conditions, could we generate parts of the file with a Puppet loop? That is to say, could we **iterate over an array or hash**, generating template content for each element? Indeed we can. This is a very powerful mechanism which enables us to generate files of arbitrary size, based on Puppet variables, or Hiera and Facter data.

Iterating over Facter data

Our first example generates part of the config file for an application which captures network packet data. To tell it which interfaces to listen on, we need to generate a list of all the live network interfaces on the node.

How can we generate this output? We know Facter can give us a list of all the network interfaces available, with `$facts['networking']['interfaces']`. This is actually a hash, where the key is the name of the interface, and the value is a hash of the interface's attributes, such as the IP address and netmask.

You may recall from *Chapter 5, Variables, expressions, and facts* that in order to iterate over a hash, we use a syntax like the following:

```
HASH.each | KEY, VALUE | {
  BLOCK
}
```

So let's apply this pattern to the Facter data and see what the output looks like (`template_iterate.epp`):

```
<% $facts['networking']['interfaces'].each |String $interface, Hash
$attrs| { -%>
interface <%= $interface %>;
<% } -%>
```

Each time round the loop, the values of `$interface` and `$attrs` will be set to the next key and value of the hash returned by `$facts['networking']['interfaces']`. As it happens, we will not be using the value of `$attrs`, but we still need to declare it as part of the loop syntax.

Each time round the loop, the value of `$interface` is set to the name of the next interface in the list, and a new output line like the following is generated:

```
interface em1;
```

At the end of the loop, we have generated as many output lines as we have interfaces, which is the desired result. Here's the final output, on a node with lots of network interfaces:

```
interface em1;
interface em2;
interface em3;
interface em4;
interface em5;
interface lo;
```

Iterating over structured facts

The next configuration data required for our application is a list of IP addresses associated with the node, which we can generate in a similar way to the previous example.

We can use more or less the same Puppet code as in the previous example, only this time we will be using each interface's `$attrs` hash to get the IP address of the associated interface.

The following example shows how this works (`template_iterate2.epp`):

```
<% $facts['networking']['interfaces'].each |String $interface, Hash
$attrs| { -%>
local_address <%= $attrs['bindings'][0]['address'] %>;
<% } -%>
```

The loop is the same as in the previous example, but this time each output line contains, not the value of `$interface`, but the value of `$attrs['bindings'][0]['address']`, which contains the IP address of each interface.

Here's the final output:

```
local_address 10.170.81.11;
local_address 75.76.222.21;
local_address 204.152.248.213;
local_address 66.32.100.81;
local_address 189.183.255.6;
local_address 127.0.0.1;
```

Iterating over Hiera data

In *Chapter 6, Managing data with Hiera* we used a Hiera array of users to generate Puppet resources for each user. Let's use the same Hiera data now to build a dynamic configuration file using iteration in a template.

The SSH daemon `sshd` can be configured to allow SSH access only by a list of named users (with the `AllowUsers` directive), and, indeed, it's good practice to do this.

Security tip

Most servers accessible from the public Internet regularly receive brute-force login attempts for random usernames, and dealing with these can use up a lot of resources. If `sshd` is configured to allow only specified users, it can quickly reject any users not in this list, without having to process the request further.

If our users are listed in Hiera, then it's easy to use a template to generate this `AllowUsers` list for the `sshd_config` file.

Just as we did when generating Puppet `user` resources, we will make a call to `lookup()` to get the array of users, and iterate over this using `each`. The following example shows what this looks like in the template (`template_hiera.epp`):

```
AllowUsers<% lookup('users').each | $user | { -%>
 <%= $user -%>
<% } %>
```

Note the leading space on the second line, which results in the usernames in the output being space-separated. Note also the use of the leading hyphen to the closing tag (`-%>`) which, as we saw earlier in the chapter, will suppress any trailing whitespace on the line.

Here's the result:

```
AllowUsers katy lark bridget hsing-hui charles
```

Working with templates

One potential problem with templates (since they can include Puppet code, variables, and Hiera data) is that it's not always clear from the Puppet manifest what **variables** the template is going to use. Conversely, it's not easy to see from the template code where any referenced variables are coming from. This can make it hard to maintain or update templates, and also to debug any problems caused by incorrect data being fed into the template.

Ideally, we would like to be able to specify in the Puppet code exactly what variables the template is going to receive, and this list would also appear in the template itself. For extra credit, we would like to be able to specify the **data type** of input variables, in just the same way that we do for classes and defined resource types (see *Chapter 8, Classes, roles, and profiles*, for more about this.)

The good news is that EPP templates allow you to declare the parameters you want passed to your template, along with the required data types, in exactly the same way as you can for classes. While it's not compulsory to declare parameters for your EPP templates, it's a very good idea to do so. With declared and typed parameters, you will be able to catch most data errors at the template compilation stage, which makes troubleshooting much easier.

Passing parameters to templates

To declare parameters for a template, list them between pipe characters (|) inside a non-printing tag, as shown in the following example (`template_params.epp`):

```
<% | String[1] $aws_access_key,
     String[1] $aws_secret_key,
| -%>
aws_access_key_id = <%= $aws_access_key %>
aws_secret_access_key = <%= $aws_secret_key %>
```

When you declare parameters in a template, you must pass those parameters explicitly, in hash form, as the second argument to the `epp()` function call. The following example shows how to do this (`epp_params.pp`):

```
file { '/root/aws_credentials':
  content => epp('/examples/template_params.epp',
    {
      'aws_access_key' => 'AKIAIAF7V6N2PTOIZVA2',
      'aws_secret_key' => '7IBpXjoYRVbJ/rCTVLaAMyud+i4co11lVt1Df1vt',
    }
  ),
}
```

This form of the `epp()` function call takes two parameters: the path to the template file, and a hash containing all the required template parameters. The keys to the hash are the parameter names, and the values are the values. (These need not be literal values; they could be Hiera lookups, for example.)

It's very likely that you will be using Hiera data in templates, and although in our previous `AllowUsers` example we called `lookup()` directly from the template to look up the data, this isn't really the best way to do it. Now that we know how to declare and pass parameters to templates, we should do the same thing with Hiera data.

Here is an updated version of the `AllowUsers` example where we do the Hiera lookup in the manifest, as part of the `epp()` call. First, we need to declare a `$users` parameter in the template (`template_hiera_params.epp`):

```
<% | Array[String] $users | -%>
AllowUsers<% $users.each | $user | { -%>
 <%= $user -%>
<% } %>
```

Then, when we compile the template with `epp()`, we pass in the Hiera data by calling `lookup()` in the parameters hash (`epp_hiera.pp`):

```
file { '/tmp/sshd_config_example':
  content => epp('/examples/template_hiera_params.epp',
    {
      'users' => lookup('users'),
    }
  ),
}
```

If you have declared a parameter list in the template, you must pass it exactly those parameters in the `epp()` call, and no others. EPP templates declare parameters in the same way as classes do: parameters can be given default values, and any parameter without a default value is mandatory.

It's clear from the previous example that declaring parameters makes it much easier to see what information the template is going to use from the calling code, and we now have the benefit of automated checking of the parameters and their types.

Note, however, that even templates with a parameter list can still access any Puppet variable or fact in the template body; Puppet does not prevent the template from using variables which have not been declared as parameters, or getting data directly from Hiera. It should be clear by now, though, that bypassing the parameter checking machinery in this way is a bad idea.

Best practices

Use EPP templates for dynamically-generated files, declare typed parameters in the template, and pass those parameters as a hash to the `epp()` function. To make your template code easier to understand and maintain, always pass data explicitly to the template. If the template needs to look up Hiera data, do the lookup in your Puppet manifest and have the template declare a parameter to receive the data.

Validating template syntax

We've seen in this chapter that templates can contain complex logic and iteration that can generate almost any output required. The downside of this power and flexibility is that it can be difficult to read and debug template code.

Fortunately, Puppet includes a tool to check and validate your templates on the command line: `puppet epp validate`. To use it, run the following command against your template file:

```
puppet epp validate /examples/template_params.epp
```

If there is no output, the template is valid. If the template contains an error, you will see an error message, something like the following:

```
Error: Syntax error at '%' at /examples/template_params.epp:3:4
Error: Errors while validating epp
Error: Try 'puppet help epp validate' for usage
```

Rendering templates on the command line

As any programmer knows, even programs with valid syntax don't necessarily produce the correct results. It can be very useful to see exactly what output the template is going to produce, and Puppet also provides a tool to do this: `puppet epp render`.

To use it, run the following command:

```
puppet epp render --values "{ 'aws_access_key' => 'foo', 'aws_secret_
key' => 'bar' }" /examples/template_params.epp
aws_access_key_id = foo
aws_secret_access_key = bar
```

The `--values` argument allows you to pass in a hash of parameter-value pairs, just as you would when calling the `epp()` function in your Puppet manifest.

Alternatively, you can use the `--values_file` argument to reference a Puppet manifest file containing the hash of parameters:

```
echo "{ 'aws_access_key' => 'foo', 'aws_secret_key' => 'bar' }"
>params.pp
puppet epp render --values_file params.pp /examples/template_params.
epp
aws_access_key_id = foo
aws_secret_access_key = bar
```

You can pass parameters both on the command line with `--values`, and from a file with `--values_file`, simultaneously. Parameters given on the command line will take priority over those from the file:

```
puppet epp render --values_file params.pp --values "{ 'aws_access_key'
=> 'override' }" /examples/template_params.epp
aws_access_key_id = override
aws_secret_access_key = bar
```

You can also use `puppet epp render` to test inline template code, using the `-e` switch to pass in a literal template string:

```
puppet epp render --values "{ 'name' => 'Dave' }" -e 'Hello, <%= $name
%>'
Hello, Dave
```

Just as when testing your manifests, you can also use `puppet apply` to test your templates directly, using a command similar to the following:

```
sudo puppet apply -e "file { '/tmp/result': content => epp('/examples/
template_iterate.epp')}"
```

One advantage of this approach is that all Puppet variables, facts, and Hiera data will be available to your template.

Legacy ERB templates

You'll probably come across references to a different type of Puppet template in older code and documentation: the **ERB template**. ERB (for Embedded Ruby) was the only template mechanism provided in Puppet up until version 3.5, when EPP support was added, and EPP has now replaced ERB as Puppet's default template format.

ERB template syntax looks quite similar to EPP. The following example is a snippet from an ERB template:

```
AllowUsers <%= @users.join(' ') %><%= scope['::ubuntu'] == 'yes' ?
',ubuntu' : '' %>
```

The difference is that the template language inside the tags, is Ruby, not Puppet. Early versions of Puppet were rather limited in language features (for example, there was no `each` function to iterate over variables), so it was common to use Ruby code embedded in templates to work around this.

This required some complicated plumbing to manage the interface between Puppet and Ruby; for example, accessing variables in non-local scope in ERB templates requires the use of the `scope` hash, as in the previous example. Similarly, in order to access Puppet functions such as `strftime()`, you have to call:

```
scope.call_function('strftime', ...)
```

ERB templates also do not support declared parameters or type checking. I recommend you use only EPP templates in your own code.

Summary

In this chapter we've looked at one of the most powerful tools in Puppet's toolbox, the template file. We've examined the EPP tag syntax and seen the different kinds of tags available, including printing and non-printing tags.

We've learned that not only can you simply insert values from variables into templates, but that you can also include or exclude whole blocks of text, depending on the value of Puppet expressions, or generate templates of arbitrary size by iterating over arrays and hashes.

We've looked at some real-life examples of dynamically generating config files from Facter and Hiera data, and seen seen how to declare typed parameters in the template file, and pass in values for those parameters when calling the `epp()` function in your Puppet manifest.

We've seen how to check the syntax of templates using `puppet epp validate`, and how to render the output of a template using `puppet epp render`, passing in canned values for the template parameters using `--values` and `--values_file`, or using `puppet apply` to render the template directly.

Finally, we've touched on legacy ERB templates, where they come from, how they compare to EPP templates, and why, although you may still encounter ERB templates in the wild, you should only use EPP in your own code.

In the next chapter, we'll explore the popular topic of containers, and look at how to manage the Docker engine and Docker containers with Puppet, and deal with the vexed issue of how to manage configuration in containers.

10
Controlling containers

> *The inside of a computer is as dumb as hell but it goes like mad!*
>
> *—Richard Feynman*

In this chapter, we'll look at the emerging topic of **containers** and see how it relates to configuration management. We'll see how to use Puppet to manage the Docker daemon, as well as images and containers, and explore some different strategies for managing configuration within containers.

Understanding containers

Although the technology behind containers is at least thirty years old, it's only in the last few years that containers have really taken off (to mix a metaphor). This is largely thanks to the rise of Docker, a software platform which makes it easier to create and manage containers.

The deployment problem

The problem that Docker solves is principally one of **software deployment**: that is, making it possible to install and run your software in a wide variety of environments with minimal effort. Let's take a typical PHP web application, for example. To run the application you need at least the following to be present on a node:

- PHP source code
- PHP interpreter
- Its associated dependencies and libraries
- PHP modules required by your application
- Compiler and build tools for building native binaries for PHP modules
- Web server (for example Apache)
- Module for serving PHP apps (for example, `mod_php`)
- Config files for your application
- User to run the application
- Directories for things such as log files, images, and uploaded data

How do you manage all of this stuff? You can use a system package format, such as RPM or DEB, which uses metadata to describe its dependencies in terms of other packages, and scripts which can do much of the system configuration required.

However, this packaging is specific to a particular version of a particular operating system, and a package intended for Ubuntu 18.04, for example, will not be installable on Ubuntu 16.04 or on Red Hat Enterprise Linux. Maintaining multiple packages for several popular operating systems is a large workload on top of maintaining the application itself.

Options for deployment

One way to address this problem is for the author to provide **configuration management manifests** for the software, such as a Puppet module or a Chef recipe to install the software. However, if the intended user of the software does not use a CM tool, or uses a different tool, then this is no help. Even if they use exactly the same version of the same tool on the same operating system, they may have problems integrating the third-party module with it, and the module itself will depend on other modules and so on. It's certainly not a turnkey solution.

Another option is the **omnibus package**, a package which contains everything the software needs to run. An omnibus package for our example PHP application might contain the PHP binaries and all dependencies, plus anything else the application needs. These are necessarily quite large packages, however, and omnibus packages are still specific to a particular operating system and version, and involve a lot of maintenance effort.

Most package managers do not provide an efficient binary update facility, so even the smallest update requires re-downloading the entire package. Some omnibus packages even include their own config management tool!

Yet another solution is to provide an entire **virtual machine image**, such as a Vagrant box (the Vagrant box we've been using throughout the book is a good example). This contains not only the application plus dependencies and configuration, but the entire operating system as well. This is a fairly portable solution, since any platform which can run the virtual machine host software (for example, VirtualBox or VMware) can run the VM itself.

However, there is a performance penalty with virtual machines, and they also consume a lot of resources, such as memory and disk space, and the VM images themselves are large and unwieldy to move around a network.

While in theory you could deploy your application by building a VM image and pushing it to a production VM host, and some people do this, it's far from an efficient method of distribution.

Introducing the container

In recent years many operating systems have added facilities for self-contained execution environments, more concisely called **containers**, in which programs can run natively on the CPU, but with very limited access to the rest of the machine. A container is like a security sandbox, where anything running inside it can access files and programs inside the container, but nothing else.

This is similar in principle to a virtual machine, except that the underlying technology is quite different. Instead of running on a virtual processor, via a software emulation layer, programs in a container run directly on the underlying physical hardware. This makes containers a great deal more efficient than VMs. To put it another way, you need much less powerful hardware to run containers than you do for virtual machines of the same performance.

A single virtual machine consumes a large amount of its host's resources, which means that running more than one VM on the same host can be quite demanding. By contrast, running a process inside a container uses no more resources than running the same process natively.

Therefore, you can run a very large number of containers on a single host, and each is completely self-contained and has no access to either the host, or any other container (unless you specifically allow it). A container, at the kernel level, is really just a namespace. Processes running in that namespace cannot access anything outside it, and vice versa. All the containers on a machine use the host operating system's kernel, so although containers are portable across different Linux distributions, for example, a Linux container cannot run directly on a Windows host. Linux containers can, however, run on Windows using a virtualization layer provided by Docker for Windows.

What Docker does for containers

So if containers themselves are provided by the kernel, what is Docker for? It turns out that having an engine is not quite the same thing as having a car. The operating system kernel may provide the basic facilities for containerization, but you also need:

- A specification for how to build containers
- A standard file format for container images
- A protocol for storing, versioning, organizing, and retrieving container images
- Software to start, run, and manage containers
- Drivers to allow network traffic to and from containers
- Ways of communicating between containers
- Facilities for getting data into containers

These need to be provided by additional software. There are in fact many software frontends which allow you to manage containers: Docker, OCID, CoreOS/rkt, Apache Mesos, LXD, VMware Photon, Windows Server Containers, and so on. However, Docker is by far the market leader, and currently the majority of containers in production are running under Docker (a recent survey put the proportion at over 90%).

Deployment with Docker

The principle of deploying software with containers is very simple: the software, plus everything it needs to run, is inside the container **image**, which is like a package file, but is executable directly by the container runtime.

To run the software, all you need to do is execute a command like the following (if you have Docker installed, try it!):

```
docker run bitfield/hello
Hello, world
```

Docker will download the specified image from your configured **registry** (this could be the public registry, called Docker Hub, or your own private Docker registry) and execute it. There are thousands of Docker images available for you to use, and many software companies are increasingly using Docker images as their primary way to deploy products.

Building Docker containers

But where do these Docker images come from? Docker images are like an archive or a package file, containing the file and directory layout of all the files inside the container, including executable binaries, shared libraries, and config files. To create this image file, you use the `docker build` command.

`docker build` takes a special text file called a **Dockerfile**, which specifies what should be in the container. Usually, a new Docker image is based on an existing image with a few modifications. For example, there is a Docker image for Ubuntu Linux, which contains a fully-installed operating system ready to run.

Your Dockerfile might specify that you use the Ubuntu Docker image as a starting point, and then install the package `nginx`. The resulting Docker container contains everything that was in the stock Ubuntu image, plus the `nginx` package. You can now upload this image to a registry and run it anywhere using `docker run`.

If you wanted to package your own software with Docker, you could choose a suitable base image (such as Ubuntu) and write a Dockerfile which installs your software onto that base image. When you build the container image with `docker build`, the result will be a container with your software inside it, which anyone can run using `docker run`. The only thing they need to install is Docker.

This makes Docker a great way both for software vendors to package their products in an easy-installable format, and for users to try out different software quickly to see if it meets their needs.

The layered filesystem

The Docker filesystem has a feature called **layering**. Containers are built up in layers, so that if something changes, only the affected layer and those above it need to be rebuilt. This makes it much more efficient to update container images once they've been built and deployed.

For example, if you change one line of code in your app and rebuild the container, only the layer that contains your app needs to be rebuilt, along with any layers above it. The base image and other layers below the affected layer remain the same and can be re-used for the new container.

Managing containers with Puppet

There are a few things you need to be able to do to package and run software with Docker:

- Install, configure, and manage the Docker service itself
- Build your images
- Rebuild images when the Dockerfile changes, or a dependency is updated
- Manage the running images, their data storage, and their configuration

Unless you want to make your images public, you will also need to host an image registry for your own images.

These sound like the kinds of problems that configuration management tools can solve, and luckily, we have a great configuration management tool available. Oddly enough, while most people recognize that traditional servers need to be built and managed automatically by a tool such as Puppet, the same does not seem to be true (yet) of containers.

The trouble is, it's so easy to make a simple container and run it that many people think configuration management for containers is overkill. That may be so when you're first trying out Docker and experimenting with simple containers, but when you're running complex, multi-container services in production, at scale, things get more complicated.

First, containerizing non-trivial applications is non-trivial. They need dependencies and configuration settings and data, and ways to communicate with other applications and services, and while Docker provides you with tools to do this, it doesn't do the work for you.

Second, you need an infrastructure to build your containers, update them, store and retrieve the resulting images, and deploy and manage them in production. Configuration management for containers is very much like configuration management for traditional server-based applications, except that it's happening at a slightly higher level.

Containers are great, but they don't do away with the need for configuration management tools (remember the *Law of Conservation of Pain* from *Chapter 1, Getting started with Puppet*?):

"If you save yourself pain in one place, it pops up again in another. Whatever cool new technology comes along, it won't solve all our problems; at best, it will replace them with refreshingly different problems."

Managing Docker with Puppet

Puppet can certainly install and manage the Docker service for you, just as it can any other software, but it can also do a lot more. It can download and run Docker images, build images from Dockerfiles, mount files and directories on the container, and manage Docker volumes and networks. We'll see how to do all these things in this chapter.

Installing Docker

Before we do anything else, we'll need to install Docker on our node (using Puppet, of course). The `puppetlabs/docker_platform` module is ideal for this.

1. If you've already installed and run the `r10k` module management tool, as shown in *Chapter 7, Mastering modules*, in the *Using r10k* section, the required module will already be installed. If not, run the following commands to install it:

   ```
   cd /etc/puppetlabs/code/environments/pbg
   sudo r10k puppetfile install
   ```

2. Once the module is installed, all you need to do to install Docker on your node is to apply a manifest like the following (`docker_install.pp`):

   ```
   include docker
   ```

3. Run the following command to apply the manifest:

   ```
   sudo puppet apply --environment pbg /examples/docker_install.pp
   ```

4. To check that Docker is installed, run the following command (you may see a different version number, but that's OK):

   ```
   docker --version
   Docker version 17.05.0-ce, build 89658be
   ```

Running a Docker container

In order to run a Docker container, we first of all have to download it from a Docker registry, which is a server that stores container images. The default registry is Docker Hub, the official public Docker registry.

To do this with Puppet, you can use the `docker::image` resource (`docker_image.pp`):

```
docker::image { 'bitfield/hello':
  ensure => 'latest',
}
```

As with the `package` resource, if you specify `ensure => latest`, Puppet will check the registry every time it runs and make sure you have the latest available version of the image.

To run the image you've just downloaded, add a `docker::run` resource to your manifest (`docker_run.pp`):

```
docker::run { 'hello':
  image   => 'bitfield/hello',
  command => '/bin/sh -c "while true; do echo Hello, world; sleep 1;
done"',
}
```

Apply this manifest with the following command:

```
sudo puppet apply /examples/docker_run.pp
```

The `docker::run` resource tells Docker to fetch the image `bitfield/hello` from the local image cache and run it with the specified command, which in this case just loops forever printing `Hello, world`. (I told you containers were useful.)

The container is now running on your node, and you can check this with the following command:

```
sudo docker ps
CONTAINER ID        IMAGE               COMMAND
CREATED
STATUS              PORTS               NAMES
ba1f4aced778        bitfield/hello      „/bin/sh -c ‚while tr"    4
minutes ago        Up 4 minutes                              hello
```

The `docker ps` command shows all currently running containers (`docker ps -a` will show stopped containers too), with the following information:

- The container ID, Docker's internal identifier for the container
- The image name (`bitfield/hello` in our example)

- The currently executing command in the container
- The creation time
- Current status
- Any ports mapped by the container
- The human-readable name of the container (which is the title we gave the `docker::run` resource in our manifest)

The container is running as a service, and we can check that with the following command:

```
systemctl status docker-hello
* docker-hello.service - Daemon for hello
   Loaded: loaded (/etc/systemd/system/docker-hello.service; enabled;
vendor preset: enabled)
   Active: active (running) since Tue 2017-05-16 04:07:23 PDT; 1min 4s
ago
 Main PID: 24385 (docker)
   CGroup: /system.slice/docker-hello.service
           `-24385 /usr/bin/docker run --net bridge -m 0b --name hello
bitfield/hello...
...
```

Stopping a container

According to the Docker documentation, you can stop a container by running `sudo docker stop NAME`. However, if you try this, and then run `sudo docker ps` again, you'll see that the container is still running. What's that about?

The Puppet module assumes by default that you want to run all containers as services; that is, to configure `systemd` to keep the container running, and to start it at boot time.

Therefore, if you want to stop a container which is running as a service, you will need to do this with Puppet, by setting the `ensure` parameter on the `docker::run` resource to `absent`, as in the following example (`docker_absent.pp`):

```
docker::run { 'hello':
  ensure => absent,
  image  => 'bitfield/hello',
}
```

Alternatively, on the command line, you can use the `systemctl` command to stop the service:

```
sudo systemctl stop docker-hello
```

If you don't want your container to be managed as a service by `systemd`, specify the parameter `restart => always` to the `docker::run` resource. This tells Docker to restart the container automatically when it exits; so therefore Puppet does not need to create a `systemd` service to manage it.

Running multiple instances of a container

Of course, the true power of automation is the ability to scale. We're not limited to running a single instance of a given container; Puppet will happily start as many as you like.

Each `docker::run` resource must have a unique name, as with any other Puppet resource, so you can create them in an `each` loop, as in the following example (`docker_run_many.pp`):

```
range(1,20).each | $instance | {
  docker::run { "hello-${instance}":
    image   => 'bitfield/hello',
    command => '/bin/sh -c "while true; do echo Hello, world; sleep 1;
done"',
  }
}
```

The `range()` function comes from the `stdlib` module, and, as you might expect, `range(1,20)` returns the sequence of integers between 1 and 20 inclusive. We iterate over this sequence with the `each` function, and each time through the loop `$instance` is set to the next integer.

The `docker::run` resource title includes the value of `$instance` on each iteration, so each container will be uniquely named: `hello-1`, `hello-2`,... `hello-20`. I've chosen the number 20 at random, just as an example; you could compute the number of instances to run based on the resources available, for example the number of system CPUs or available memory.

Don't forget to stop these containers afterward (edit the example manifest to add `ensure => absent` to the `docker::run` resource and re-apply it).

Managing Docker images

Of course, it's very useful to be able to download and run public images from Docker Hub or other registries, but to unlock the real power of Docker we need to be able to build and manage our own images too.

Building images from Dockerfiles

As we saw in the previous examples, if you don't already have the specified container image on your system, Puppet's `docker::image` resource will pull it from Docker Hub for you and save it locally.

The `docker::image` resource is most useful, however, for actually **building** Docker images. This is usually done using a Dockerfile, so here is an example Dockerfile we can use to build an image (`Dockerfile.hello`):

```
FROM library/alpine:3.6
CMD /bin/sh -c "while true; do echo Hello, world; sleep 1; done"

LABEL org.label-schema.vendor="Bitfield Consulting" \
  org.label-schema.url="http://bitfieldconsulting.com" \
  org.label-schema.name="Hello World" \
  org.label-schema.version="1.0.0" \
  org.label-schema.vcs-url="github.com:bitfield/puppet-beginners-
guide.git" \
  org.label-schema.docker.schema-version="1.0"
```

The `FROM` statement tells Docker what base image to start from, of the many public images available. `FROM scratch` would start with a completely empty container. `FROM library/ubuntu` would use the official Ubuntu Docker image.

Of course, one of the key advantages of containers is that they can be as small or as large as they need to be, so downloading a 188 MB image containing all of Ubuntu is unnecessary if you simply want to run `/bin/echo`.

Alpine is another Linux distribution designed to be as small and lightweight as possible, which makes it ideal for containers. The `library/alpine` image is only 4 MB, forty times smaller than `ubuntu`; quite a saving. Also, if you build all your containers from the same base image, Docker's layer system means it only has to download and store the base image once.

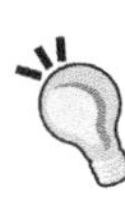

Dockerfiles can be fairly simple, as in the example, or quite complex. You can find out more about the Dockerfile format and commands from the Docker documentation:

`https://docs.docker.com/engine/reference/builder/`

The following code shows how to create a Docker image from this file (`docker_build_hello.pp`):

```
docker::image { 'pbg-hello':
  docker_file => '/examples/Dockerfile.hello',
  ensure      => latest,
}
```

Once the `docker::image` resource has been applied, the resulting `pbg-hello` image will be available for you to run as a container (`docker_run_hello.pp`):

```
docker::run { 'pbg-hello':
  image => 'pbg-hello',
}
```

Managing Dockerfiles

When you run your own apps in containers, or third-party apps in your own containers, you can manage the associated Dockerfiles with Puppet. Here's an example of a simple Dockerfile which builds a container using Nginx to serve a web page with a friendly greeting message (`Dockerfile.nginx`):

```
FROM nginx:1.13.3-alpine
RUN echo "Hello, world" >/usr/share/nginx/html/index.html

LABEL org.label-schema.vendor="Bitfield Consulting" \
  org.label-schema.url="http://bitfieldconsulting.com" \
  org.label-schema.name="Nginx Hello World" \
  org.label-schema.version="1.0.0" \
  org.label-schema.vcs-url="github.com:bitfield/puppet-beginners-
guide.git" \
  org.label-schema.docker.schema-version="1.0"
```

Here's the Puppet manifest which manages this Dockerfile, and builds an image from it (`docker_build_nginx.pp`):

```
file { '/tmp/Dockerfile.nginx':
  source => '/examples/Dockerfile.nginx',
  notify => Docker::Image['pbg-nginx'],
}

docker::image { 'pbg-nginx':
  docker_file => '/tmp/Dockerfile.nginx',
  ensure      => latest,
}
```

Run the following command to apply this manifest:

```
sudo puppet apply /examples/docker_build_nginx.pp
```

Whenever the contents of the Dockerfile change, applying this manifest will cause the image to be rebuilt.

For the purposes of this example we are building and running the container on the same node. In practice, though, you should build your containers on a dedicated build node and upload the resulting images to the registry, so that your production nodes can download and run them.

Here's the manifest to run the container we just built (`docker_run_nginx.pp`):

```
docker::run { 'pbg-nginx':
  image         => 'pbg-nginx:latest',
  ports         => ['80:80'],
  pull_on_start => true,
}
```

Note the `pull_on_start` attribute, which tells Puppet to always download the latest available version of the container when starting or restarting it.

If you worked through *Chapter 7, Mastering modules*, the Apache web server will be running and listening on port `80`, so you will need to run the following commands to remove it before applying this manifest:

```
sudo apt-get -y --purge remove apache2
sudo service docker restart
sudo puppet apply --environment pbg /examples/docker_run_nginx.pp
```

You can check that the container is working by browsing to the following URL on your local machine:

`http://localhost:8080`

You should see the text `Hello, world`.

If you're using the Vagrant box, port `8080` on your local machine is automatically mapped to port `80` on the VM, which is then mapped by Docker to port `80` on the `pbg-nginx` container. If for some reason you need to change this port mapping, edit your Vagrantfile (in the Puppet Beginner's Guide repo) and look for the following line:

```
config.vm.network "forwarded_port", guest: 80,
host: 8080
```

Change these settings as required, and run the following command on your local machine in the PBG repo directory:

```
vagrant reload
```

If you're not using the Vagrant box, the container's port `80` will be exposed at your local port `80`, so the URL will simply appear as follows:

`http://localhost`

Building dynamic containers

Although Dockerfiles are a fairly powerful and flexible way of building containers, they are only static text files, and very often you will need to pass information into the container to tell it what to do. We might call such containers—whose configuration is flexible and based on data available at build time—**dynamic containers**.

Configuring containers with templates

One way to configure containers dynamically is to use Puppet to manage the Dockerfile as an EPP template (see *Chapter 9, Managing files with templates*), and interpolate the required data (which could come from Hiera, Facter, or directly from Puppet code).

Let's upgrade our previous `Hello, world` example to have Nginx serve any arbitrary text string, supplied by Puppet at build time.

Here's the manifest to generate the Dockerfile from a template and run the resulting image (`docker_template.pp`):

```
file { '/tmp/Dockerfile.nginx':
  content => epp('/examples/Dockerfile.nginx.epp',
    {
      'message' => 'Containers rule!'
    }
  ),
```

```
    notify => Docker::Image['pbg-nginx'],
  }

  docker::image { 'pbg-nginx':
    docker_file => '/tmp/Dockerfile.nginx',
    ensure      => latest,
    notify      => Docker::Run['pbg-nginx'],
  }

  docker::run { 'pbg-nginx':
    image         => 'pbg-nginx:latest',
    ports         => ['80:80'],
    pull_on_start => true,
  }
```

Apply this manifest with the following commands:

```
sudo puppet apply --environment pbg /examples/docker_template.pp
```

When you have applied the manifest and built the container, you will find that if you change the value of `message` and reapply, the container will be rebuilt with the updated text. The `docker::image` resource uses `notify` to tell the `docker::run` resource to restart the container when the image changes.

> Templating the Dockerfile like this is a powerful technique. Since you can have Puppet put any arbitrary data into a Dockerfile, you can configure anything about the container and its build process: the base image, the list of packages to install, files and data that should be added to the container, and even the command entry point for the container.

Self-configuring containers

Let's take this idea even further and use Puppet to dynamically configure a container which can fetch its data from Git. Instead of serving static text supplied at build time, we will have the container itself check out a Git repo for the website.

Most of the code from the previous example remains unchanged, except for the Dockerfile resource (`docker_website.pp`):

```
  file { '/tmp/Dockerfile.nginx':
    content => epp('/examples/Dockerfile.website.epp',
      {
        'git_url' => 'https://github.com/bitfield/pbg-website.git'
      }
    ),
```

```
  notify  => Docker::Image['pbg-nginx'],
}

docker::image { 'pbg-nginx':
  docker_file => '/tmp/Dockerfile.nginx',
  ensure      => latest,
  notify      => Docker::Run['pbg-nginx'],
}

docker::run { 'pbg-nginx':
  image         => 'pbg-nginx:latest',
  ports         => ['80:80'],
  pull_on_start => true,
}
```

The Dockerfile itself is a little more complicated, because we need to install Git in the container and use it to check out the supplied Git repo (`Dockerfile.website.epp`):

```
<% | String $git_url | -%>
FROM nginx:1.13.3-alpine
RUN apk update \
  && apk add git \
  && cd /usr/share/nginx \
  && mv html html.orig \
  && git clone <%= $git_url %> html

LABEL org.label-schema.vendor="Bitfield Consulting" \
  org.label-schema.url="http://bitfieldconsulting.com" \
  org.label-schema.name="Nginx Git Website" \
  org.label-schema.version="1.0.0" \
  org.label-schema.vcs-url="github.com:bitfield/puppet-beginners-
guide.git" \
  org.label-schema.docker.schema-version="1.0"
```

When you apply this manifest and browse to `http://localhost:8080`, you should see the text:

```
Hello, world!
This is the demo website served by the examples in Chapter 10,
'Controlling containers', from the Puppet Beginner's Guide.
```

Although we supplied the `git_url` parameter directly to the Dockerfile template, that data could of course come from anywhere, including Hiera. With this technique, you can build a container to serve any website simply by changing the Git URL passed to it.

Using the iteration pattern we saw in the `docker_run_many` example earlier in this chapter, you could build a set of containers like this from an array of `git_url` values, each serving a different website. Now we're really starting to exploit the power of Docker-plus-Puppet.

Run the following command to stop the container before going on to the next example:

```
sudo docker stop pbg-nginx
```

There's one slight problem with this idea. Although it's good to have the container be able to serve content from a Git repo determined at build time, every time the container is started or restarted, it will have to run the `git clone` process again. This takes time, and if the repo or the network is unavailable for some reason, it can stop the container from working.

A better solution would be to serve the content from persistent storage, and we'll see how to do that in the next section.

Persistent storage for containers

Containers are designed to be transient; they run for a while, and then disappear. Anything inside the container disappears with it, including files and data created during the container's run. This isn't always what we want, of course. If you're running a database inside a container, for example, you usually want that data to persist when the container goes away.

There are two ways of persisting data in a container: the first is to mount a directory from the host machine inside the container, known as a **host-mounted volume**, and the second is to use what's called a **Docker volume**. We'll look at both of these in the following sections.

Host-mounted volumes

If you want a container to be able to access files on the host machine's filesystem (such as application code that you're working on and you want to test, for example), the easiest way to do that is to mount a directory from the host on the container. The following example shows how to do this (`docker_mount.pp`):

```
docker::run { 'mount_test':
  image    => 'library/alpine:3.6',
  volumes  => ['/tmp/container_data:/mnt/data'],
  command  => '/bin/sh -c "echo Hello, world >/mnt/data/hello.txt"',
}
```

The `volumes` attribute specifies an array of volumes to attach to the container. If the volume is of the form `HOST_PATH:CONTAINER_PATH`, Docker will assume you want to mount the directory `HOST_PATH` on the container. The path inside the container will be `CONTAINER_PATH`. Any files which already exist in the mounted directory will be accessible to the container, and anything the container writes to the directory will still be available once the container has stopped.

If you apply this example manifest, the container will mount the host machine's `/tmp/container_data/` directory (this will be created if it doesn't exist) as `/mnt/data/` in the container.

The `command` attribute tells the container to write the string `Hello, world` to the file `/mnt/data/hello.txt`.

Run the following command to apply this manifest:

```
sudo puppet apply /examples/docker_mount.pp
```

The container will start, write the data, and then exit. If all has gone well, you'll see that the file `/tmp/container_data/hello.txt` is now present and contains the data written by the container:

```
cat /tmp/container_data/hello.txt
Hello, world
```

Host-mounted volumes are very useful when a container needs to access or share data with applications running on the host machine. For example, you could use a host-mounted volume with a container which runs syntax checks, lint, or continuous integration tests on your source code directory.

However, containers using host-mounted volumes are not portable, and they rely on a specific directory being present on the host machine. You can't specify a host-mounted volume in a Dockerfile, so you can't publish a container which relies on one. While host-mounted volumes can be useful for testing and development, a better solution in production is to use Docker volumes.

Docker volumes

A more portable way of adding persistent storage to containers is to use a **Docker volume**. This is a persistent data object which lives in Docker's storage area and can be attached to one or more containers.

The following example shows how to use `docker::run` to start a container with a Docker volume (`docker_volume.pp`):

```
docker::run { 'volume_test':
  image   => 'library/alpine:3.6',
  volumes => ['pbg-volume:/mnt/volume'],
  command => '/bin/sh -c "echo Hello from inside a Docker volume >/
mnt/volume/index.html"',
}
```

The `volumes` attribute is a little different from the previous example. It has the form `VOLUME_NAME:CONTAINER_PATH`, which tells Docker that this is not a host-mounted volume, but a Docker volume named `VOLUME_NAME`. If the value before the colon is a path, Docker assumes you want to mount that path from the host machine, but otherwise, it assumes you want to mount a Docker volume with the specified name.

As in the previous example, the container's `command` argument writes a message to a file on the mounted volume.

If you apply this manifest, once the container has exited, you can see that the volume is still present by running the following command:

```
sudo docker volume ls
DRIVER              VOLUME NAME
local               pbg-volume
```

A Docker volume is a good way to store data that you need to keep even when the container is not running (a database, for example). It's also a good way to make data available to containers without having to load it into each container every time it starts.

In the website example earlier in the chapter, instead of each container checking out its own copy of the Git repo, you could check out the repo into a Docker volume, and then have each container mount this volume when it starts.

Let's test that idea with the following manifest (`docker_volume2.pp`):

```
docker::run { 'volume_test2':
  image   => 'nginx:alpine',
  volumes => ['pbg-volume:/usr/share/nginx/html'],
  ports   => ['80:80'],
}
```

This is the same `nginx` container we used earlier in the chapter, which serves whatever is in its `/usr/share/nginx/html` directory as a website.

The `volumes` attribute tells the container to mount the `pbg-volume` volume on `/usr/share/nginx/html`.

Run the following commands to apply this manifest:

```
sudo docker stop pbg-nginx
sudo puppet apply /examples/docker_volume2.pp
```

If everything works as we expect, we should able to browse to the following URL on the local machine: `http://localhost:8080/`

We should see the following text:

```
Hello from inside a Docker volume
```

This is a very powerful feature of containers. They can read, write, and modify data created by other containers, maintain persistent storage of their own, and share data with other running containers, all using volumes.

A common pattern for running applications in Docker is to use multiple, communicating containers, each providing a single specific service. For example, a web application might use an Nginx container to serve an application to users, while storing its session data in a MySQL container mounting a persistent volume. It could also use a linked Redis container as an in-memory key-value store.

Apart from sharing data via volumes, though, how do these containers actually communicate over the network? We'll see the answer to that in the next section.

Networking and orchestration

We started off the chapter by saying that containers are completely self-contained, and have no access to each other, even if they're running on the same host. But to run real applications, we need containers to communicate. Fortunately, there is a way to do this: the **Docker network**.

Connecting containers

A Docker network is like a private chat room for containers: all the containers inside the network can talk to each other, but they can't talk to containers outside it or in other networks, and vice versa. All you need to do is have Docker create a network, give it a name, and then you can start containers inside that network and they will be able to talk to each other.

Let's develop an example to try this out. Suppose we want to run the Redis database inside a container, and send data to it from another container. This is a common pattern for many applications.

In our example, we're going to create a Docker network, and start two containers inside it. The first container is a public Docker Hub image that will run the Redis database server. The second container will install the Redis client tool, and write some data to the Redis server container. Then, to check it worked, we can try to read the data back from the server.

Run the following command to apply the Docker network example manifest:

```
sudo puppet apply /examples/docker_network.pp
```

If everything worked as it should, our Redis database should now contain a piece of data named `message` containing a friendly greeting, proving that we've passed data from one container to another over the Docker network.

Run the following command to connect to the client container and check that this is the case:

```
sudo docker exec -it pbg-redis redis-cli get message
"Hello, world"
```

So how does it all work? Let's take a look at the example manifest. First of all, we create the network for the two containers to run in, using the `docker_network` resource in Puppet (`docker_network.pp`):

```
docker_network { 'pbg-net':
  ensure => present,
}
```

Now, we run the Redis server container, using the public `redis:4.0.1-alpine` image.

```
docker::run { 'pbg-redis':
  image => 'redis:4.0.1-alpine',
  net   => 'pbg-net',
}
```

Did you notice that we supplied the `net` attribute to the `docker::run` resource? This specifies the Docker network that the container should run in.

Next, we build a container which has the Redis client (`redis-cli`) installed so that we can use it to write some data to the Redis container.

Here's the Dockerfile for the client container (`Dockerfile.pbg-demo`):

```
FROM nginx:1.13.3-alpine
RUN apk update \
  && apk add redis

LABEL org.label-schema.vendor="Bitfield Consulting" \
  org.label-schema.url="http://bitfieldconsulting.com" \
  org.label-schema.name="Redis Demo" \
  org.label-schema.version="1.0.0" \
  org.label-schema.vcs-url="github.com:bitfield/puppet-beginners-
guide.git" \
  org.label-schema.docker.schema-version="1.0"
```

We build this container in the usual way using `docker::image`:

```
docker::image { 'pbg-demo':
  docker_file => '/examples/Dockerfile.pbg-demo',
  ensure      => latest,
}
```

Finally, we run an instance of the client container with `docker::run`, passing in a command to `redis-cli` to write some data to the other container.

```
docker::run { 'pbg-demo':
  image   => 'pbg-demo',
  net     => 'pbg-net',
  command => '/bin/sh -c "redis-cli -h pbg-redis set message \"Hello,
world\""',
}
```

As you can see, this container also has the attribute `net => 'pbg-net'`. It will therefore run in the same Docker network as the `pbg-redis` container, so the two containers will be able to talk to each other.

When the container starts, the `command` attribute calls `redis-cli` with the following command:

```
redis-cli -h pbg-redis set message "Hello, world"
```

The `-h pbg-redis` argument tells Redis to connect to the host `pbg-redis`.

> How does using the `pbg-redis` name connect to the right container? When you start a container inside a network, Docker automagically configures DNS lookups within the container to find other containers in the network by name. When you reference a container name (the title of the container's `docker::run` resource, which in our example is `pbg-redis`), Docker will route the network connection to the right place.

The command `set message "Hello, world"` creates a Redis key named `message`, and gives it the value `"Hello, world"`.

We now have all the necessary techniques to containerize a real application: using Puppet to manage multiple containers, built from dynamic data, pushed to a registry, updated on demand, communicating over the network, listening on ports to the outside world, and persisting and sharing data via volumes.

Container orchestration

We've seen a number of ways to manage individual containers in this chapter, but the question of how to provision and manage containers at scale, and across multiple hosts—what we call container **orchestration**—remains.

For example, if your app runs in a container, you probably won't be running just one instance of the container: you need to run multiple instances, and route and load-balance traffic to them. You also need to be able to distribute your containers across multiple hosts, so that the application is resilient against the failure of any individual container host.

What is orchestration?

When running containers across a distributed cluster, you also need to be able to deal with issues such as networking between containers and hosts, failover, health monitoring, rolling out updates, service discovery, and sharing configuration data between containers via a key-value database.

Although container orchestration is a broad task, and different tools and frameworks focus on different aspects of it, the core requirements of orchestration include:

- **Scheduling**: Running a container on the cluster and deciding which containers to run on which hosts to provide a given service
- **Cluster management**: Monitoring and marshalling the activity of containers and hosts across the cluster, and adding or removing hosts
- **Service discovery**: Giving containers the ability to find and connect to the services and data they need to operate

What orchestration tools are available?

Google's Kubernetes and Docker's Swarm are both designed to orchestrate containers. Another product, Apache Mesos, is a cluster management framework which can operate on different kinds of resources, including containers.

Most containers in production today are running under one of these three orchestration systems. Kubernetes has been around the longest and has the biggest user base, but Swarm, though a relatively new arrival, is part of the official Docker stack, so is being rapidly adopted.

Because all these products are necessarily rather complicated to set up and operate, there is also the option of **Platform-as-a-Service** (**PaaS**) orchestration: essentially, running your containers on a managed cloud platform. **Google Container Engine** (**GKE**) is Kubernetes as a service; Amazon's **EC2 Container Service** (**ECS**) is a proprietary, Kubernetes-like system.

As yet, Puppet integration with container orchestrators is somewhat limited and at an early stage, though, given the popularity of containers, this is likely to advance rapidly. There is some elementary support for generating Kubernetes configuration from Puppet resources, and some for managing Amazon ECS resources, but it's fair to say that automating container orchestration at scale with Puppet is so far still in its infancy. Watch this space, however.

Running Puppet inside containers

If a container can contain a whole operating system, such as Ubuntu, you might be wondering: "can't I just run Puppet inside the container?"

You can, and some people do take this approach to managing containers. It also has a number of advantages:

- You can use your existing Puppet manifests, or Forge modules; no need to write complex Dockerfiles
- Puppet will keep the container continuously updated; no need to rebuild when something changes

Of course, there are a few disadvantages too:

- Installing Puppet inflates the image size considerably, and pulls in all sorts of dependencies
- Running Puppet slows down the build process, and also consumes resources in the running container

There are also some hybrid options, such as running Puppet in the container during the build stage, and then removing Puppet and its dependencies, plus any intermediate build artifacts, before saving the final image.

Puppet's `image_build` module is a promising new way of building containers directly from Puppet manifests, and I expect to see rapid progress in this space in the near future.

Are containers mini VMs or single processes?

Which option you favor probably depends on your basic approach to containers. Do you see them as mini-virtual machines, not too different from the servers you're already managing? Or do you see them as transient, lightweight, single-process wrappers?

If you treat containers as mini-VMs, you'll probably want to run Puppet in your containers, in the same way as you do on your physical and virtual servers. On the other hand, if you think a container should just run a single process, it doesn't seem appropriate to run Puppet in it. With single-process containers there's very little to configure.

I can see arguments in favor of the mini-VM approach. For one thing, it makes it much easier to transition your existing applications and services to containers; instead of running them in a VM, you just move the whole thing (application, support services, and database) into a container, along with all your current management and monitoring tools.

However, while this is a valid approach, it doesn't really make the most of the inherent advantages of containers: small image sizes, quick deployment, efficient rebuilding, and portability.

Configuring containers with Puppet

Personally, I'm a container minimalist: I think the container should contain only what it needs to do the job. Therefore, I prefer to use Puppet to manage, configure, and build my containers from the outside, rather than from the inside, and that's why I've used that approach in this chapter.

That means generating Dockerfiles from templates and Hiera data, as we've seen in the examples, as well as templating config files which the container needs. You can have the Dockerfile copy these files into the container during the build, or mount individual files and directories from the host onto the container.

As we've seen, a good way to handle shared data is to have Puppet write it into a Docker volume or a file on the host which is then mounted (usually read-only) by all running containers.

The advantage of this is that you don't need to rebuild all your containers following a config change. You can simply have Puppet write the changes to the config volume, and trigger each container to reload its configuration using a `docker::exec` resource, which executes a specified command on a running container.

Containers need Puppet too

At the risk of laboring a point, containerization is not an alternative to using configuration management tools such as Puppet. In fact, the need for configuration management is even greater, because you not only have to build and configure the containers themselves, but also store, deploy, and run them: all of which requires an infrastructure.

As usual, Puppet makes this sort of task easier, more pleasant, and—most importantly—more scalable.

Summary

In this chapter, we've examined some of the problems associated with software deployment, some of the options for solving them, and the advantages of the container solution. We've briefly introduced the basics of container technology and Docker, in particular, and seen that containers are another kind of configuration management problem which Puppet can help solve.

We've installed the `docker_platform` module, and used it to set up Docker on our VM, and build and run simple Docker containers. We've seen how to automatically rebuild the container image when the underlying Dockerfile changes, and how to use Puppet to configure a Dockerfile dynamically at build time.

We've introduced the topic of persistent storage for containers, including host-mounted volumes and Docker volumes, and how to manage these with Puppet. We've set up a Docker network with two communicating containers exchanging data over network ports.

We've looked at the advantages and disadvantages of running Puppet inside containers, as opposed to using Puppet to configure and build containers from the outside, and also suggested a hybrid strategy where Puppet manages configuration data on a volume attached to running containers.

Finally, we've covered some of the issues involved in container orchestration, and introduced some of the most popular platforms and frameworks available.

In the next chapter, we'll learn how to use Puppet to manage cloud computing resources, with an in-depth example developing a software-defined Amazon EC2 infrastructure.

11
Orchestrating cloud resources

Rest is not idleness, and to lie sometimes on the grass under trees on a summer's day, listening to the murmur of the water, or watching the clouds float across the sky, is by no means a waste of time.

—John Lubbock

In this chapter you'll learn how to use the `puppetlabs/aws` module to create and manage Amazon AWS cloud instances, and associated resources such as subnets, security groups, and VPCs. You'll also learn how to build your entire cloud infrastructure directly from Hiera data.

Introducing the cloud

Before exploring the advantages of cloud computing, perhaps we should define what it is. In the pre-cloud days, if you needed computing power, you bought an actual, physical computer. But from the customer's point of view, we don't necessarily want a computer: we just want to compute. We would like to be able to buy as much or as little compute resource as we happen to need at a given time, without paying a large fixed cost for a dedicated computer.

Enter **virtualization**. A single physical server can provide a large number of virtual servers, each of which is (in theory) completely isolated from the others. The hosting provider builds a platform (consisting of many physical servers networked together) which provides, from the customer's point of view, a large intangible **cloud** of virtual compute resources (hence the term).

Automating cloud provisioning

Creating new cloud instances is cheaper and easier than buying physical hardware, but you still have choices to make: how much CPU or memory the instance has, how much disk space, what kind of disks (physical, solid-state, network-attached storage), what operating system should be installed, whether the instance has a public IP address, what firewall rules it should have, and so on.

If you've read the book this far in the book, you should now recognize this as a **configuration management** problem. You will also probably have some idea what I'm going to recommend in order to solve it, but first let's look at a few of the available options.

Using CloudFormation

CloudFormation is a template language specific to **Amazon Web Services** (**AWS**). It describes AWS resources in a declarative way, rather like Puppet resources. You upload your CloudFormation template to the AWS portal (or API), apply it, and AWS will create all the resources specified. The following example shows a snippet of CloudFormation code:

```
"Resources" : {
   "EC2Instance" : {
     "Type" : "AWS::EC2::Instance",
     "Properties" : {
       "InstanceType" : { "Ref" : "InstanceType" },
       "SecurityGroups" : [ { "Ref" : "InstanceSecurityGroup" } ],
       "KeyName" : { "Ref" : "KeyName" },
       "ImageId" : { "Fn::FindInMap" : [ "AWSRegionArch2AMI", { "Ref"
: "AWS::Region" },
```

```
                            { "Fn::FindInMap" : [
"AWSInstanceType2Arch", { "Ref" : "InstanceType" }, "Arch" ] } ] }
      }
    },
```

Frankly, it's not much fun to program in. While it may technically be infrastructure as code, it's pretty basic. Nonetheless, it still represents an advance on manually setting up AWS infrastructure with a web browser.

Using Terraform

Terraform is a rather more sophisticated tool for provisioning cloud resources. It allows you to describe your resources in a declarative way, like CloudFormation, but at a slightly higher level of abstraction, which is not AWS-specific. The following example shows what Terraform code looks like:

```
resource "aws_instance" "web" {
  ami           = "${data.aws_ami.ubuntu.id}"
  instance_type = "t2.micro"

  tags {
    Name = "HelloWorld"
  }
}
```

Terraform is a promising technology, but it's fair to say it's at an early stage of development.

Using Puppet

Stand-alone tools for managing cloud infrastructure are fine, but if we're doing everything else with Puppet, it seems a shame to introduce a whole new tool just for that. So could we use Puppet to manage cloud resources instead?

Fortunately, Puppet provides an excellent Forge module (`puppetlabs/aws`) which does exactly this. In the rest of this chapter, we'll work through some examples of how to use `puppetlabs/aws` to manage AWS cloud resources.

Setting up an Amazon AWS account

If you already have an AWS account, skip to the next section. Otherwise, you can follow these instructions to set up a new account and get the credentials you need to start building infrastructure with Puppet.

Creating an AWS account

Follow these steps to create a new AWS account:

1. Browse to the following URL:

   `https://aws.amazon.com/`

2. Click **Sign In to the Console**.
3. Follow the instructions to create and verify your account.

To manage AWS resources using Puppet, we will create an additional AWS user account specifically for Puppet, using Amazon's **Identiy and Access Management** (**IAM**) framework. We'll see how to do this in the following sections.

Creating an IAM policy

Before we create the user account for Puppet, we need to grant specific permissions for the things it needs to do, such as read and create EC2 instances. This involves creating an **IAM policy**, which is a set of named permissions you can associate with a user account.

IAM policies are expressed as a JSON-format document. There is a policy JSON file in the example repo, named `/examples/iam_policy.json`. Open this file and copy the contents, ready to paste into your web browser.

Follow these steps to create the policy and associate it with the Puppet user:

1. In the AWS console, select **Services** | **IAM**.
2. Select **Policies**.
3. Click **Create Policy**.
4. On the **Create Policy** screen, select **Create Your Own Policy**.
5. Enter **Policy Name** (for example, `puppet`).
6. In the **Policy Document** textbox, paste the text you copied from the `iam_policy.json` file.
7. Click **Create Policy** at the bottom to save this.

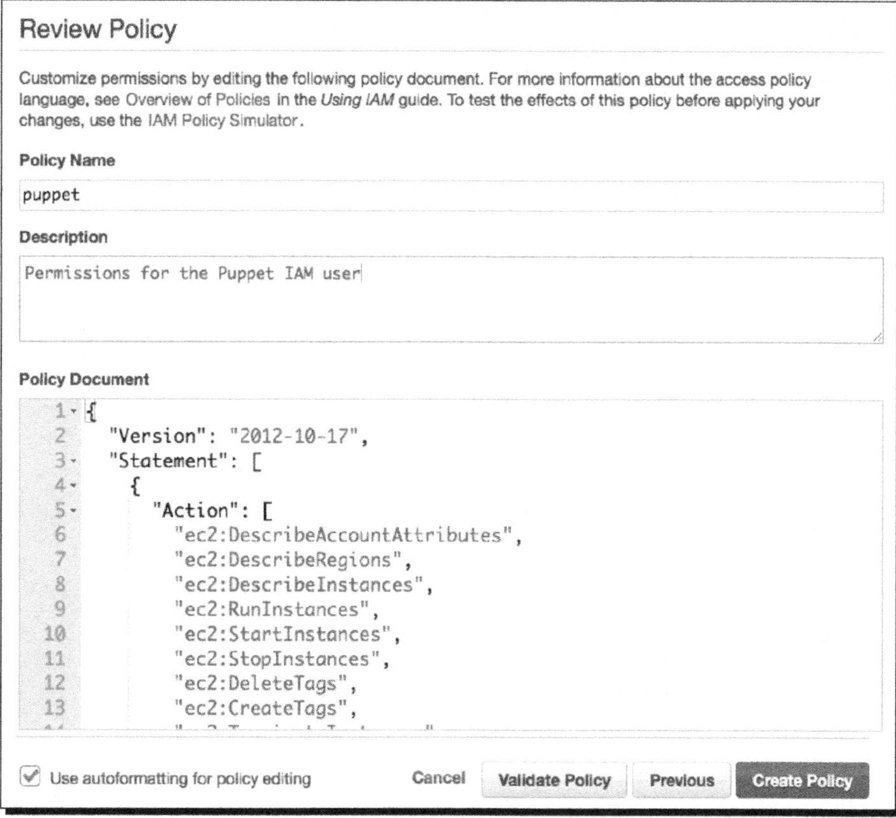

Creating an IAM user

To create the Puppet IAM user and associate it with the policy, follow these steps:

1. Sign in to the AWS console.
2. Select **Services** | **IAM** | **Users**.
3. Click **Add user**.
4. Enter the username you want to use for this account (for example, `puppet`).

5. In the **Access type** section, select **Programmatic access**.

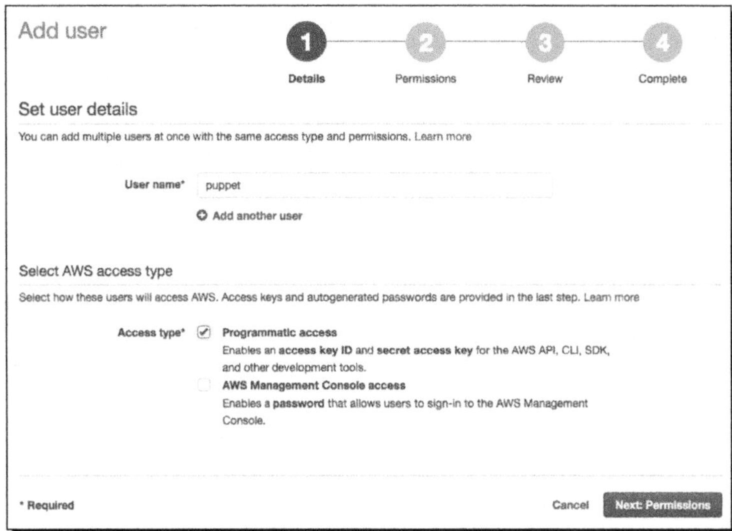

6. Click **Next: Permissions**.
7. Click **Attach existing policies directly**.
8. Type `puppet` in the **Policy Type** search box and press *Enter*.

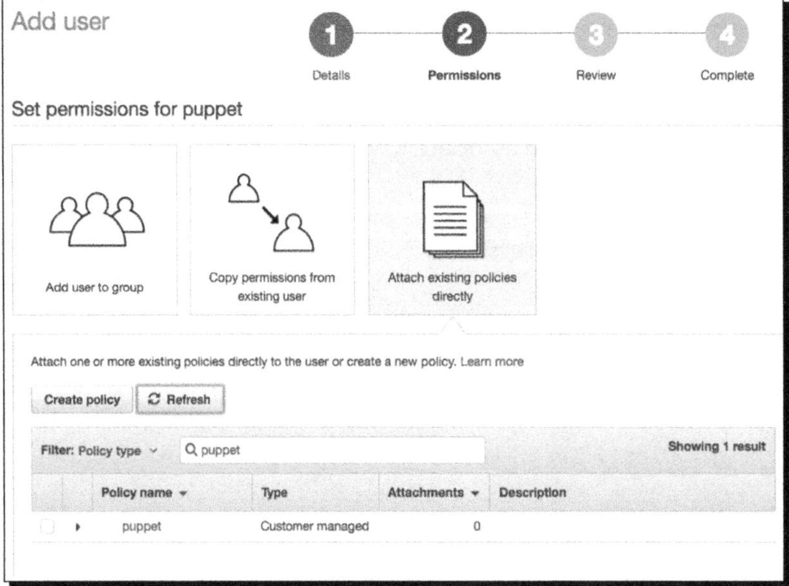

9. You should see the policy we created in the previous section, so check the box next to it and click **Next: Review**.
10. Check that the settings are correct and click **Create user**.

When you finish creating the IAM user and policy, you should see the **Success** screen, which lists your access credentials. Copy the access key ID and the secret access key (click **Show** to see the secret access key). You will need these credentials for the next steps (but keep them safe).

Storing your AWS credentials

Follow these steps to configure your VM for access to AWS with your newly-generated credentials:

1. On your Vagrant VM, run the following command to create the directory to hold your credentials file:

```
mkdir /home/ubuntu/.aws
```

2. Create a file named `/home/ubuntu/.aws/credentials` with the following contents (substitute your Access Key ID and Secret Access Key values from the AWS console screen):

```
[default]
aws_access_key_id = AKIAINSZUVFYMBFDJCEQ
aws_secret_access_key = pghia0r5/GjU7WEQj2Hr7Yr+MFkf+mqQdsBk0BQr
```

Creating the file manually is fine for this example, but for production use, you should manage the credentials file with Puppet using encrypted Hiera data, as shown in the *Managing secret data* section in *Chapter 6, Managing data with Hiera*.

Getting ready to use puppetlabs/aws

In the following sections, we'll see how to generate an SSH key pair to connect to your EC2 instances, and also install the `puppetlabs/aws` module with its dependencies.

Creating a key pair

You'll need an SSH key pair in order to connect to any EC2 instances you create. We will generate and download your key pair in this section.

1. In the AWS console, go to the **EC2** section and select **Key pairs** under **Network & Security** in the left pane.
2. Click the **Create Key Pair** button.

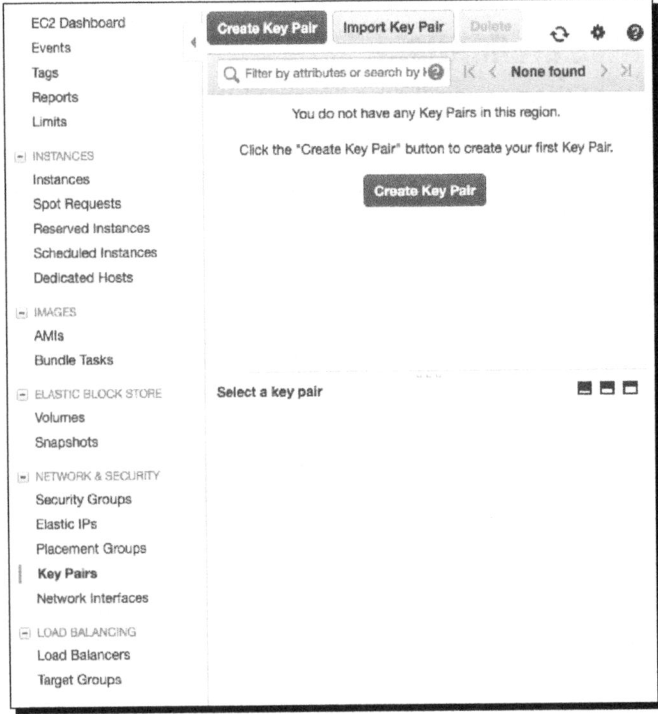

3. You will be prompted for the name of your key pair. Enter `pbg` for this example.
4. A file named `pbg.pem` will be automatically downloaded by your browser. Move this file to your `~/.ssh` directory on your own computer (or copy it to the `ubuntu` user's `~/.ssh` directory on the Vagrant VM, if you'd rather access your AWS instances from there).
5. Set the correct permissions on the key file with the following command:

```
chmod 600 ~/.ssh/pbg.pem
```

Installing the puppetlabs/aws module

Follow these steps to install the `puppetlabs/aws` module:

If you've already set up the `r10k` module management tool, as shown in *Chapter 7, Mastering modules*, the required module will already be installed. If not, run the following commands to install it:

```
cd /etc/puppetlabs/code/environments/pbg
sudo r10k puppetfile install
```

Installing the AWS SDK gem

The `puppetlabs/aws` module requires a couple of gems, which we can install easily using Puppet, with the following manifest (`aws_sdk.pp`):

```
ensure_packages([
  'aws-sdk-core',
  'retries'
],
  { provider => puppet_gem })
```

> Notice the `provider => puppet_gem` in that example? You might remember from *Chapter 4, Understanding Puppet resources*, that `puppet_gem` installs a Ruby gem in Puppet's context (as opposed to the system Ruby context, which is completely separate). Gems which are required by Puppet modules need to be installed in this way or Puppet won't be able to load them.

1. Apply the manifest with the following command:

   ```
   sudo puppet apply --environment pbg /examples/aws_sdk.pp
   ```

2. Create the `/home/ubuntu/.aws/config` file with the following contents:

   ```
   [default]
   region=us-east-1
   ```

Creating EC2 instances with Puppet

Although you can manage many different types of AWS resources with Puppet, the most important is the EC2 instance (the virtual server). In this section, we'll see how to create your first EC2 instance.

Choosing an Amazon Machine Image (AMI)

In order to run an EC2 instance, which is to say an AWS virtual machine, you need to choose which virtual machine to run out of the many thousands available. Each virtual machine snapshot is called an **Amazon Machine Image** (**AMI**) and has a unique ID. It's this ID that you will add to your Puppet manifest to tell it what kind of instance to start.

It doesn't matter much for the purposes of this example which AMI you choose, but we'll be using an official Ubuntu image. To find one, follow these steps:

1. Browse to the following URL:

   `https://cloud-images.ubuntu.com/locator/ec2/`

2. In the **Search** box, enter `us-east-1 xenial`
3. You should see a list of Ubuntu Xenial AMIs in the `us-east-1` region, of various instance types, looking something like the following screenshot:

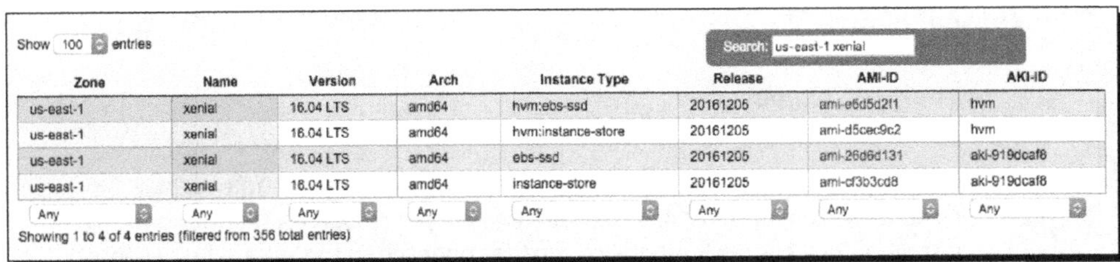

Show 100 entries
Search: us-east-1 xenial

Zone	Name	Version	Arch	Instance Type	Release	AMI-ID	AKI-ID
us-east-1	xenial	16.04 LTS	amd64	hvm:ebs-ssd	20161205	ami-e6d5d2f1	hvm
us-east-1	xenial	16.04 LTS	amd64	hvm:instance-store	20161205	ami-d5cec9c2	hvm
us-east-1	xenial	16.04 LTS	amd64	ebs-ssd	20161205	ami-26d6d131	aki-919dcaf8
us-east-1	xenial	16.04 LTS	amd64	instance-store	20161205	ami-cf3b3cd8	aki-919dcaf8
Any	Any	Any	Any	Any	Any	Any	Any

Showing 1 to 4 of 4 entries (filtered from 356 total entries)

4. Find an AMI in the list whose **Instance Type** is `ebs-ssd`. In the preceding screenshot, the third AMI in the list (`ami-26d6d131`) is suitable.

The hexadecimal code in the `AMI-ID` column, starting `ami-` is the AMI ID. Make a note of this for later. Click the link to see the AWS instance type selection page, and check that the AMI you've selected has a label saying **Free tier eligible**; these AMIs do not incur charges. If you start an instance of a non-free-tier AMI, you will be charged for it.

Creating the EC2 instance

Now we have chosen a suitable AMI, we're ready to create an EC2 instance with Puppet.

Before we can do that, however, we need to make a couple of changes to the AWS settings, so follow these steps:

1. In the AWS console, select **VPC** from the **Services** menu.
2. Select **Your VPCs** in the left pane.

3. There will be only one VPC listed. Click in the **Name** field and set its name to `default-vpc`
4. Select **Subnets** in the left pane.
5. There will be several subnets listed, one for each availability zone. Find the one associated with the `us-east-1a` availability zone.
6. Click in the subnet's **Name** field and set the name to `default-subnet`

> Why do we have to set names for the VPC and subnet before running the example? The `puppetlabs/aws` module refers to resources by their 'name', which is an arbitrary string, rather than their ID, which is a long hexadecimal code like the AMI ID. Although AWS creates a default VPC and subnet for you automatically, it doesn't assign them a name, which means we can't refer to them in Puppet code until we've set names for them. It doesn't matter what the names actually are so long as the name in your Puppet code is the same as the name assigned in the AWS control panel. We'll find out more about what VPCs and subnets do, and how to use them, later in the chapter.

7. Edit the file `/examples/aws_instance.pp`, and change the value of `$ami` in the first line to the AMI ID you picked earlier (in our example, `ami-26d6d131`):

   ```
   sudo vi /examples/aws_instance.pp
   $ami = 'ami-26d6d131'
   ```

8. Save the file, and run the following command:

   ```
   sudo puppet apply --environment pbg /examples/aws_instance.pp
   ```

9. You should see some output from Puppet like the following:

   ```
   Notice: /Stage[main]/Main/Ec2_securitygroup[pbg-sg]/ensure:
   created
   Notice: /Stage[main]/Main/Ec2_instance[pbg-demo]/ensure: changed
   absent to running
   ```

10. If you check the **EC2** section of the AWS console, you should see that your new instance's status is **Initializing**, and it will soon be ready to use.

Accessing your EC2 instance

Once the status of the newly-launched instance has changed from **Initializing** to **Running** (you may need to click the refresh button on the AWS console), you can connect to it using SSH and the key file you downloaded earlier.

1. In the AWS console, look for the **Public IP** address of the instance and copy it.
2. From your own machine (or from the Vagrant VM if you copied the `pbg.pem` file to it) run the following command (replace `YOUR_INSTANCE_IP` with the public IP of the instance):

```
ssh -i ~/.ssh/pbg.pem -l ubuntu YOUR_INSTANCE_IP
The authenticity of host 'YOUR_INSTANCE_IP (YOUR_INSTANCE_IP)'
can't be established.
ECDSA key fingerprint is SHA256:T/
pyWVJYWys2nyASJVHmDqOkQf8PbRGru3vwwKH71sk.
Are you sure you want to continue connecting (yes/no)? yes
Warning: Permanently added 'YOUR_INSTANCE_IP' (ECDSA) to the list
of known hosts.
Welcome to Ubuntu 16.04.3 LTS (GNU/Linux 4.4.0-1030-aws x86_64)
```

Now that you have SSH access to the instance, you can bootstrap it with Puppet in the same way as for physical nodes, or just install Puppet and Git manually and check out the manifest repo. (We'll develop a complete, automated bootstrap process in *Chapter 12, Putting it all together*.)

Congratulations! You've just created your first EC2 instance with Puppet. In the next section, we'll look at the code and examine the resources in detail.

VPCs, subnets, and security groups

Let's go through the example manifest and see how it works. But first, we need to know something about AWS resources.

An EC2 **instance** lives inside a **subnet**, which is a self-contained virtual network. All instances within the subnet can communicate with each other. Subnets are partitions of a **Virtual Private Cloud** (**VPC**), which is a private internal network specific to your AWS account.

An instance also has a **security group**, which is a set of firewall rules governing network access to the instance.

When you create an AWS account, you get a default VPC, divided into subnets for each AWS **availability zone** (**AZ**). We are using the default VPC and one of the default subnets for the example instance, but since we also need a security group, we create that first in Puppet code.

The ec2_securitygroup resource

The first part of the example manifest creates the required `ec2_securitygroup` resource (`aws_instance.pp`):

```
ec2_securitygroup { 'pbg-sg':
  ensure      =>  present,
  description => 'PBG security group',
  region      => $region,
  vpc         => 'default-vpc',
  ingress     => [
    {
      description => 'SSH access from world',
      protocol    => 'tcp',
      port        => 22,
      cidr        => '0.0.0.0/0',
    },
    {
      description => 'Ping access from world',
      protocol    => 'icmp',
      cidr        => '0.0.0.0/0',
    },
  ],
}
```

First of all, an `ec2_securitygroup` has a title (`pbg-sg`) which we will use to refer to it from other resources (such as the `ec2_instance` resource). It also has a `description`, which is just to remind us what it's for.

It is part of a `region` and a `vpc`, and has an array of `ingress` rules. These are your firewall rules. Each firewall port or protocol you want to allow needs a separate ingress rule.

Each ingress rule is a hash like the following:

```
{
  description => 'SSH access from world',
  protocol    => 'tcp',
  port        => 22,
  cidr        => '0.0.0.0/0',
}
```

The `protocol` specifies the type of traffic (`tcp`, `udp`, and so on).

The `port` is the port number to open (`22` is the SSH port, which we'll need in order to log in to the instance).

Finally, the `cidr` key specifies the range of network addresses to allow access to. (`0.0.0.0/0` means 'all addresses'.)

The ec2_instance resource

The `ec2_instance` resource, as you'd expect, manages an individual EC2 instance. Here's the relevant section of the example manifest (`aws_instance.pp`):

```
ec2_instance { 'pbg-demo':
  ensure                      => present,
  region                      => $region,
  subnet                      => 'default-subnet',
  security_groups             => 'pbg-sg',
  image_id                    => $ami,
  instance_type               => 't1.micro',
  associate_public_ip_address => true,
  key_name                    => 'pbg',
}
```

First, `ensure => present` tells AWS that the instance should be running. (You can also use `running` as a synonym for `present`.) Setting `ensure => absent` will terminate and delete the instance (and any ephemeral storage attached to it).

EC2 instances can also be in a third state, `stopped`. Stopped instances preserve their storage and can be restarted. Because AWS bills by the instance-hour, you don't pay for instances that are stopped, so it's a good idea to stop any instances that don't need to be running right now.

The instance is part of a `region` and a `subnet`, and has one or more `security_groups`.

The `image_id` attribute tells AWS which AMI ID to use for the instance.

The `instance_type` attribute selects from AWS's large range of types, which more or less correspond to the computing power of the instance (different types vary in memory size and the number of virtual CPUs, and a few other factors).

As we're inside a private network, instances will not be reachable from the Internet unless we assign them a public IP address. Setting `associate_public_ip_address` to `true` enables this feature. (You should set this to `false` unless the instance actually needs to expose a port to the Internet.)

Finally, the instance has a `key_name` attribute which tells AWS which SSH key we are going to use to access it. In this case, we're using the key we created earlier in the chapter, named `pbg`.

Before going on to the next example, terminate your instance to avoid using up your free hours. You can do this by selecting the instance in the AWS control panel and clicking **Actions | Instance State | Terminate**, or reapplying your Puppet manifest with the instance's `ensure` attribute set to `absent`.

Managing custom VPCs and subnets

In the previous example, we used the pre-existing default VPC and subnet to create our instance. That's fine for demonstration purposes, but in production you'll want to use a dedicated VPC for your Puppet-managed resources, to keep it separate from any other resources in your AWS account, and from other Puppet-managed VPCs. You could, for example, have a staging VPC and a production VPC.

By default, a new VPC has no access to the Internet; we'll also need an **Internet gateway** (which routes Internet traffic to and from the VPC) and a **route table** (which tells a given subnet to send non-local traffic to the gateway). The `puppetlabs/aws` module provides Puppet resources to create and manage each of these entities.

Creating an instance in a custom VPC

In this section, we'll use a more sophisticated example manifest to create a new VPC and subnet, with an associated Internet gateway and route table, then add a security group and EC2 instance.

Follow these steps to apply the manifest:

1. Edit the file `/examples/aws_vpc.pp` and change the value of `$ami` in the first line to the AMI ID you picked earlier (in our example, `ami-26d6d131`):

   ```
   sudo vi /examples/aws_vpc.pp
   $ami = 'ami-26d6d131'
   ```

2. Save the file and run the following command:

   ```
   sudo puppet apply --environment pbg /examples/aws_vpc.pp
   ```

3. You should see some output from Puppet like the following:

   ```
   Notice: /Stage[main]/Main/Ec2_vpc[pbg-vpc]/ensure: created
   Notice: /Stage[main]/Main/Ec2_vpc_internet_gateway[pbg-igw]/
   ensure: created
   Notice: /Stage[main]/Main/Ec2_vpc_routetable[pbg-rt]/ensure:
   created
   Notice: /Stage[main]/Main/Ec2_vpc_subnet[pbg-vpc-subnet]/ensure:
   created
   ```

```
Notice: /Stage[main]/Main/Ec2_securitygroup[pbg-vpc-sg]/ensure:
created
Notice: /Stage[main]/Main/Ec2_instance[pbg-vpc-demo]/ensure:
changed absent to running
```

4. If you check the **EC2** section of the AWS console, you should see that your new instance status is **Initializing**, and it will soon be ready to use.

The ec2_vpc resource

Let's look at the example manifest in detail. Here's the `ec2_vpc` resource (`aws_vpc.pp`):

```
ec2_vpc { 'pbg-vpc':
  ensure     => present,
  region     => $region,
  cidr_block => '10.99.0.0/16',
}
```

The VPC requires a `region` attribute and `cidr_block`, which is the range of network addresses that the VPC will use. (Actually, this isn't required, as AWS will allocate you one at random if you don't specify it. We specify one here just for the demonstration.)

It doesn't matter what your network range actually is, as it's entirely internal. However, it's good practice to use one of the address ranges officially assigned to private networks, such as `10.x.y.z`. To make it less likely that your range will conflict with any other assigned in your organization, pick a random number for `x` (we've used `99` in the example).

The ec2_vpc_internet_gateway resource

We saw earlier that a VPC, by default, is not connected to the Internet. There are various ways to get Internet traffic into the VPC, including VPNs and Amazon **Elastic Load Balancers** (**ELB**), but for this example, we'll use an `ec2_vpc_internet_gateway` resource, which looks like the following:

```
ec2_vpc_internet_gateway { 'pbg-igw':
  ensure => present,
  region => $region,
  vpc    => 'pbg-vpc',
}
```

The gateway has a title (`pbg-igw`), and it is associated with a particular `region` and `vpc`.

The ec2_vpc_routetable resource

Having provisioned an ec2_vpc_internet_gateway, we now need to set up a route table to determine which traffic to send to it. Here is the ec2_vpc_routetable resource from the example:

```
ec2_vpc_routetable { 'pbg-rt':
  ensure => present,
  region => $region,
  vpc    => 'pbg-vpc',
  routes => [
    {
      destination_cidr_block => '10.99.0.0/16',
      gateway                => 'local'
    },
    {
      destination_cidr_block => '0.0.0.0/0',
      gateway                => 'pbg-igw'
    },
  ],
}
```

As usual, a route table has a title, region, and vpc. It also has an array of one or more routes.

A **route** is like a road sign for network packets. It says, "if you're heading for this destination, take this junction." Each route in the array is a hash containing a destination_cidr_block and gateway key.

The first route in our example is for local traffic (destined for the 10.99.0.0/16 network, which is the network we assigned to our VPC):

```
{
  destination_cidr_block => '10.99.0.0/16',
  gateway                => 'local'
}
```

This tells traffic for the 10.99.0.0/16 network that it is local; that is, there's no need to use a gateway, because it's already on the desired network.

The second route is for all other traffic:

```
{
  destination_cidr_block => '0.0.0.0/0',
  gateway                => 'pbg-igw'
}
```

The network address `0.0.0.0/0` matches all possible network addresses (traffic for `10.99.0.0/16` will already have been filtered out by the previous route, so we are left with all other traffic, which must be for the Internet). The designated gateway is `pbg-igw`, which is the `ec2_vpc_internet_gateway` we created earlier.

So this route table equates to the following instructions for routing traffic:

- Traffic for `10.99.0.0/16`, stay on this network
- All other traffic, please proceed to the `pbg-igw` gateway

These routes will suffice for a single VPC; if you have a more complicated network setup in AWS, you will need a more complicated route table, but the principles will be the same.

The ec2_vpc_subnet resource

A subnet, as we've seen, is a subdivision of the VPC network, which enables you to logically partition your VPC for different groups of resources. For example, you might have one subnet which is accessible from the Internet for public-facing nodes, and another for internal resources such as database or log servers.

In the example we just have one subnet:

```
ec2_vpc_subnet { 'pbg-vpc-subnet':
  ensure            => present,
  vpc               => 'pbg-vpc',
  region            => $region,
  cidr_block        => '10.99.0.0/24',
  availability_zone => "${region}a",
  route_table       => 'pbg-rt',
}
```

It has a title, `vpc`, and `region`. Because it is a subdivision of the VPC network, it also needs a `cidr_block` specifying exactly which part of the network address space it occupies. This must be a subdivision of the network address you assigned to the containing VPC, as indeed it is in this example.

A subnet exists within an AWS availability zone (equivalent to a data center). These are named after their region; for example, the `us-east-1` region has availability zones `us-east-1a`, `us-east-1b`, and so on. This allows you to provision redundant resources in different availability zones, so that if one should fail, the other can take over. For this example, however, we're using just one availability zone, `us-east-1a`, which we pass to the `availability_zone` attribute.

By default, resources in a subnet can only communicate within the subnet. To allow traffic in and out of the subnet, we need to associate it with `route_table`. By using the `pbg-rt` route table we created earlier, we can send Internet traffic via the `pbg-igw` gateway.

And that's it. The `ec2_securitygroup` and `ec2_instance` resources are more or less the same as in our earlier example, except for using the new subnet.

Other AWS resource types

Puppet is not limited to managing EC2 instances; the `puppetlabs/aws` module also supports ELB load balancers, Cloudwatch alarms, auto scaling groups, Elastic IPs, DHCP, VPNs, IAM users and policies, RDS databases, S3 storage buckets, SQS queues, Route 53 DNS management, and the **EC2 Container Service** (**ECS**). Due to constraints of space, time, and energy, I have not provided examples for all of these, but you can consult the module's admirably comprehensive documentation at this URL:

`https://forge.puppet.com/puppetlabs/aws`

Provisioning AWS resources from Hiera data

There's nothing wrong with managing AWS resources directly in the code, as we've done in the previous examples, but we can do just a little bit better.

In *Chapter 6, Managing data with Hiera*, we saw how to create Puppet resources directly from Hiera data. In that example (*Building resources from Hiera hashes*), we stored all the users for our infrastructure in a Hiera hash called `users`, and then used the `each` keyword to iterate over that hash, creating a user resource for each user. Here's the example code again (`hiera_users2.pp`):

```
lookup('users2', Hash, 'hash').each | String $username, Hash $attrs |
{
  user { $username:
    * => $attrs,
  }
}
```

The magic `*` character (the **attribute splat operator**) tells Puppet to use the contents of the `$attrs` hash as the attributes of the resource.

The advantage of describing resources as Hiera data is that when we come to add a new user, or change the details for an existing user, we don't need to touch Puppet code at all. Everything is defined in Hiera.

Iterating over Hiera data to create resources

Alert readers may be wondering, "Couldn't we do the same thing with all these AWS resources? Can we just define everything in a Hiera hash and have Puppet iterate over it to create the resources?"

Indeed we can. The manifest to create all these resources is surprisingly concise (`aws_hiera.pp`):

```
$aws_resources = lookup('aws_resources', Hash, 'hash')
$aws_resources.each | String $r_type, Hash $resources | {
  $resources.each | String $r_title, Hash $attrs | {
    Resource[$r_type] { $r_title:
      * => $attrs,
    }
  }
}
```

To apply the manifest, follow these steps:

1. Edit the Hiera data file `aws.yaml` and change the value of the `ami:` setting in the first line to the AMI ID you picked earlier (in our example, `ami-26d6d131`):

   ```
   sudo vi /etc/puppetlabs/code/environments/pbg/data/aws.yaml
   ami: 'ami-26d6d131'
   ```

2. Save the file and run the following command:

   ```
   sudo puppet apply --environment pbg /examples/aws_hiera.pp
   ```

If you've already run the previous example and the AWS resources are still present, you'll see no output from Puppet, because the resources are exactly the same.

Remember, if the state of the system is already the same as the desired state expressed in the manifest, Puppet will do nothing.

If you want to prove to yourself that the example manifest really works, delete the resources using the AWS control panel (or use Puppet to delete them by changing `present` to `absent` in the Hiera data) and reapply the manifest.

If you compare the manifest to that from the Hiera users example, you can see that instead of a single loop, it consists of two nested loops. The outer loop iterates over the contents of the `$aws_resources` hash:

```
$aws_resources = lookup('aws_resources', Hash, 'hash')
$aws_resources.each | String $r_type, Hash $resources | {
  ...
  }
}
```

Each key of the `$aws_resources` hash is the name of a Puppet resource type. Here's the first one (from `hiera_aws.yaml`):

```
'ec2_vpc':
    ...
```

So the first time round this loop, the value of `$r_type` will be `ec2_vpc`, and the value of `$resources` will be this hash:

```
'pbg-vpc':
  ensure: present
  region: "%{lookup('region')}"
  cidr_block: '10.99.0.0/16'
```

Now we enter the inner loop, which creates all the resources of type `$r_type`:

```
$resources.each | String $r_title, Hash $attrs | {
  Resource[$r_type] { $r_title:
    * => $attrs,
  }

}
```

As it happens, there is only one `ec2_vpc` resource, so the first time round the inner loop, the value of `$r_title` will be `pbg-vpc`, and the value of `$attrs` will be this hash:

```
ensure: present
region: "%{lookup('region')}"
cidr_block: '10.99.0.0/16'
```

So Puppet will create this resource:

```
ec2_vpc { 'pbg-vpc':
  ensure     => present,
  region     => 'us-east-1',
  cidr_block => '10.99.0.0/16',
}
```

This is identical to the `ec2_vpc` resource in the previous example, and as we go round the outer loop we will create the other resources in the same way.

What's `Resource[$r_type]`? This is a bit of Puppet wizardry. The problem is that we need to declare a Puppet resource whose type we don't know yet; it will be supplied by the `$r_type` variable. You might at first try using a syntax like the following:

```
$r_type = 'ec2_vpc'
$r_type { 'pbg-vpc':
  ...
}
```

Unfortunately, Puppet doesn't allow this syntax, but there is a way to get round the problem. The abstract data type `Resource` matches any resource type (you can read more about Puppet data types in *Chapter 8, Classes, roles, and profiles*).

We can make `Resource` more specific by including the actual resource type in square brackets: `Resource['ec2_vpc']`. This is valid syntax for declaring a resource.

So this is how we declare a resource whose type comes from a variable:

```
$r_type = 'ec2_vpc'
Resource[$r_type] { 'pbg-vpc':
  ...
}
```

Now that your AWS resources are described by Hiera data, it should be much easier to maintain and extend them as you use Puppet in production.

Cleaning up unused resources

To close down your EC2 instance, and thus avoid using up your free hours or being billed for the instance, edit your Hiera data to set `ensure: absent` on the `ec2_instance` resource:

```
'ec2_instance':
  'pbg-vpc-demo':
    ensure: absent
    region: "%{lookup('region')}"
    subnet: 'pbg-vpc-subnet'
    security_groups: 'pbg-vpc-sg'
    image_id: "%{lookup('ami')}"
    instance_type: 't1.micro'
    associate_public_ip_address: true
    key_name: 'pbg'
```

When you reapply the manifest, Puppet will stop the instance. You can leave other resources in place, as they don't incur charges.

Summary

In this chapter, we've introduced the basic idea of cloud computing, and looked at some options for managing cloud resources, including CloudFormation and Terraform, before meeting the `puppetlabs/aws` module.

We've worked through the process of creating an AWS account, setting up an IAM user and policy, generating credentials and SSH keys, installing the AWS SDK gem, and choosing a suitable AMI (Amazon Machine Image).

Using Puppet, we've created an EC2 instance and security group, and seen how to connect to the running instance with SSH. Going further, we've created a whole VPC from scratch, complete with subnets, Internet gateway, route table, security group, and EC2 instance.

Lastly, we've seen how to build all these cloud resources directly from Hiera data, which is the most flexible and powerful way to describe Puppet resources.

In the next and final chapter, we'll draw together ideas and techniques from all the previous chapters in this book to create a complete, working example Puppet infrastructure which you can use as a basis for your own.

12

Putting it all together

> *Manhood is patience. Mastery is nine times patience.*
>
> *—Ursula K. Le Guin, 'A Wizard of Earthsea'*

In this chapter, we will apply ideas from all the previous chapters to see what a complete, working Puppet infrastructure looks like, using a demonstration repo which illustrates all the principles explained in this book. You can use it as the basis of your own Puppet codebase, adapting and expanding it as needed.

Getting the demo repo

The demo repo is available on GitHub, and you can clone it in the same way as for the example repo for this book by running this command:

```
git clone -b production https://github.com/bitfield/control-repo-3
```

It contains everything you'll need to manage nodes with Puppet:

- User accounts and SSH keys
- SSH and `sudoers` config
- Time zone and NTP settings
- Hiera data
- Automatic Puppet update and apply scripts
- Bootstrap script for new nodes

It also includes a Vagrantfile so you can try out the repo on a Vagrant virtual machine.

Copying the repo

If you are going to use the demo repo as the basis for your own Puppet repo, you need to make a copy of it so that you can edit and maintain it yourself.

You can do this in two ways. One is to *fork* the repo to your own GitHub account. To do this, log in to GitHub and browse to the demo repo URL:

`https://github.com/bitfield/control-repo-3.git`

Look for the **Fork** button at the top right of the page and click it. This will create a new repo under your account that will contain all the code and history from the demo repo.

Alternatively, you can follow these steps:

1. Create a new repo in your GitHub account (name it `puppet`, `control-repo`, or whatever you prefer).
2. Make a note of the repo URL.
3. Clone the demo repo to your personal machine:
   ```
   git clone -b production https://github.com/bitfield/control-repo-3
   cd control-repo-3
   ```
4. Rename the original repository remote (so you can get updates in future):
   ```
   git remote rename origin upstream
   ```

5. Add your new repo as the `origin` remote (using the URL for your repo you noted earlier):

   ```
   git remote add origin YOUR_GIT_URL
   ```

6. Push to the new remote:

   ```
   git push origin production
   ```

Your repo now contains a complete copy of the demo repo, which you can edit and customize just as you like.

As the original repo is updated in the future, you will be able to pull these changes into your own version. To get changes from upstream, run the following commands:

```
git fetch upstream
git rebase upstream/production
```

Understanding the demo repo

It's now time to see how all the ideas from the previous chapters fit together. It should be helpful for you to see how a complete Puppet infrastructure works, and you can also use this repo as a basis for your own projects. We'll see how you can do that later in the chapter, but first, a word or two about the overall structure of the repo.

The control repo

A **control repo** is a Puppet codebase which contains no modules, or only site-specific modules, and it's a good way to organize your Puppet code.

In *Chapter 7, Mastering modules* we learned about using the `r10k` tool to manage modules with a Puppetfile. The Puppetfile specifies which modules we use, with their exact versions, and their sources (usually Puppet Forge, but they can also come from remote Git repos).

Therefore, our Puppet repo needs to contain only a Puppetfile, along with our Hiera data, and the `role` and `profile` modules.

Module management

Because `r10k` expects to manage everything in the `modules/` directory using the Puppetfile, our **site-specific modules** are kept in a separate directory in the control repo named `site-modules/`.

To enable this, we need to add the following setting to the `environment.conf` file:

```
modulepath = "modules:site-modules:$basemodulepath"
```

This adds `site-modules/` to the list of places Puppet will look for modules.

As detailed in *Chapter 7, Mastering modules*, we will be using `r10k` and a Puppetfile to manage all third-party modules. Accordingly, there is no `modules/` directory in the demo repo: `r10k` will create this when it installs the required modules.

Here's the Puppetfile with the list of modules we need for the initial repo. Of course, as you adapt the repo to your own needs, you'll be adding more modules to this list (`Puppetfile`):

```
forge "http://forge.puppetlabs.com"

# Modules from the Puppet Forge
mod 'puppetlabs/accounts', '1.1.0'
mod 'puppetlabs/ntp', '6.2.0'
mod 'puppetlabs/stdlib', '4.19.0'
mod 'saz/sudo', '4.2.0'
mod 'saz/timezone', '3.5.0'
mod 'stm/debconf', '2.0.0'
```

We'll see how these modules are used in the following sections.

Every so often, use the `generate-puppetfile` tool to automatically update your module versions and dependencies (see *Chapter 7, Mastering modules* for more about this). Run the following command in the repo directory:

```
generate-puppetfile -p Puppetfile
```

Copy and paste the output back into your Puppetfile, replacing the existing `mod` statements.

Classes

As you may recall from *Chapter 8, Classes, roles, and profiles*, we use Hiera data to determine which classes and resources should be applied to the node. The common classes are listed in `common.yaml`, and there is a per-node data file for the `demo` node which includes the `role::demo` class. These classes are included by the following line in `manifests/site.pp`:

```
include(lookup('classes', Array[String], 'unique'))
```

Roles

Role classes identify by name what the function of the node is, and define what profile classes should be included (see *Chapter 8, Classes, roles, and profiles* for more about this).

It's common practice to keep your role classes in a `role` module, and as this is a site-specific module, it's filed under `site-modules/`.

Here's the `role::demo` role manifest (`site-modules/role/manifests/demo.pp`):

```
# Be the demo node
class role::demo {
  include profile::common
}
```

Profiles

A **profile class** identifies by name some specific piece of software or functionality required for a role, and declares the necessary resources to manage it (refer to *Chapter 8, Classes, roles, and profiles* for a more detailed explanation of profiles).

Often, there are profiles which are common to all nodes: our user accounts, for example, and a few others. It's logical to keep these in the `common.yaml` Hiera data file, so that these profiles will be included by all nodes.

Here are the classes included in `common.yaml`:

```
classes:
- profile::ntp
- profile::puppet
- profile::ssh
- profile::sudoers
- profile::timezone
- profile::users
```

We'll see what each of these profiles do in the following sections.

In the Hiera data, classes are listed in alphabetical order: this can be helpful when you have many classes included, and can make it easier to see whether or not a given class is already in the list. When you add new classes, make sure you keep the list in alphabetical order.

Users and access control

The `puppetlabs/accounts` module provides a standard way to handle user accounts with the `accounts::user` class. Accordingly, we will use this to manage our users in the `profile::users` class.

If you prefer to manage user accounts directly in Puppet using the `user` and `ssh_authorized_key` resources, see *Chapter 4, Understanding Puppet resources* for more information.

You could just list the required users as literal resources in your Puppet manifest, of course. But instead let's take the data-driven approach described in *Chapter 6, Managing data with Hiera*, and define our users with Hiera data.

This is what the data structure looks like (`data/common.yaml`):

```
users:
  'john':
    comment: 'John Arundel'
    uid: '1010'
    sshkeys:
      - 'ssh-rsa AAAA ...'
  'bridget':
    comment: 'Bridget X. Zample'
    uid: '1011'
    sshkeys:
      - 'ssh-rsa AAAA ...'
```

Here's the code in the `users` profile to read the data and create the corresponding `accounts::user` resources (`site-modules/profile/manifests/users.pp`):

```
# Set up users
class profile::users {
  lookup('users', Hash, 'hash').each | String $username, Hash $attrs |
{
    accounts::user { $username:
      * => $attrs,
    }
  }
}
```

As you can see, we fetch all the user data into a single `$users` hash with a call to `lookup()`. We iterate over the hash, declaring an `accounts::user` resource for each user, whose attributes are loaded from the hash data.

Note that when using the `accounts::user` resource, the `sshkeys` attribute must contain an array of authorized SSH public keys for the user.

SSH configuration

It's good security practice to restrict SSH logins to a set of named users, using the `AllowUsers` directive in `/etc/ssh/sshd_config`. We used a Puppet template to build this config file in *Chapter 9, Managing files with templates*. In that example, we got the list of allowed users from Hiera, and we will do the same here.

Here's the template for the `sshd_config` file (`site-modules/profile/templates/ssh/sshd_config.epp`):

```
<%- | Array[String] $allow_users | -%>
# File is managed by Puppet

AcceptEnv LANG LC_*
ChallengeResponseAuthentication no
GSSAPIAuthentication no
PermitRootLogin no
PrintMotd no
Subsystem sftp internal-sftp
AllowUsers <%= join($allow_users, ' ') %>
UseDNS no
UsePAM yes
X11Forwarding yes
```

We declare that the template takes an `$allow_users` parameter which is an Array of String values. Because the `AllowUsers` parameter in `sshd_config` expects a space-separated list of users, we call the `join()` function from the standard library to create this list from the Puppet array (see *Chapter 7, Mastering modules*, for more about this and other standard library functions).

Here's the relevant Hiera data (`data/common.yaml`):

```
allow_users:
  - 'john'
  - 'bridget'
  - 'ubuntu'
```

We could have just constructed the list from the `$users` hash, which contains all known users, but we don't necessarily want everyone on that list to be able to log in to every node. Conversely, we may need to allow logins for some accounts which are not managed by Puppet. An example is the `ubuntu` account, which is required by Vagrant in order to manage the VM properly. If you're not using Vagrant boxes, you can remove the `ubuntu` user from this list.

The code to read this Hiera data and populate the template is as follows (`site-modules/profile/manifests/ssh.pp`):

```
# Manage sshd config
class profile::ssh {
  ensure_packages(['openssh-server'])

  file { '/etc/ssh/sshd_config':
    content => epp('profile/ssh/sshd_config.epp', {
      'allow_users' => lookup('allow_users', Array[String],
        'unique'),
    }),
    notify  => Service['ssh'],
  }

  service { 'ssh':
    ensure => running,
    enable => true,
  }
}
```

This is a package-file-service pattern, which you may remember from *Chapter 2, Creating your first manifests*.

First, we install the `openssh-server` package (this is usually already installed, but it's good style to declare the package anyway, since we rely on it for what follows).

Next, we manage the `/etc/ssh/sshd_config` file with a template, which we populate using Hiera data from a call to `lookup('allow_users', Array[String], 'unique')`. This file notifies the `ssh` service whenever it changes.

Finally, we declare the `ssh` service and specify that it should be running and enabled at boot time.

Sudoers configuration

The `sudo` command is the standard Unix mechanism for controlling **user privileges**. It's usually used to allow normal users to run commands with the privileges of the `root` user.

Using `sudo` is preferable to allowing people to log in and run a shell as `root`, and `sudo` also audits and records which user ran which commands. You can also specify very fine-grained permissions, such as allowing a user to run only a certain command as `root`, but no others.

The most popular Forge module for managing `sudo` permissions is `saz/sudo`, and that's what we'll use here. Here's the Hiera data listing the users with `sudo` access (`data/common.yaml`):

```
sudoers:
  - 'john'
  - 'bridget'
  - 'ubuntu'
```

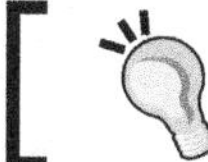

If you're not using Vagrant, you can remove the `ubuntu` user from this list.

Here's the `profile` class which reads the data (`site-modules/profile/manifests/sudoers.pp`):

```
# Manage user privileges
class profile::sudoers {
  sudo::conf { 'secure_path':
    content  => 'Defaults      secure_path="/usr/local/sbin:/usr/
local/bin:/usr/sbin:/usr/bin:/sbin:/bin:/opt/puppetlabs/puppet/bin:/
opt/puppetlabs/bin"',
    priority => 0,
  }
  $sudoers = lookup('sudoers', Array[String], 'unique', [])
  $sudoers.each | String $user | {
    sudo::conf { $user:
      content  => "${user} ALL=(ALL) NOPASSWD: ALL",
      priority => 10,
    }
  }
}
```

This allows us to run commands like `sudo` puppet, as a normal user. That's what this part of the manifest does:

```
  sudo::conf { 'secure_path':
    content  => 'Defaults      secure_path="/usr/local/sbin:/usr/
local/bin:/usr/sbin:/usr/bin:/sbin:/bin:/opt/puppetlabs/puppet/bin:/
opt/puppetlabs/bin"',
    priority => 0,
  }
```

The `sudo::conf` resource, provided by the `saz/sudo` module, allows us to write arbitrary `sudoers` config as a string: in this case, setting the `secure_path` variable.

The remainder of the profile is concerned with configuring passwordless `sudo` privileges for each user named in the Hiera array `sudoers`. As usual, we get the array from Hiera and proceed to iterate over it with `each`, creating a `sudo::conf` resource for each named user.

Time zone and clock synchronization

There is a handy Forge module for managing server time zones: `saz/timezone`. Here's our `timezone` profile which uses that module to set all nodes to UTC (`site-modules/profile/manifests/timezone.pp`):

```
# Set the time zone for all nodes
class profile::timezone {
  class { 'timezone':
    timezone => 'Etc/UTC',
  }
}
```

It may seem tempting to set the node's time zone to your own local time zone, instead of UTC. However, this idea doesn't scale. When you have nodes in multiple time zones, or all over the world, they will all be in different time zones, this will lead to very confusing results when you try to compare timestamps from different log files. Always set the node's time zone to UTC, and then you'll never be confused (at least, not about that).

Similarly, we want to make sure that the clocks on all our nodes are synchronized, not only with each other, but with the global time standard as a whole. We will be using the `puppetlabs/ntp` module for this, and here is the relevant profile (`site-modules/profile/manifests/ntp.pp`):

```
# Synchronize with NTP
class profile::ntp {
  include ::ntp
}
```

As it happens, there's no special configuration to do for NTP (though you could, if you wanted, specify a list of time servers to contact, for example).

Puppet configuration

We need to configure a regular cron job which pulls any updates from the Git repo and runs Puppet to apply the updated manifest.

The `profile::puppet` class sets this up (`site-modules/profile/manifests/puppet.pp`):

```
# Set up Puppet config and cron run
class profile::puppet {
  service { ['puppet', 'mcollective', 'pxp-agent']:
    ensure => stopped, # Puppet runs from cron
    enable => false,
  }

  cron { 'run-puppet':
    ensure  => present,
    command => '/usr/local/bin/run-puppet',
    minute  => '*/10',
    hour    => '*',
  }

  file { '/usr/local/bin/run-puppet':
    source => 'puppet:///modules/profile/puppet/run-puppet.sh',
    mode   => '0755',
  }

  file { '/usr/local/bin/papply':
    source => 'puppet:///modules/profile/puppet/papply.sh',
    mode   => '0755',
  }
}
```

There are a fair number of resources in this profile, so let's look at each of them in turn.

First, we stop and disable some of the services started by the Puppet package, which we won't need:

```
service { ['puppet', 'mcollective', 'pxp-agent']:
  ensure => stopped, # Puppet runs from cron
  enable => false,

}
```

Next follows the cron job which carries out the regular Git updates and Puppet runs. The `run-puppet` script looks like this (`site-modules/profile/files/run-puppet.sh`):

```
#!/bin/bash
cd /etc/puppetlabs/code/environments/production && git pull
/opt/puppetlabs/puppet/bin/r10k puppetfile install
/opt/puppetlabs/bin/puppet apply --environment production manifests/
```

Here's the `cron` resource which runs the script:

```
cron { 'run-puppet':
  ensure  => present,
  command => '/usr/local/bin/run-puppet',
  minute  => '*/10',
  hour    => '*',
}
```

The job is set to run every 10 minutes, but you can adjust this if you need to.

This looks very much like the `run-puppet` script you may recall from *Chapter 3, Managing your Puppet code with Git*. The only difference is the extra step to run `r10k puppetfile install` (in case you added any new external modules in to the Puppetfile) and the addition of the `--environment` switch to `puppet apply`.

The next resource in `profile::puppet` deploys a convenience script named `papply`, which saves you from having to type the whole `puppet apply` command manually (`site-modules/profile/files/papply.sh`):

```
#!/bin/bash
environment=${PUPPET_ENV:-production}
/opt/puppetlabs/puppet/bin/r10k puppetfile install
/opt/puppetlabs/bin/puppet apply --environment ${environment}
--strict=warning /etc/puppetlabs/code/environments/${environment}/
manifests/ $*
```

Just running `papply` from the command line will apply Puppet immediately, without pulling any Git changes.

If you want to test Puppet changes from a different environment (for example, if you have a staging branch checked out at `/etc/puppetlabs/code/environments/staging`), you can control this with the `PUPPET_ENV` variable, as follows:

```
PUPPET_ENV=staging papply
```

Note that `papply` passes its command-line arguments on to Puppet (with `$*`), so you can add any arguments supported by the `puppet apply` command:

```
papply --noop --show_diff
```

We also supply the flag `--strict=warning` to the `puppet apply` command, which will cause Puppet to alert you if any potentially problematic code is encountered (such as referencing a variable which has not yet been defined). If you want Puppet to be really strict, set `--strict=error` instead, which will prevent the manifest being applied until all such problems are fixed.

The bootstrap process

In order to prepare a new node for Puppet management using the demo repo, we need to do a number of things:

- Install Puppet
- Clone the Git repo
- Run Puppet for the first time

In *Chapter 3, Managing your Puppet code with Git*, we performed these steps manually, but the demo repo automates this process (usually known as **bootstrap**). Here is the bootstrap script (`scripts/bootstrap.sh`):

```
#!/bin/bash
PUPPET_REPO=$1
HOSTNAME=$2
BRANCH=$3
if [ "$#" -ne 3 ]; then
  echo "Usage: $0 PUPPET_REPO HOSTNAME BRANCH"
  exit 1
fi
hostname ${HOSTNAME}
echo ${HOSTNAME} >/etc/hostname
source /etc/lsb-release
```

```
apt-key adv --fetch-keys http://apt.puppetlabs.com/DEB-GPG-KEY-puppet
wget http://apt.puppetlabs.com/puppetlabs-release-${DISTRIB_CODENAME}.
deb
dpkg -i puppetlabs-release-${DISTRIB_CODENAME}.deb
apt-get update
apt-get -y install git puppet-agent
cd /etc/puppetlabs/code/environments
mv production production.orig
git clone ${PUPPET_REPO} production
cd production
git checkout ${BRANCH}
/opt/puppetlabs/puppet/bin/gem install r10k --no-rdoc --no-ri
/opt/puppetlabs/puppet/bin/r10k puppetfile install --verbose
/opt/puppetlabs/bin/puppet apply --environment=production /etc/
puppetlabs/code/environments/production/manifests/
```

It expects to be run with three arguments (we'll see how this is done in a moment): `PUPPET_REPO`, the Git URL for the Puppet repo to clone, `HOSTNAME`, the desired hostname for the node, and `BRANCH`, the branch of the Puppet repo to use.

First, the script sets the specified hostname:

```
hostname ${HOSTNAME}
echo ${HOSTNAME} >/etc/hostname
```

Next, it looks at the `/etc/lsb-release` file to find out the version of Ubuntu installed.

This script is Ubuntu-specific, but you can easily modify it to work with a different Linux distribution if you need to.

The appropriate Puppet Labs APT repository package is downloaded with `wget` and installed. Then the `puppet-agent` package is installed along with `git`:

```
source /etc/lsb-release
apt-key adv --fetch-keys http://apt.puppetlabs.com/DEB-GPG-KEY-puppet
wget http://apt.puppetlabs.com/puppetlabs-release-${DISTRIB_CODENAME}.
deb
dpkg -i puppetlabs-release-${DISTRIB_CODENAME}.deb
apt-get update && apt-get -y install git puppet-agent
```

The next step in the bootstrap process is to clone the Git repo into the place where Puppet expects to find its manifests:

```
cd /etc/puppetlabs/code/environments
mv production production.orig
```

```
git clone ${PUPPET_REPO} production
cd production
git checkout ${BRANCH}
```

Next, we install `r10k` (in Puppet's gem context, using the Puppet-specific `gem` command) and run `r10k puppetfile install`, to install all the required modules listed in the `Puppetfile`:

```
/opt/puppetlabs/puppet/bin/gem install r10k --no-rdoc --no-ri
/opt/puppetlabs/puppet/bin/r10k puppetfile install --verbose
```

Now we can run Puppet for the first time, which will configure everything else we need:

```
/opt/puppetlabs/bin/puppet apply --environment=production /etc/
puppetlabs/code/environments/production/manifests/
```

Of course, in order to run this script on the target node, we have to copy it there first. This step is performed by the `puppify` script (`scripts/puppify`):

```
#!/bin/bash
PUPPET_REPO=https://github.com/bitfield/control-repo-3.git
IDENTITY="-i /Users/john/.ssh/pbg.pem"
if [ "$#" -lt 2 ]; then
  cat <<USAGE
Usage: $0 TARGET HOSTNAME [BRANCH]
Install Puppet on the node TARGET (IP address or DNS name) and run
the bootstrap process. Set the hostname to HOSTNAME, and optionally
use
the control repo branch BRANCH.
USAGE
  exit 1
fi
TARGET=$1
HOSTNAME=${2}
BRANCH=${3:-production}
OPTIONS="-oStrictHostKeyChecking=no"
echo -n "Copying bootstrap script... "
scp ${IDENTITY} ${OPTIONS} $(dirname $0)/bootstrap.sh
ubuntu@${TARGET}:/tmp
echo "done."
echo -n "Bootstrapping... "
ssh ${IDENTITY} ${OPTIONS} ubuntu@${TARGET} "sudo bash /tmp/bootstrap.
sh ${PUPPET_REPO} ${HOSTNAME} ${BRANCH}"
echo "done."
```

First, the script sets the URL of the Git repo to clone (you'll need to change this to your own URL when you adapt the demo repo for your own use):

```
PUPPET_REPO=https://github.com/bitfield/control-repo-3.git
```

Next, we specify the key file used to connect to the target node via SSH (again, modify this to use your own key):

```
IDENTITY="-i /Users/john/.ssh/pbg.pem"
```

After the usage message and processing the command-line arguments, the script proceeds to copy the `bootstrap.sh` file to the target node:

```
scp ${IDENTITY} ${OPTIONS} $(dirname $0)/bootstrap.sh
ubuntu@${TARGET}:/tmp
```

The final step is to run the bootstrap script on the node, passing it the required command-line arguments:

```
ssh ${IDENTITY} ${OPTIONS} ubuntu@${TARGET} "sudo bash /tmp/bootstrap.
sh ${PUPPET_REPO} ${HOSTNAME} ${BRANCH}"
```

Adapting the repo for your own use

You will need to change some of the data and settings in the demo repo to be able to use it yourself. To get you started, here is a table showing which files to change and what information you'll need to supply, with more detailed explanations in the following sections:

File	What to change
`data/common.yaml`	`users`: Users and SSH keys common to all nodes `allow_users`: Users allowed to log in to all nodes `sudoers`: Users allowed to use `sudo` on all nodes `classes`: Classes included by all nodes
`data/nodes/[NODE NAME].yaml`	`users`: Users and SSH keys that only exist on this node `allow_users`: Users allowed to log in to only this node `sudoers`: Users allowed to use `sudo` on only this node `classes`: Classes included only by this node
`site-modules/role/manifests/`	Role classes for your nodes (include `profile::common` in each one)

File	What to change
scripts/puppify	PUPPET_REPO: Git URL of your Puppet repo IDENTITY: Path to the SSH key for initial bootstrap of nodes, if you need one

Configuring users

As we saw earlier in this chapter, the user accounts managed by Puppet are configured from Hiera data. Edit the data/common.yaml file, which looks like this:

```
users:
  'john':
    comment: 'John Arundel'
    uid: '1010'
    sshkeys:
      - 'ssh-rsa AAAA... john@susie'
...
```

Replace the existing users with the user accounts you want to create on nodes (at first it may just be one account, for yourself). Add any SSH keys you want to use with them to the sshkeys array.

The list of allowed users on each node is controlled by the allow_users array. Replace the users listed there with your own users.

The list of users with sudo privileges is controlled by the sudoers array. Replace the users listed there with those of your own users which you want to have root privileges.

Adding per-node data files and role classes

Per-node Hiera data, including classes, is kept in the data/nodes/ directory. When you add a new node, add a data file for it named data/nodes/NODE_NAME.yaml, replacing NODE_NAME with the node's hostname.

Include role classes suitable to the node (see *Chapter 8, Classes, roles, and profiles* for more information about this). If you don't specify any classes in the per-node file, the node will just include the classes listed in common.yaml. This will be enough to set your node up with your SSH account and key, and validate that the bootstrap process works properly. Later, you can start adding role classes to the per-node file to get actual work done.

Add your role classes to the site-modules/role/manifests/ directory, along the lines of role::demo.

If there are users which you only need on a specific node, and you don't want them to exist on all the nodes, list them under `users` in the per-node data file. If they need to log in via SSH, add them to `allow_users` too. Similarly, if you need a user to have `sudo` rights only on this node, list them under `sudoers` in the per-node data file.

Modifying the bootstrap credentials

In the `scripts/puppify` file, edit the `PUPPET_REPO` setting to the URL of your own Git repo. If you need an SSH key to connect to the target node (for example, if you're using Amazon EC2, in which case you'll have a `.pem` file containing your key which you downloaded from the AWS console), add its location to the `IDENTITY` variable.

Bootstrapping a new node

If you'd like to try out the demo repo on a Vagrant box, there is a suitable Vagrantfile included within the repo directory.

If you don't have Vagrant installed, follow the instructions in the *Installing VirtualBox and Vagrant* section of *Chapter 1, Getting Started with Puppet* first.

Bootstrapping a Vagrant VM

Run the following command in the repo directory to start your Vagrant VM:

```
scripts/start_vagrant.sh
```

Bootstrapping physical or cloud nodes

Alternatively, you can bootstrap a physical or cloud node using the repo. All you will need is the IP address or DNS name of the target node.

Run the following command from the Puppet repo, replacing `TARGET_SERVER` with the address or name of the node, and `HOSTNAME` with the hostname that you want to set (for example `demo`):

```
scripts/puppify TARGET_SERVER HOSTNAME
```

You will see some output related to copying the bootstrap script, installing the Puppet package, cloning the repo, installing the Forge modules, and running Puppet for the first time. Once this is completed, the node should be ready, and you can try logging in to it using your own SSH account.

Using other distributions and providers

The `puppify` and `bootstrap` scripts included with the demo repo will work for an Ubuntu node on Amazon EC2, but you can modify them to work with any Linux distribution or server provider.

For example, if you're using a **Google Compute Engine** (**GCE**) instance, you can edit the `puppify` script to replace the `ssh` command with `gcloud compute ssh`. If you're using a Digital Ocean droplet, you can add your SSH key to the droplet when you provision it via the web interface, and you can modify the `puppify` script to log in as the `root` user instead of `ubuntu`.

If you're managing nodes on several different platforms, you may find it more convenient to use a customized `puppify` script for each one, naming them (for example) `puppify_ec2`, `puppify_linode`, and so on.

If you're not using Ubuntu or Debian, you may need to make some changes to the `bootstrap.sh` script. For example, if you're using Red Hat Linux or CentOS, you'll need to have the script install Puppet via `yum` instead of `apt`. Again, if you're managing nodes on multiple OS distributions, you may need to maintain a custom bootstrap script for each one.

Summary

In this chapter we've introduced the example control repo and seen how to download it. We've explained the control repo pattern, and how it works with `r10k` and the Puppetfile to manage third-party and local modules. We've learned how to fork the repo and pull changes from upstream.

We've looked at the example role and profile classes, and seen how Puppet can use Hiera data to configure user accounts, SSH keys, allowed users, and `sudoers` privileges. We've covered the use of Forge modules to manage time zone setting and NTP synchronization. Additionally, we've explored the resources and scripts necessary to control automatic Puppet updates and runs.

The demo repo contains bootstrap scripts to help you put a freshly-provisioned node under Puppet control, and we've examined how these scripts work in detail.

Finally, we've learned how to adapt the demo repo for your own site, and outlined how to add your own users and access settings, and your own common profiles, and per-node role classes. We 've seen how to plug in your own information to the bootstrap scripts and how to use them to bootstrap a new node.

The beginning

I hope you've enjoyed this book and have learned something useful from it; I certainly learned a lot from writing it. However, there's only so much you can learn from books. As Proust wrote, "We don't receive wisdom; we must discover it for ourselves after a journey that no one can take for us or spare us."

It's good to have a friend point us in the right direction and come with us a little way for moral support, but then we need to walk on by ourselves. I hope that this book will be the beginning of your journey, not the end.

The world-famous classical guitarist John Williams was once asked how long it took him to learn to play the guitar. "I'm still learning," he said.

Index

A

B

C

D

E

F

G

H

I

L

M

N

O

P

R

S

T

U

V

Y

Made in the USA
Middletown, DE
28 October 2018